Lecture Notes in Computer Science   16149

Founding Editors

Gerhard Goos
Juris Hartmanis

Editorial Board Members

Elisa Bertino, *Purdue University, West Lafayette, IN, USA*
Wen Gao, *Peking University, Beijing, China*
Bernhard Steffen, *TU Dortmund University, Dortmund, Germany*
Moti Yung, *Columbia University, New York, NY, USA*

The series Lecture Notes in Computer Science (LNCS), including its subseries Lecture Notes in Artificial Intelligence (LNAI) and Lecture Notes in Bioinformatics (LNBI), has established itself as a medium for the publication of new developments in computer science and information technology research, teaching, and education.

LNCS enjoys close cooperation with the computer science R & D community, the series counts many renowned academics among its volume editors and paper authors, and collaborates with prestigious societies. Its mission is to serve this international community by providing an invaluable service, mainly focused on the publication of conference and workshop proceedings and postproceedings. LNCS commenced publication in 1973.

M. Emre Celebi · Johanna Paula Müller ·
Catarina Barata · Allan Halpern ·
Philipp Tschandl · Marc Combalia · Yuan Liu ·
Kumar Abhishek ·
Joanna Jaworek-Korjakowska · Moi Hoon Yap ·
Katharina Breininger · Maximilian Lindholz ·
Jana Hutter · Richard Ruppel · Smiti Tripathy ·
Franziska Mathis-Ullrich · Stefanie Burghaus ·
Matthias May
Editors

Skin Image Analysis, and Computer-Aided Pelvic Imaging for Female Health

10th International Workshop, ISIC 2025
and First International Workshop, CAPI 2025
Held in Conjunction with MICCAI 2025
Daejeon, South Korea, September 23, 2025
Proceedings

Editors
M. Emre Celebi
Department of Computer Science and Mathematics
University of Central Arkansas
Conway, AR, USA

Catarina Barata
Instituto Superior Técnico
Lisboa, Portugal

Philipp Tschandl
Medical University of Vienna
Vienna, Austria

Yuan Liu
Google
Mountain View, CA, USA

Joanna Jaworek-Korjakowska
AGH University of Kraków
Kraków, Poland

Katharina Breininger
University of Wuerzburg
Würzburg, Germany

Jana Hutter
Smart Imaging Lab
Erlangen, Germany

Smiti Tripathy
Smart Imaging Lab
Erlangen, Germany

Stefanie Burghaus
University Hospital Erlangen
Erlangen, Germany

Johanna Paula Müller
University of Erlangen-Nuremberg
Erlangen, Germany

Allan Halpern
Memorial Sloan Kettering Cancer Center
New York, NY, USA

Marc Combalia
Hospital Clinic of Barcelona
Barcelona, Barcelona, Spain

Kumar Abhishek
Simon Fraser University
Burnaby, BC, Canada

Moi Hoon Yap
Manchester Metropolitan University
Manchester, UK

Maximilian Lindholz
Charité-Universitätsmedizin Berlin
Berlin, Germany

Richard Ruppel
Charité - University Medicine Berlin
Berlin, Germany

Franziska Mathis-Ullrich
University of Erlangen-Nuremberg
Erlangen, Germany

Matthias May
University Hospital Erlangen
Erlangen, Germany

ISSN 0302-9743 ISSN 1611-3349 (electronic)
Lecture Notes in Computer Science
ISBN 978-3-032-05824-9 ISBN 978-3-032-05825-6 (eBook)
https://doi.org/10.1007/978-3-032-05825-6

© The Editor(s) (if applicable) and The Author(s), under exclusive license
to Springer Nature Switzerland AG 2026

This work is subject to copyright. All rights are solely and exclusively licensed by the Publisher, whether the whole or part of the material is concerned, specifically the rights of translation, reprinting, reuse of illustrations, recitation, broadcasting, reproduction on microfilms or in any other physical way, and transmission or information storage and retrieval, electronic adaptation, computer software, or by similar or dissimilar methodology now known or hereafter developed.
The use of general descriptive names, registered names, trademarks, service marks, etc. in this publication does not imply, even in the absence of a specific statement, that such names are exempt from the relevant protective laws and regulations and therefore free for general use.
The publisher, the authors and the editors are safe to assume that the advice and information in this book are believed to be true and accurate at the date of publication. Neither the publisher nor the authors or the editors give a warranty, expressed or implied, with respect to the material contained herein or for any errors or omissions that may have been made. The publisher remains neutral with regard to jurisdictional claims in published maps and institutional affiliations.

This Springer imprint is published by the registered company Springer Nature Switzerland AG
The registered company address is: Gewerbestrasse 11, 6330 Cham, Switzerland

If disposing of this product, please recycle the paper.

ISIC 2025 Preface

The Tenth International Skin Imaging Collaboration (ISIC) Workshop on Skin Image Analysis was held at the Daejeon Conference Center, Daejeon, South Korea on September 23, 2025, in conjunction with the 28th International Conference on Medical Image Computing and Computer Assisted Intervention (MICCAI).

Skin is the largest organ of the human body, and the first area of a patient assessed by clinical staff. The skin delivers numerous insights into a patient's underlying health: for example, pale or blue skin suggests respiratory issues, unusually yellowish skin can signal hepatic issues, or certain rashes can be indicative of autoimmune issues. In addition, dermatological complaints are the most prevalent reason that patients seek primary care. Images of the skin are the most easily captured form of medical image in healthcare, and the domain shares qualities with standard computer vision datasets, serving as a natural bridge between standard computer vision tasks and medical applications. However, significant and unique challenges still exist in this domain. For example, there is remarkable visual similarity across disease conditions, and compared to other medical imaging domains, varying genetics, disease states, imaging equipment, and imaging conditions can significantly change the appearance of the skin, making localization and classification in this domain unsolved tasks.

This workshop served as a venue to facilitate advancements and knowledge dissemination in the field of skin image analysis, raising awareness and interest for these socially valuable tasks. The invited speakers were major influencers in computer vision and skin image analysis.

Authors were asked to submit full-length manuscripts for double-blind peer review. A total of 23 submissions were received, and with a Program Committee composed of 23 experts in the field, reviewed by at least three reviewers. Based on the feedback and critiques, six of the best papers (26%) were selected for oral presentation at the workshop, and included this Springer LNCS volume.

We thank the authors for submitting their excellent work, our reviewers for their timely and detailed reviews, our invited speakers, and all our attendees. We sincerely hope that the efforts coming together to make this workshop possible will help advance the field and have a positive impact on health care worldwide.

September 2025

M. Emre Celebi
Catarina Barata
Allan Halpern
Philipp Tschandl
Marc Combalia
Yuan Liu
Kumar Abhishek
Joanna Jaworek-Korjakowska
Moi Hoon Yap

ISIC 2025 Organization

Steering Committee

Noel C. F. Codella	Microsoft, USA
Anthony Hoogs	Kitware, USA
Yun Liu	Google Health, USA
Dale Webster	Google Health, USA

Workshop Chairs

M. Emre Celebi	University of Central Arkansas, USA
Catarina Barata	Instituto Superior Técnico, Portugal
Allan Halpern	Memorial Sloan Kettering Cancer Center, USA
Philipp Tschandl	Medical University of Vienna, Austria
Marc Combalia	Kenko AI, Spain
Yuan Liu	Google, USA
Kumar Abhishek	Simon Fraser University, Canada
Joanna Jaworek-Korjakowska	AGH University of Kraków, Poland
Moi Hoon Yap	Manchester Metropolitan University, UK

Program Committee

Euijoon Ahn	James Cook University, Australia
Sandra Avila	University of Campinas, Brazil
Nourhan Bayasi	University of British Columbia, Canada
Lei Bi	University of Sydney, Australia
Siyi Du	Imperial College London, UK
Ghassan Hamarneh	Simon Fraser University, Canada
Jeremy Kawahara	AIP Labs, Hungary
Jinman Kim	University of Sydney, Australia
Sinan Kockara	Rice University, USA
Kivanc Kose	Memorial Sloan Kettering Cancer Center, USA
Tim K. Lee	University of British Columbia, Canada
Carlos Santiago	Instituto Superior Técnico, Portugal
Janet Wang	Tulane University, USA
Yuheng Wang	University of British Columbia, Canada
Fengying Xie	Beihang University, China

CAPI 2025 Preface

Women's health and particularly the application of sophisticated imaging and analysis tools to the female pelvis has recently attracted fast-growing interest. Large-scale funding calls, e.g. from NIH's Eunice Kennedy Shriver National Institute of Child Health and Human Development (NICHD) and the National Institute of Biomedical Imaging and Bioengineering co-leading a 3 m$ challenge on improving diagnosis of endometriosis, the foundation of a dedicated organisation (Fondation pour la Recherche sur l'Endométriose) in France, and dedicated funding calls from the Ministry of Education and Research in Germany, are examples of the changing and growing funding landscape in this area and reflect the growing public interest and realization of the need to improve diagnosis and therapy. Taking endometriosis as an example, often referred to as the chameleon disease, research and improvements in care are clearly required: "Endometriosis is one of the most common gynecological diseases, but it can take up to 10 years to get a diagnosis [..] Roughly 10 percent globally—of reproductive-age women and girls have endometriosis." Diana W. Bianchi, M.D., NICHD Director. Further common diseases affecting women specifically are cervical cancer, endometrial cancers, ovarian cancer, and fibroids, among others.

However, the female reproductive organs display an extraordinary variability, both between individuals (e.g. retroverted/anteverted uteri), within the same individual at different stages of the menstrual cycle (e.g. uterine lining, ovarian appearance) and even more dramatically over the female patient's life span - from the appearance reflecting the stage of sexual maturation, to reproductive age, to pregnancy and postpartum changes, to postmenstrual women, where the endometrium and ovaries undergo progressive involution. The influence of hormones and the requirement to assess any imaging with respect to the phase to differentiate between normal and pathological findings further complicate diagnosis and decision making. A recent study highlights the urgent need for standardization in gynecological imaging. It found that common features used to diagnose adenomyosis, a prevalent pelvic disorder, are often not reproducible and frequently misapplied, revealing critical clinical gaps and the need for substantial research efforts. Furthermore, the pelvis is an area of extraordinary dynamic events, from natural peristalsis, to breathing motion, to the influence of surrounding tissues such as the bowel on the imaging process. Both diagnosis and therapies often include laparoscopic interventions, amplifying the challenges stated above and placing further emphasis on the need for individualized imaging and analysis techniques. This area is thus becoming increasingly relevant as well to the interventional part of MICCAI ("CAI") as robotic surgeries are becoming more complex and new surgical developments lead to highly specialized tools and advanced methods for surgical planning.

This area therefore poses excellent challenges, both on the image acquisition side as well as on the analysis side, calling for expertise in advanced methods in these areas, which are perfectly represented in the MICCAI community. At the main MICCAI conference, various directly related papers have been presented in a range of sections, but this workshop complements the main MICCAI conference by providing a focused discussion of women's reproductive health imaging on future directions for research and clinical requirements from the user's and patient's perspective that are not possible within the main conference, including early-stage research in a field which has only recently received this level of attention. It furthermore aims to grow this application within the MICCAI community - by raising awareness of both the clinical need and the fascinating challenges present. CAPI aspires to become a prime platform for research into women's reproductive health by linking the growing community with researchers working in Computer Assisted Intervention.

We received nine paper submissions covering the full scope of medical image analysis applied to women's reproductive health, from early detection and diagnosis, to computer-aided diagnosis, to handling data, labels, annotations and segmentations, evaluation methods, clinical validity like performance metrics, multimodal approaches, AI-based anomaly detection, and more. At least three reviewers, highly knowledgeable in their field, commented in the traditional double-blind MICCAI process on each paper, the committee carefully evaluated these reviews, and we were delighted to be able to accep seven full paper submissions as well as one abstract.

August 2025

Johanna Paula Müller
Katharina Breininger
Maximilian Lindholz
Jana Hutter
Richard Ruppel
Smiti Tripathy
Franziska Mathis-Ullrich
Stefanie Burghaus
Matthias May

Acknowledgments

The workshop organizers thank and the MICCAI society, and the MICCAI 2025 organizers, particularly the workshop chairs, for their work and for providing a platform for this first edition of the CAPI workshop. We also thank the reviewers for providing us with high-quality reviews.

CAPI 2025 Organization

Program Committee Chairs

Johanna P. Müller	Friedrich-Alexander Universität Erlangen-Nürnberg, Germany
Katharina Breininger	Julius-Maximilians-Universität Würzburg, Germany
Maximilian Lindholz	Charité-Universitätsmedizin Berlin, Germany
Jana Hutter	University Hospital Erlangen and Friedrich-Alexander Universität Erlangen-Nürnberg, University Hospital Erlangen, Germany
Richard Ruppel	Charité-Universitätsmedizin Berlin, Germany
Smiti Tripathy	University Hospital Erlangen and Friedrich-Alexander Universität Erlangen-Nürnberg, Germany
Franziska Mathis-Ullrich	Friedrich-Alexander Universität Erlangen-Nürnberg, Germany
Stefanie Burghaus	University Hospital Erlangen, Germany
Matthias May	University Hospital Erlangen, Germany

Steering Committee

Jana Hutter	University Hospital Erlangen and Friedrich-Alexander Universität Erlangen-Nürnberg, University Hospital Erlangen, Germany
Matthias May	University Hospital Erlangen, Germany
Katharina Breininger	Julius-Maximilians-Universität Würzburg, Germany
Tobias Penzkofer	Charité-Universitätsmedizin Berlin, Germany
Franziska Mathis Ulrich	Friedrich-Alexander Universität Erlangen-Nürnberg, Germany
Maximilian Lindholz	Charité-Universitätsmedizin Berlin, Germany
Stefanie Burghaus	University Hospital Erlangen, Germany
Smiti Tripathy	University Hospital Erlangen and Friedrich-Alexander Universität Erlangen-Nürnberg, Germany

Richard Ruppel	Charité-Universitätsmedizin Berlin, Germany
Johanna P. Müller	Friedrich-Alexander Universität Erlangen-Nürnberg, Germany
Jasmin Arjomandi	Friedrich-Alexander Universität Erlangen-Nürnberg, Germany

Program Committee

Jonas Alle	University of Bamberg, Germany
Jordina Aviles Verdera	King's College London, UK & University Hospital Erlangen and Friedrich-Alexander Universität Erlangen-Nürnberg, Germany
Matthew Baugh	Imperial College London, UK
Deepak Bhatia	University Hospital Erlangen and Friedrich-Alexander Universität Erlangen-Nürnberg, Germany
Isabelle Bloch	Sorbonne Université, France
Hannah Braun	Friedrich-Alexander Universität Erlangen-Nürnberg, Germany
Katharina Breininger	Julius-Maximilians-Universität Würzburg, Germany
Francesco Di Salvo	University of Bamberg, Germany
Sebastian Doerrich	University of Bamberg, Germany
Anika Knupfer	University Hospital Erlangen and Friedrich-Alexander Universität Erlangen-Nürnberg, Germany
Roxane Licandro	Medical University of Vienna, Austria
Matthias May	University Hospital Erlangen, Germany
Raghav Mehta	Imperial College London, UK
Richard Ruppel	Charité-Universitätsmedizin Berlin, Germany
Vanya Saksena	Friedrich-Alexander Universität Erlangen-Nürnberg, Germany
Andrzej Skalski	AGH University Krakow, Poland
Omar Todd	Imperial College London, UK
Smiti Tripathy	University Hospital Erlangen and Friedrich-Alexander Universität Erlangen-Nürnberg, Germany
Marc Vornehm	Friedrich-Alexander Universität Erlangen-Nürnberg, Germany

Publicly Available Female Pelvis MRI Datasets: Current Resources and Limitations for Image-Based Research

Maximilian Lindholz[1], Tillmann Arlt[1], Richard Ruppel[1], Robin Schmidt[1], Yasmin El-Nahry[1], Sylvia Mechsner[1], Sophia Elisabeth Ellen Schulze-Weddige[1], Georg Lukas Baumgärtner[1], Charlie Alexander Hamm[1], Lynn Jeanette Savic[1], Sebastian Arndt[2], Lisa Siegler[2], Leonard Stepansky[2], Matthias May[2], and Tobias Penzkofer[1]

[1] Charité – Universitätsmedizin Berlin, Berlin, Germany
{maximilian.lindholz,tillmann.arlt,richard.ruppel,robin.schmidt,
yasmin.el-nahry,sylvia.mechsner,sophia.schulze-weddige,
georg.baumgaertner,charlie.hamm,lynn-jeanette.savic,
tobias.penzkofer}@charite.de

[2] Universitätsklinikum Erlangen, Erlangen, Germany
{sebastian.arndt,lisa.siegler,matthias.may}@uk-erlangen.de,
leonard.stepansky@fau.de

M. Lindholz and T. Arlt — These authors contributed equally to this work.

Introduction: Gynecologic research relies on accurate imaging, with MRI offering excellent soft tissue contrast and serving as the imaging gold standard for diagnosing conditions such as uterine myomas [8]. However, open-source imaging datasets show a gender imbalance, with female participants and diseases being underrepresented [9].

Methods: We conducted a keyword-based search, including among other sources PubMed, Huggingface, and Google Scholar (e.g., "pelvic MRI dataset", "uterine MRI dataset"), followed by a review of relevant citations. Datasets were included based on three criteria: (1) online accessibility, (2) MRI modality, and (3) representation of female pelvic anatomy. Clinical and technical metadata were automatically extracted from DICOM and NIFTI formats along with complementary files and then verified through manual review.

Results: Seven publicly available female pelvic MRI datasets could be identified [6, 1, 7, 5, 3, 2, 8, 4], one of which could be separated into two subsets. Table 1 in the appendix summarizes the key characteristics of all included datasets. The datasets consistently lack essential clinical metadata such as hormonal status, menstrual cycle phase, and medication. The imaging protocols varied in orientation, sequence type (cf. Tables 1 and 2 in the appendix), magnetic field strength (1.5 to 3 T), slice thickness (4 to 15 mm), and resolution (64 × 64 to 1152 × 1152 pixels). Annotations were mostly absent or limited, with consistent segmentations found only in the UMD dataset [8].

Discussion: This analysis highlights a significant gap in publicly available female pelvic MRI imaging data, with only seven datasets meeting our inclusion criteria. None

Table 1 Comparison of publicly accessible female pelvic MRI datasets. Sequence types are detailed in Table 2;'N/A' signifies missing data (meaning data not available). Only participants with available MRI data were included, which could lead to varying patient numbers compared to those reported in the original studies

	CCTH [6, 1]	CPTAC-UCEC [7]	TCGA-CESC [5]	TCGA-OV [3]	TCGA-UCEC [2]	UMD [8, 9]	UT-Endo-MRI 1 [4]	UT-Endo-MRI 2 [4]
Patient Age	54.29 ± 11.67 years	63.07 ± 10.53 years	50.90 ± 13.22 years	61.00 ± 0.00 years	57.24 ± 17.04 years	49.06 ± 12.91 years	N/A	N/A
Number of Patients	23	36	54	1	8	300	51	81
Health Status	Cervical cancer	Endometrial carcinoma	Cervical squamous cell carcinoma, Endocervical adenocarcinoma	Ovarian cancer	Endometrial carcinoma	Uterine myoma	Endo- metriosis	Endo- metriosis
Hormonal Status	N/A	N/A	N/A	N/A	N/A	N/A	N/A	N/A
Cycle Phase	N/A	N/A	N/A	N/A	N/A	N/A	N/A	N/A
Medication	N/A	N/A	N/A	N/A	N/A	N/A	N/A	N/A
Associated Clinical Data	Follow-up, classification	Histo-pathology, whole slide image	Whole slide image	Proteo-genomics, radiogenomics	Genomic, digitized histo-pathology	Age	N/A	N/A
Sequence Type	1–4	1–4	1–4	1–4	1–4	2	1–2	1–2
Magnetic Field Strength	1.5 T	1.5 T	3 T, 1.5 T	1.5 T	3 T, 1.5 T	3 T, 1.5 T	3 T, 1.5 T	3 T, 1.5 T
Scanner Manufacturer	SIEMENS, Philips, GE Medical	SIEMENS, GE Medical	SIEMENS, Philips, GE Medical	SIEMENS	Philips, GE Medical	Philips	SIEMENS, Philips, GE Medical	SIEMENS, Philips, GE Medical
Min. Image Resolution	128 × 128	108 × 162	64 × 64	112 × 128	64 × 64	480 × 480	157 × 143	224 × 224
Max. Image Resolution	640 × 640	576 × 576	1024 × 1024	512 × 512	512 × 512	1152 × 1152	880 × 880	640 × 640
Number of Resolutions	10	34	39	9	3	13	48	15
Slice Thickness [mm]	4.36 ± 0.48	9.26 ± 33.97	5.23 ± 4.71	15.16 ± 21.23	5.82 ± 1.60	5.05 ± 0.87	4.06 ± 1.65	4.90 ± 1.68
Slice Gap [mm]	0.31 ± 0.56	0.55 ± 0.98	1.49 ± 2.56	0.76 ± 1.31	0.38 ± 2.16	0.55 ± 0.16	N/A	N/A
Voxel Size [mm3]	1.08 ± 0.54 × 1.08 ± 0.54 × 4.36 ± 0.48	1.03 ± 0.45 × 1.03 ± 0.45 × 9.26 ± 33.97	0.80 ± 0.74 × 0.80 ± 0.74 × 5.23 ± 4.71	1.13 ± 0.48 × 1.13 ± 0.48 × 15.16 ± 21.23	1.11 ± 1.33 × 1.11 ± 1.33 × 5.82 ± 1.60	0.49 ± 0.11 × 0.49 ± 0.11 × 5.08 ± 0.93	0.50 ± 0.00 × 0.50 ± 0.00 × 4.06 ± 1.65	0.84 ± 0.18 × 0.84 ± 0.18 × 4.90 ± 1.68
Image Annotations and Segmentations	None	Uterus, uterus seed point	None	None	None	Uterine wall, uterine cavity, uterine myoma, nabothian cyst	Ovary, uterus, endometrioma, cyst, cul de sac	Ovary, uterus, endometrioma, cyst, cul de sac
License	CC BY 4.0	CC BY 3.0	CC BY 3.0	CC BY 3.0	CC BY 3.0	CC BY 4.0	CC BY 4.0	CC BY 4.0

of these datasets included essential clinical details such as medication use or menstrual cycle phase.

Conclusion: Larger, more diverse, and contextualized public pelvic MRI datasets are needed to advance gynecologic imaging research.

Keywords: Pelvic MRI · Uterus · Public datasets · Metadata quality · Medical imaging · Annotation gaps

Acknowledgments. This study was funded by "NUM 2.0" (FKZ: 01KX2121).

Table 2. Available MRI sequences in the included datasets

Num	Group	Key Descriptors
1	T1-weighted	Pre/post contrast, FSPGR, FLASH
2	T2-weighted	TSE, TSER, frFSE, HASTE, TRUFI
3	DWI/ADC	Diffusion sequences and ADC maps
4	DCE/Perfusion	Dynamic contrast, multi-phase

References

1. Bowen, S.R., Yuh, W.T., Hippe, D.S., et al.: Tumor radiomic heterogeneity: multiparametric functional imaging to characterize variability and predict response following cervical cancer radiation therapy. J. Magn. Reson. Imaging **47**(5), 1388–1396 (2018). https://doi.org/10.1002/jmri.25874
2. Erickson, B.J., Mutch, D., Lippmann, L., Jarosz, R.: The cancer genome atlas uterine corpus endometrial carcinoma collection (tcga-ucec) (version 4) (2016). data set, The Cancer Imaging Archive. https://doi.org/10.7937/K9/TCIA.2016.GKJ0ZWAC
3. Holback, C., Jarosz, R., Prior, F., et al.: The cancer genome atlas ovarian cancer collection (tcga-ov) (version 4) (2016). dataset, The Cancer Imaging Archive. https://doi.org/10.7937/K9/TCIA.2016.NDO1MDFQ
4. Liang, X., Alpuing Radilla, L.A., Khalaj, K., et al.: Uthealth - endometriosis mri dataset (ut-endomri) (2025). https://doi.org/10.5281/zenodo.15750762
5. Lucchesi, F.R., Aredes, N.D.: The cancer genome atlas cervical squamous cell carcinoma and endocervical adenocarcinoma collection (tcga-cesc) (version 3) (2016). dataset, The Cancer Imaging Archive. https://doi.org/10.7937/K9/TCIA.2016.SQ4M8YP4
6. Mayr, N., Yuh, W.T.C., Bowen, S., et al.: Cervical cancer – tumor heterogeneity: Serial functional and molecular imaging across the radiation therapy course in advanced cervical cancer (version 1) (2023). data set, The Cancer Imaging Archive. https://doi.org/10.7937/ERZ5-QZ59
7. National Cancer Institute Clinical Proteomic Tumor Analysis Consortium (CPTAC): The clinical proteomic tumor analysis consortium uterine corpus endometrial carcinoma collection (cptac-ucec) (version 13) (2019). dataset, The Cancer Imaging Archive. https://doi.org/10.7937/k9/tcia.2018.3r3juisw
8. Pan, H., Chen, M., Bai, W., et al.: Large-scale uterine myoma mri dataset covering all figo types with pixel-level annotations. Sci. Data **11**, 410 (2024). https://doi.org/10.1038/s41597-024-03170-x
9. Tripathi, S., et al.: Understanding biases and disparities in radiology ai datasets: a review. J. Am. Coll. Radiol. **20**(9), 836–841 (2023). https://doi.org/10.1016/j.jacr.2023.06.015

Contents

Proceedings of the Tenth International Skin Imaging Collaboration Workshop (ISIC 2025)

LesionGen: A Concept-Guided Diffusion Model for Dermatology Image Synthesis 3
  Jamil Fayyad, Nourhan Bayasi, Ziyang Yu, and Homayoun Najjaran

Fitzpatrick Thresholding for Skin Image Segmentation 13
  Duncan Stothers, Lia Gracey, Sophia Xu, and Carlie Reeves

What Can We Learn from Inter-Annotator Variability in Skin Lesion Segmentation? 23
  Kumar Abhishek, Jeremy Kawahara, and Ghassan Hamarneh

Topology-Aware Deep Models for Skin Lesion Classification 34
  Sayoni Chakraborty, Philmore Koung, and Baris Coskunuzer

Retrieval-Augmented VLMs for Multimodal Melanoma Diagnosis 46
  Jihyun Moon and Charmgil Hong

Lightweight Dual-Task Framework for Semi-supervised Lesion Segmentation with Knowledge Distillation from SAM 57
  Xuan-Loc Huynh, Huy-Thach Pham, Anh Mai Vu, Thanh-Minh Nguyen, Tran Quang Khai Bui, Tat-Bach Nguyen, Quan Nguyen, Minh Huu Nhat Le, and Phat K. Huynh

Proceedings of Computer-Aided Pelvic Imaging for Female Health (CAPI)

UteroVAE: A Shape-Informed Variational Autoencoder for Uterine MRI Encoding in Adenomyosis, Fibroids, and Healthy Uteri 71
  Richard Ruppel, Maximilian Lindholz, Robin Schmidt, Yasmin El-Nahry, Sylvia Mechsner, Sophia Elisabeth Ellen Schulze-Weddige, Georg Lukas Baumgärtner, Tillmann Arlt, Charlie Alexander Hamm, Sebastian Arndt, Lisa Siegler, Leonard Stepansky, Jana Hutter, Matthias May, and Tobias Penzkofer

Delineation Uncertainty from Clinician Ranges in Cervical Cancer
Radiotherapy Planning 82
    Omar Todd, Sooha Kim, Katherine Mackay, Raghav Mehta,
    Fabio De Sousa Ribeiro, David Bernstein, Alexandra Taylor,
    and Ben Glocker

Diffusing the Blind Spot: Uterine MRI Synthesis with Diffusion Models 93
    Johanna P. Müller, Anika Knupfer, Pedro Blöss,
    Edoardo Berardi Vittur, Bernhard Kainz, and Jana Hutter

Multi-step Segmentation of Pelvic Fractures: Handling Variable Fracture
Counts Through Anatomical and Surface Analysis 103
    Artur Jurgas, Maciej Stanuch, Marek Wodziński, and Andrzej Skalski

Visionerves: Automatic and Reproducible Hybrid AI for Peripheral
Nervous System Recognition Applied to Endometriosis Cases 113
    Giammarco La Barbera, Enzo Bonnot, Thomas Isla,
    Juan Pablo de la Plata, Joy-Rose Dunoyer de Segonzac, Jennifer Attali,
    Cécile Lozach, Alexandre Bellucci, Louis Marcellin, Laure Fournier,
    Sabine Sarnacki, Pietro Gori, and Isabelle Bloch

A Prospective Dual-Modality Tool for Monitoring Uterine Peristalsis:
Integrating Dynamic MRI and Electrohysterography 125
    Maria Camila Bustos Vivas, Smiti Tripathy, and Jana Hutter

Real-Time Automated Analysis and Reporting of Uterine MRI 137
    Deepak Bhatia, Jordina Aviles Verdera, Michael Kitzberger,
    Smiti Tripathy, Maria Camila Bustos Vivas, Lieselotte Kratzsch,
    Anika Knupfer, and Jana Hutter

Author Index 149

Proceedings of the Tenth International Skin Imaging Collaboration Workshop (ISIC 2025)

`LesionGen`: A Concept-Guided Diffusion Model for Dermatology Image Synthesis

Jamil Fayyad[1]([✉]), Nourhan Bayasi[2], Ziyang Yu[3], and Homayoun Najjaran[1]

[1] University of Victoria, Victoria, Canada
`jfayyad@uvic.ca`
[2] University of British Columbia, Vancouver, Canada
[3] University of Toronto, Toronto, Canada

Abstract. Deep learning models for skin disease classification require large, diverse, and well-annotated datasets. However, such resources are often limited due to privacy concerns, high annotation costs, and insufficient demographic representation. While text-to-image diffusion probabilistic models (`T2I-DPMs`) offer promise for medical data synthesis, their use in dermatology remains underexplored, largely due to the scarcity of rich textual descriptions in existing skin image datasets. In this work, we introduce `LesionGen`, a clinically informed `T2I-DPM` framework for dermatology image synthesis. Unlike prior methods that rely on simplistic disease labels, `LesionGen` is trained on structured, concept-rich dermatological captions derived from expert annotations and pseudo-generated, concept-guided reports. By fine-tuning a pretrained diffusion model on these high-quality image-caption pairs, we enable the generation of realistic and diverse skin lesion images conditioned on meaningful dermatological descriptions. Our results demonstrate that models trained solely on our synthetic dataset achieve classification accuracy comparable to those trained on real images, with notable gains in worst-case subgroup performance. Code and data are available here.

Keywords: Synthetic Data Generation · Text-to-Image Diffusion Models · Dermatology · Skin Lesion Classification

1 Introduction

Deep learning (DL) has revolutionized medical image analysis, offering unprecedented accuracy in disease detection [24] and classification [2–5,8,10]. However, these models are inherently data-hungry, requiring vast amounts of high-quality, diverse training images to generalize well [9,11]. In dermatology, this need is particularly acute because skin disease classification relies on nuanced visual cues that can vary across demographics, lighting conditions, and disease progression. Yet, real-world medical datasets are often limited due to privacy concerns, ethical restrictions, and the high cost of expert annotations. The scarcity of diverse, labeled skin disease images presents a significant barrier to developing robust DL models.

To address this issue, synthetic data generation has emerged as a promising solution, with generative models offering a powerful tool for augmenting medical datasets. Among these, diffusion probabilistic models (DPMs) [13] have demonstrated outstanding capabilities in generating high-fidelity images across diverse domains, including image synthesis [14,25], translation [16], classification [17] and segmentation [23]. Particularly noteworthy are text-to-image diffusion models (T2I-DPMs), which leverage natural language descriptions to generate realistic images aligned with specific conditions, achieving state-of-the-art performance. For instance, de Wilde et al. [7] adapted pre-trained T2I-DPMs to medical imaging through textual inversion, successfully generating diagnostically accurate images across a range of modalities. Similarly, Chen et al. [6] introduced EyeDiff, a T2I-DPM trained on a variety of ophthalmic datasets, demonstrating its effectiveness in generating images of rare eye diseases to address the critical issue of data imbalance in diagnostic models.

However, despite the promising potential of T2I-DPMs in medical imaging, their application to dermatology faces a significant limitation: unlike other medical modalities, where images are typically accompanied by detailed textual reports [22], skin disease datasets often lack such structured descriptions. This absence of rich textual metadata makes it challenging to fully leverage T2I-DPMs for data synthesis in dermatology. To date, only two studies have applied T2I-DPMs to skin lesion synthesis [1,19], but both relied on overly simplistic textual descriptions limited to disease labels; e.g., 'an image of <label-only>', where <label-only> is replaced by the name of the corresponding skin disease. This approach is insufficient, as it fails to capture the rich, nuanced visual features that define each condition, such as variations in texture, color, shape, and progression. These features are critical for accurate lesion classification and diagnosis, and without them, the generated images lack the diversity and specificity needed to enhance model performance effectively.

In this work, we propose LesionGen, a novel T2I-DPM framework for concept-driven skin image synthesis, primarily aimed at improving worst-case performance across subgroups. Our method generates rich image–caption pairs by producing structured, clinically meaningful descriptions of dermatological images. Specifically, we employ two concept-based text generation strategies to create these captions: (1) a strategy based on expert dermatological descriptions, where each image is annotated with seven clinically relevant diagnostic attributes; and (2) a strategy using pseudo-generated dermatological descriptions, where a vision-language model is guided to produce detailed medical text conditioned on these dermatological concepts. These concept-grounded captions are paired with their corresponding images to form high-quality training data for LesionGen, enabling conditional image generation. Our results demonstrate that models trained solely on this synthetic data achieve competitive classification accuracy, with notable improvements in worst-case subgroup performance.

2 Methodology

We propose LesionGen, a dermatology image synthesis using a fine-tuned T2I-DPM. As shown in Fig. 1, the framework constructs image–caption pairs from

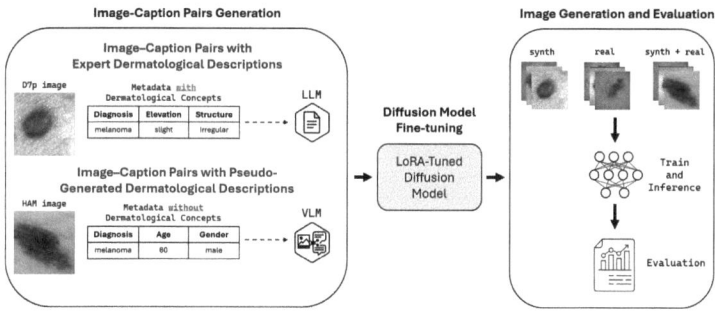

Fig. 1. Overview of LesionGen. Lesion images are paired with either expert dermatological descriptions transformed into text by an LLM, or pseudo-captions generated from image features using a VLM, forming a unified multimodal dataset. A LoRA-tuned diffusion model is trained on the multimodal dataset, and the trained model generates diverse, class-consistent images, which are then evaluated in the downstream classification task.

expert annotations and pseudo-generated descriptions, then fine-tunes the diffusion model on these pairs for image generation and downstream evaluation.

2.1 Training Data Construction

Image–Caption Pairs with Expert Dermatological Descriptions. To construct clinically grounded pairs, we use the D7P dataset [15], which contains 1,926 dermoscopic images spanning six diagnostic classes: nv, mel, bcc, df, bkl, and vasc. Each image is paired with structured metadata describing seven clinically meaningful attributes (referred to as *concepts*), including pigmentation, lesion elevation, and structure. To transform this metadata into natural language, we prompt an LLM model with a structured template (Fig. 2–top), generating dermatologist-style captions that serve as conditioning text for diffusion training.

Image–Caption Pairs with Pseudo-Generated Dermatological Descriptions. The HAM10000 (HAM) dataset [21] is a widely used benchmark in dermatology, comprising over 10,000 dermoscopic images across seven diagnostic classes (the six from D7P, plus akiec). Although HAM includes basic metadata, such as patient age, gender, lesion type, and anatomical location, it lacks corresponding textual descriptions and, critically, does not provide annotations for key dermatological concepts, as in D7P, that are important to clinical diagnosis. To address this, we leverage a VLM model to generate structured dermatological descriptions that draw on both the available metadata (e.g., lesion label, patient age, gender) and the visual content of each image. Rather than prompting the VLM to produce free-form clinical descriptions, we craft targeted prompts that explicitly instruct the model to describe each image using the seven diagnostic concepts defined in the D7P dataset (e.g., pigmentation, elevation, structure). Although these attributes are not explicitly annotated in HAM, our prompt-

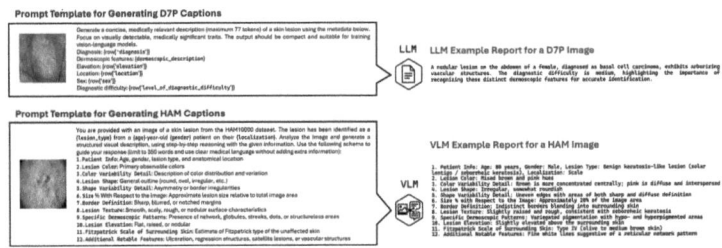

Fig. 2. Prompt templates and example outputs for dermatological caption generation from (top) expert-annotated D7P data and (bottom) pseudo-generated HAM data.

ing strategy enables the VLM to generate clinically meaningful, concept-based descriptions that enhance the dataset's utility for diffusion model fine-tuning. Figure 2-bottom illustrates the prompting strategy and an example output.

2.2 Diffusion Model Fine-Tuning

We fine-tune a pretrained DPM using a combined set of expert and pseudo-generated image–caption pairs from D7P and HAM. The resulting model, LesionGen, is trained to generate realistic and diverse skin lesion images conditioned on dermatological descriptions. To improve alignment between medical language and visual features, we leverage CLIP for text conditioning and apply Low-Rank Adaptation (LoRA) for efficient fine-tuning. Formally, LesionGen samples an image x_0 given a text embedding c as $x_0 \sim p_\theta(x_0 \mid c)$, where c encodes the structured dermatological description.

3 Experiments and Results

We evaluate how synthetic skin lesion images generated by LesionGen affect downstream classification performance. Specifically, we ask: (1) How effective are these synthetic images for training a CNN classifier (e.g., ResNet18 [12])? and (2) How does prompt design influence the utility of generated images?

3.1 Experimental Setup

We fine-tune a pretrained Stable Diffusion v1.4 model [18] on our multi-modal dataset of image–caption pairs (see Sect. 2), which makes our LesionGen model. In our main experimental setting, we use **rich and balanced prompts** as input to LesionGen during image generation. We refer to this configuration as LesionGen-R&B. Rich refers to the prompts being identical to those used during diffusion model fine-tuning, whereas balanced refers to addressing class imbalance during image generation by ensuring each lesion class is associated with an equal number of prompts. Since some classes are underrepresented in the original dataset, we use GPT-4o to generate paraphrased versions of existing prompts for those classes. These paraphrases retain the original clinical meaning while introducing linguistic variation; e.g., turning 'A nodular melanoma featuring diffuse irregular pigmentation, irregular dots' into 'A nodular melanoma showing uneven pigmentation, scattered dots'. Using LesionGen-R&B, we generate a class-balanced synthetic dataset with 500 samples per class. A ResNet18 classifier is then trained on different combinations of the synthetic and real data, and evaluated on held-out real test sets from D7P and HAM.

3.2 Baseline and Competing Method

We compare LesionGen-R&B against two baselines. The first is a **real-only (upper bound)** configuration, where the ResNet18 classifier is trained solely on real images. The second is a prior SOTA method [1], referred to as **p-SOTA**, in which the diffusion model is both **fine-tuned and sampled** using only static prompts that only include the label (e.g., melanoma) without any descriptive captions.

3.3 Implementation Details

Prompt Generation. We use GPT-4o in two modes: text-only for D7P (from structured metadata) and vision–language for HAM (using base64-encoded images with structured instructions). Prompts are generated with temperature 0.3 and a 77-token limit to comply with CLIP's tokenization limits.

Diffusion Model Fine-Tuning. We use Stable Diffusion v1.4, pretrained on the LAION-2B dataset [20], and fine-tune it using LoRA (Low-Rank Adaptation) on our image-caption dataset. The LoRA training uses a rank of 64, learning rate of 1e-5, and a constant scheduler. Training is performed for 15,000 steps using mixed precision (fp16), gradient checkpointing, and image augmentations like cropping and horizontal flipping. The output resolution is 256×256. We qualitatively monitor progress by evaluating validation prompts every five epochs.

Downstream Classification. The downstream classifier is a ResNet18 trained from scratch. Input images are resized to 224×224, normalized with a mean and standard deviation of 0.5, and randomly flipped during training. We use stochastic gradient descent with momentum 0.9, initial learning rate 0.01, and step decay (factor 0.1 every 10 epochs). Training uses a batch size of 32 and early stopping with patience of 5 epochs. Our code is implemented in PyTorch using the HuggingFace Diffusers library and OpenAI APIs.

3.4 Main Results

We train the ResNet18 model on a combined dataset consisting of up to 250 real images per class (when available), supplemented with synthetic images generated by LesionGen-R&B to reach a total of 500 training samples per class. This setup is referred to as (**synth+real**). The classification performance measured by overall accuracy and per-class precision on the D7P and HAM test sets is reported in Tables 1 and 2, respectively.

Table 1. Classification performance on the D7P test set. We report overall accuracy and per-class precision. The best results are **bolded** in green-shaded cells.

Experiment	Overall Accuracy	bcc	bkl	df	mel	nv	vasc
p-SOTA (synth+real)	0.450	**0.333**	0.125	0.250	0.627	0.712	0.250
real-only	0.650	0.214	**0.333**	0.000	0.636	0.678	0.000
Ours							
LesionGen-R&B (synth+real)	**0.653**	0.188	0.316	**0.500**	**0.658**	**0.721**	**0.251**

Table 2. Classification performance on the HAM test set. We report overall accuracy and per-class precision. The best results are **bolded** in green-shaded cells.

Experiment	Overall Accuracy	akiec	bcc	bkl	df	mel	nv	vasc
p-SOTA (synth+real)	0.587	0.231	0.364	0.343	0.077	0.313	**0.954**	0.434
real-only	0.737	0.273	**0.488**	0.527	0.000	0.594	0.812	**1.000**
Ours								
LesionGen-R&B (synth+real)	**0.756**	**0.375**	0.421	**0.538**	**0.418**	**0.622**	0.807	0.315

On the **D7P test set** (Table 1), the classifier trained on LesionGen-R&B-generated data achieves the highest overall accuracy (65.3%), slightly outperforming the real-only model (65.0%) and significantly surpassing the p-SOTA baseline (45.0%). Beyond overall accuracy, our method yields major improvements in worst-class performance. Notably, the precision for the df class increases from 0.000 (real-only) and 0.250 (p-SOTA) to 0.500 with LesionGen-R&B, demonstrating that our rich and balanced generation strategy enables the classifier to recover performance on previously underrepresented classes. Additionally, LesionGen-R&B provides the highest precision in 4 out of 6 classes, including mel and nv, which are critical in clinical diagnosis.

On the **HAM test set** (Table 2), the classifier achieves the best overall accuracy (75.6%) with our approach, outperforming the real-only (73.7%) and p-SOTA (58.7%) scenarios. The improvements in rare or challenging classes are particularly notable: df improves from 0.000 (real-only) and 0.077 (p-SOTA) to 0.418 with our method, and akiec rises from 0.273 to 0.375. Our method also leads to the best precision in 5 out of 7 classes, showing that LesionGen-R&B-generated data improves class-wise consistency without overfitting to majority classes. While vasc and nv show a slight drop compared to real-only, they remain strong overall, and this trade-off results in a more balanced and robust classifier.

3.5 Ablation Studies

We conduct ablation studies to answer three questions: (A) Can synthetic data alone yield strong performance? (B) What is the impact of prompt balancing on class-wise and overall accuracy? and (C) How much does prompt enrichment improve results over static, label-only prompts?

Table 3. Ablation study results on the D7P test set, reporting overall accuracy and per-class precision. The best results in each ablation are **bolded** in green-shaded cells.

Experiment	Overall Accuracy	bcc	bkl	df	mel	nv	vasc
Ablation A: Impact of Using Synthetic Data Alone							
p-SOTA (synth only)	0.446	0.056	0.113	0.000	0.636	**0.715**	**0.111**
LesionGen-R&B (synth only)	**0.551**	**0.100**	**0.143**	0.000	**0.652**	0.690	0.056
Ablation B: Impact of Removing Prompt Balancing							
LesionGen-R (synth only)	0.577	0.000	**0.250**	**0.059**	**0.623**	0.651	0.050
LesionGen-R (synth+real)	**0.611**	**0.250**	0.067	0.000	0.596	**0.670**	**0.125**
Ablation C: Impact of Using Static, Label-Only Prompts							
LesionGen-S (synth only)	0.324	0.000	0.047	0.028	0.280	0.692	0.067
LesionGen-S (synth+real)	**0.637**	**0.077**	**0.222**	**0.300**	**0.597**	**0.733**	**0.300**

Table 4. Ablation study results on the HAM test set, reporting overall accuracy and per-class precision. The best results in each ablation are **bolded** in green-shaded cells.

Experiment	Overall Accuracy	akiec	bcc	bkl	df	mel	nv	vasc
Ablation A: Impact of Using Synthetic Data Alone								
p-SOTA (synth only)	0.315	0.009	0.126	0.130	0.000	0.236	**0.978**	**0.091**
LesionGen-R&B (synth only)	**0.524**	**0.145**	**0.188**	**0.210**	**0.045**	**0.489**	0.681	0.080
Ablation B: Impact of Removing Prompt Balancing								
LesionGen-R (synth only)	0.428	0.000	0.078	0.169	0.000	0.164	0.927	**1.000**
LesionGen-R (synth+real)	**0.585**	**0.230**	**0.389**	**0.312**	0.000	**0.298**	**0.938**	0.475
Ablation C: Impact of Using Static, Label-Only Prompts								
LesionGen-S (synth only)	0.176	0.011	0.211	0.068	0.000	0.214	**1.000**	0.000
LesionGen-S (synth+real)	**0.608**	**0.239**	**0.370**	**0.405**	**0.065**	**0.326**	0.942	**0.512**

Ablation A: Impact of Using Synthetic Data Alone. In ablation study A, we remove all real training images and train the ResNet18 model solely on synthetic data generated by either p-SOTA or LesionGen-R&B. As shown in Tables 3 and 4, this leads to a clear drop in both overall accuracy and worst-class precision compared to the synth+real setting (Tables 1 and 2). For instance, on the HAM dataset, training on p-SOTA synthetic images results in just 31.5% accuracy, whereas synthetic images from LesionGen-R&B yield a significantly higher 52.4%. While performance still falls short of configurations that include real data, these results indicate that our concept-driven generation approach produces higher-quality and more informative samples than prior methods. Overall, this ablation confirms that synthetic data alone is not sufficient, but can be highly effective when used in combination with real samples.

Ablation B: Impact of Removing Prompt Balancing. In this ablation, we generate synthetic data using rich, concept-guided prompts but without applying prompt balancing for underrepresented classes. As shown in Tables 3 and 4, removing balancing results in a decline in overall accuracy and highly

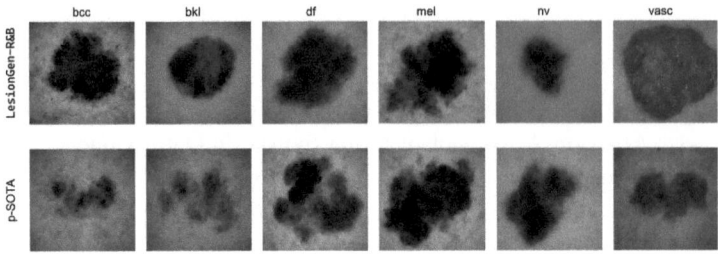

Fig. 3. Examples of synthetic skin lesion images generated from LesionGen-R&B (top) and p-SOTA (bottom) across six classes.

inconsistent class-wise performance, particularly when compared to the full LesionGen-R&B setting (Tables 1 and 2) where balancing was applied. Furthermore, the classifier performs well on majority classes; e.g., on HAM, precision for nv reaches 93.8% in the synth+real setting, and vasc reaches 100% even with synthetic data alone. However, performance on minority classes could collapse entirely; e.g., df.

Ablation C: Impact of Using Static, Label-Only Prompts. Finally, we test the necessity of the rich prompts by replacing them with static, label-only prompts. In the synth-only setting, performance deteriorates markedly, with accuracy dropping to 32.4% on D7P (Table 3) and 17.6% on HAM (Table 4), with multiple classes exhibiting zero or near-zero precision. Even in the synth+real setting, performance lags behind the rich and balanced prompts configuration (Tables 1 and 2), demonstrating that label-only prompts lack the semantic richness needed to guide the diffusion model toward clinically meaningful generation.

3.6 Visualization Results

Figure 3 shows samples from LesionGen-R&B (top) and p-SOTA (bottom). Despite visual similarity, our method's superior classification performance suggests it captures subtle, clinically relevant features beyond human perception.

4 Conclusion

In this work, we demonstrate the effectiveness of combining text-to-image diffusion models with concept-guided dermatological prompts for generating high-quality synthetic skin lesion images. Unlike prior approaches that rely on simple label-based conditioning, our method leverages rich, structured descriptions aligned with clinical concepts, and balances class representation through prompt paraphrasing. This design enables the generation of semantically diverse and class-balanced datasets that complement real-world dermatology benchmarks. Training a ResNet18 on LesionGen's outputs significantly boosts classification performance, especially for underrepresented groups, outperforming the baselines. Future work includes expanding to skin tone diversity, interactive refinement, and multi-modal conditioning.

References

1. Akrout, M., et al.: Diffusion-based data augmentation for skin disease classification: impact across original medical datasets to fully synthetic images. In: MICCAI 2023, pp. 99–109. Springer, Cham (2023). https://doi.org/10.1007/978-3-031-53767-7_10
2. Bayasi, N., Du, S., Hamarneh, G., Garbi, R.: Continual-GEN: continual group ensembling for domain-agnostic skin lesion classification. In: Celebi, M.E., et al. (eds.) MICCAI 2023. LNCS, vol. 14393, pp. 3–13. Springer, Cham (2023). https://doi.org/10.1007/978-3-031-47401-9_1
3. Bayasi, N., Fayyad, J., Bissoto, A., Hamarneh, G., Garbi, R.: BiasPruner: debiased continual learning for medical image classification. In: Linguraru, M.G., et al. (eds.) MICCAI 2024. LNCS, vol. 15010, pp. 90–101. Springer, Cham (2024). https://doi.org/10.1007/978-3-031-72117-5_9
4. Bayasi, N., Hamarneh, G., Garbi, R.: Culprit-prune-net: efficient continual sequential multi-domain learning with application to skin lesion classification. In: de Bruijne, M., et al. (eds.) MICCAI 2021. LNCS, vol. 12907, pp. 165–175. Springer, Cham (2021). https://doi.org/10.1007/978-3-030-87234-2_16
5. Bayasi, N., Hamarneh, G., Garbi, R.: Continual-zoo: leveraging zoo models for continual classification of medical images. In: Proceedings of the IEEE/CVF Conference on Computer Vision and Pattern Recognition, pp. 4128–4138 (2024)
6. Chen, R., et al.: Eyediff: text-to-image diffusion model improves rare eye disease diagnosis. arXiv preprint arXiv:2411.10004 (2024)
7. De Wilde, B., Saha, A., de Rooij, M., Huisman, H., Litjens, G.: Medical diffusion on a budget: textual inversion for medical image generation. Med. Imaging Deep Learn. (MIDL) (2023)
8. Elkhayat, M., Mahmoud, M., Fayyad, J., Bayasi, N.: Foundation models as class-incremental learners for dermatological image classification. arXiv preprint arXiv:2507.14050 (2025)
9. Fayyad, J.: Out-of-distribution detection using inter-level features of deep neural networks. Ph.D. thesis, University of British Columbia (2023)
10. Fayyad, J., Alijani, S., Najjaran, H.: Empirical validation of conformal prediction for trustworthy skin lesions classification. Comput. Methods Programs Biomed. **253**, 108231 (2024)
11. Fayyad, J., Gupta, K., Mahdian, N., Gruyer, D., Najjaran, H.: Exploiting classifier inter-level features for efficient out-of-distribution detection. Image Vis. Comput. **142**, 104897 (2024)
12. He, K., Zhang, X., Ren, S., Sun, J.: Deep residual learning for image recognition. In: Proceedings of the IEEE Conference on Computer Vision and Pattern Recognition, pp. 770–778 (2016)
13. Ho, J., Jain, A., Abbeel, P.: Denoising diffusion probabilistic models. In: Advances in Neural Information Processing Systems (NeurIPS), vol. 33, pp. 6840–6851 (2020)
14. Jiang, L., Mao, Y., Wang, X., Chen, X., Li, C.: Cola-diff: conditional latent diffusion model for multi-modal MRI synthesis. In: Greenspan, H., et al. (eds.) MICCAI 2023. LNCS, vol. 14229, pp. 398–408. Springer, Cham (2023). https://doi.org/10.1007/978-3-031-43999-5_38
15. Kawahara, J., Daneshvar, S., Argenziano, G., Hamarneh, G.: Seven-point checklist and skin lesion classification using multitask multimodal neural nets. IEEE J. Biomed. Health Inform. **23**(2), 538–546 (2018)

16. Kui, X., et al.: Med-LVDM: medical latent variational diffusion model for medical image translation. Biomed. Signal Process. Control **106**, 107735 (2025)
17. Prusty, M.R., Sudharsan, R.M., Anand, P.: Enhancing medical image classification with generative AI using latent denoising diffusion probabilistic model and wiener filtering approach. Appl. Soft Comput. **161**, 111714 (2024)
18. Rombach, R., Blattmann, A., Lorenz, D., Esser, P., Ommer, B.: High-resolution image synthesis with latent diffusion models (2022)
19. Sagers, L.W., et al.: Augmenting medical image classifiers with synthetic data from latent diffusion models. arXiv preprint arXiv:2308.12453 (2023)
20. Schuhmann, C., et al.: Laion-5b: an open large-scale dataset for training next generation image-text models. Adv. Neural. Inf. Process. Syst. **35**, 25278–25294 (2022)
21. Tschandl, P., Rosendahl, C., Kittler, H.: The HAM10000 dataset, a large collection of multi-source dermatoscopic images of common pigmented skin lesions. Sci. Data **5**(1), 1–9 (2018)
22. Wang, X., Peng, Y., Lu, L., Lu, Z., Bagheri, M., Summers, R.M.: Chestx-ray8: Hospital-scale chest x-ray database and benchmarks on weakly-supervised classification and localization of common thorax diseases. In: Proceedings of the IEEE Conference on Computer Vision and Pattern Recognition, pp. 2097–2106 (2017)
23. Wu, J., et al.: Medsegdiff: medical image segmentation with diffusion probabilistic model. In: Medical Imaging with Deep Learning (MIDL), pp. 1623–1639 (2024)
24. Xie, J., et al.: Multi-disease detection in retinal images guided by disease causal estimation. In: Linguraru, M.G., et al. (eds.) MICCAI 2024. LNCS, vol. 15001, pp. 743–753. Springer, Cham (2024). https://doi.org/10.1007/978-3-031-72378-0_69
25. Yellapragada, S., Graikos, A., Prasanna, P., Kurc, T., Saltz, J., Samaras, D.: Pathldm: text conditioned latent diffusion model for histopathology. In: Proceedings of the IEEE/CVF Winter Conference on Applications of Computer Vision (WACV), pp. 5182–5191 (2024)

Fitzpatrick Thresholding for Skin Image Segmentation

Duncan Stothers[1(✉)]📷, Lia Gracey[2]📷, Sophia Xu[3], and Carlie Reeves[4]

[1] San Francisco, CA, USA
duncanstothers@alumni.harvard.edu
[2] Ascension Medical Group – Seton Dermatology, Austin, TX, USA
[3] Vagelos College of Physicians and Surgeons, Columbia University, New York, NY, USA
sx2400@cumc.columbia.edu
[4] University of Mississippi Medical Center, Jackson, MS, USA
CReeves4@umc.edu

Abstract. Accurate estimation of the body surface area (BSA) involved by a rash, such as psoriasis, is critical for assessing rash severity, selecting an initial treatment regimen, and following clinical treatment response. Attempts at segmentation of inflammatory skin disease such as psoriasis perform markedly worse on darker skin tones, potentially impeding equitable care. We assembled a psoriasis dataset sourced from six public atlases, annotated for Fitzpatrick skin type, and added detailed segmentation masks for every image. Reference models based on U-Net, ResU-Net, and SETR-small are trained without tone information. On the tuning split we sweep decision thresholds and select (i) global optima and (ii) per Fitzpatrick skin tone optima for Dice and binary IoU. Adapting Fitzpatrick specific thresholds lifted segmentation performance for the darkest subgroup (Fitz VI) by up to +31 % bIoU and +24 % Dice on UNet, with consistent, though smaller, gains in the same direction for ResU-Net (+25 % bIoU, +18 % Dice) and SETR-small (+17 % bIoU, +11 % Dice). Because Fitzpatrick skin tone classifiers trained on Fitzpatrick-17k now exceed 95 % accuracy, the cost of skin tone labeling required for this technique has fallen dramatically. Fitzpatrick thresholding is simple, model-agnostic, requires no architectural changes, no re-training, and is virtually cost free. We demonstrate the inclusion of Fitzpatrick thresholding as a potential future fairness baseline.

Keywords: Fitzpatrick · Psoriasis · Segmentation · BSA

1 Background

1.1 Significance

Skin rashes remain one of the most frequent reasons for new primary-care encounters, accounting for more than 13 million office visits annually in the

---

D. Stothers—Independent Researcher. Present address: Vancouver, Canada.

United States and rising [3]. Diagnostic accuracy is unevenly distributed: both practicing dermatologists and trainees perform noticeably worse on images of darker skin tones [4,8]. The accurate assessment of body surface area (BSA) affected by skin conditions, such as rashes, is crucial for clinical decision-making. Yet, physicians still rely on the outdated "1 palm = 1% BSA" method where BSA involved with a rash is estimated using the patient's palm size. This subjective measurement can lead to under- or over-treatment in the clinic. Additionally, a minimum threshold of BSA involvement is a criterion for payors in insurance coverage decisions, which makes accurate calculations imperative for a patient to be eligible for more advanced biologic treatments and for following treatment response. More specifically, BSA is an important calculation in the widely used Psoriasis Area and Severity Index that is most often deployed in clinical trial settings to assess baseline and treatment response for new therapeutics; these common measures are subjective and prone to human error [2]. No widely used tools exist to automate these important assessments in all skin types [16,21,26]. Any systematic error in segmenting lesions on dark skin therefore propagates directly into PASI scores, treatment eligibility, and ultimately patient outcomes.

1.2 Previous Work

Early ISIC Analyses Highlight Tone Bias. The first wave of ISIC challenge papers demonstrated that convolutional networks trained almost exclusively on Fitzpatrick I–III images attained dermatologist-level accuracy on similarly light-skinned test sets, yet their performance degraded noticeably on darker tones [11,13]. Follow-up studies on ISIC 2018, Fitzpatrick-17k, and DDI quantified AUROC and sensitivity gaps of 10–35 pp favoring light skin [5,11,13]. The consensus emerging from this literature is that distributional shift in pigmentation, not just lesion morphology, drives a substantial share of the error.

From Complex Debiasing Schemes to Stratified Operating Points. Most responses to the documented bias have focused on sophisticated data- or model-centric fixes—balanced resampling, adversarial representation learning, group-adaptive batch normalization, or fairness-guided pruning [17,24,25]. A conceptually simpler alternative, rooted in the equalized-odds post-processing of Hardt's 2016 approach [12], is to select a *separate decision threshold* for each Fitzpatrick group so that error rates align across tones.

The FPR–TPR Trade-Off in Binary Classification. Applying stratified thresholds to binary classification is not trivial: raising sensitivity for an underserved group often worsens its false-positive rate, and—by impossibility results—one cannot simultaneously satisfy perfect calibration and equalized odds once prevalence differs [14,18]. Consequently, dermatology researchers have tended to pursue fairness during training [17,24,25], where the utility–equity trade-off is perceived as more controllable, rather than post-hoc calibration.

Segmentation: A Setting Where Tone-Specific Optima Exist. Segmentation changes the landscape. Each image yields a dense probability map, and there is, in principle, a threshold that maximizes Dice or bIoU for every subgroup. If the score distributions for Fitzpatrick V–VI are shifted left—as empirical histograms repeatedly show [1] —a universal cut-off under-segments dark skin. Calibrating per-tone thresholds can therefore improve both subgroup Dice and *overall* performance, because each group operates closer to its own theoretical optimum. This observation motivates the present study, which evaluates Fitzpatrick-specific thresholding in the clinically consequential task of psoriasis BSA estimation.

1.3 Clinical Relevance of Precise BSA Estimation

Psoriasis management provides an ideal test-bed for tone-aware segmentation because small changes in the BSA assessment directly translate to different treatment pathways. The PASI scoring rubric weights percent-involved BSA in each anatomical region; a 5–10%-point error may erroneously move a patient into a different disease severity category. In a recent review of machine learning BSA estimators, skin tone discussion was omitted from all segmentation approaches [15], with the sole exception that in one study it was shown that error modes exist where healthy darker skin regions are sometimes mis-classified as lesional [10]. Demonstrating that Fitzpatrick-specific thresholding can reduce this bias would offer a pragmatic, model-agnostic fairness intervention with potential uses both in clinical trials and photo-based tele-dermatology.

2 Methodology

2.1 Data Collection

We assembled a large publicly available psoriasis dataset by sourcing from six open dermatology repositories: Derm Atlas Brazil [20], DermIS [7], DermNet NZ [22], the Hellenic Dermatology Atlas [6], the Interactive Dermatology Atlas [23], and Fitzpatrick-17k [11]. Subtypes of psoriasis that were excluded included pustular variants and isolated nail disease, filtered out by keyword rules and manual dermatologist review. Duplicates were removed, and patient IDs were assigned to prevent leakage between train, tune, and test sets. The final dataset contained 754 psoriasis images from 631 patients.

2.2 Skin-Tone Annotation and Segmentation Labels

Each retained image was independently labeled with a Fitzpatrick type (I–VI) by a board-certified dermatologist. Pixel-level diseased-skin masks were produced using the VIA Image Annotator tool [9]. Three assistants (medical student, resident physician, and graduate research assistant) drew initial polygon masks; a board-certified MD–PhD dermatologist specializing in psoriasis revised every mask to ensure high quality segmentation masks, especially on difficult cases such as low contrast lesions on darker skin tones (Fig. 1, Table 1).

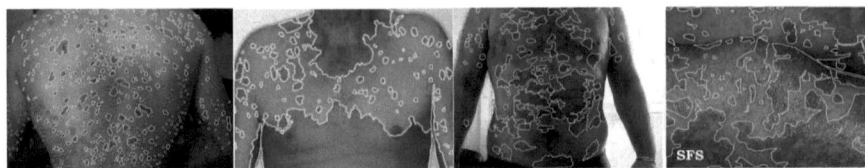

Fig. 1. Examples of high detail manual skin-disease labeling employed in the study.

Table 1. Per-dataset image counts by Fitzpatrick skin-type

Dataset	I	II	III	IV	V	VI	Total
Brazil	0	2	29	40	40	4	115
DermIS	22	67	2	3	3	0	97
DermNetNZ	27	171	68	32	7	5	310
Fitzpatrick 17k	35	57	8	11	7	1	119
Hellenic	1	29	16	6	0	0	52
Interactive	0	24	22	4	5	6	61
Column total	**85**	**350**	**145**	**96**	**62**	**16**	**754**

2.3 Data Split

Patient-level IDs were stratified by Fitzpatrick skin tone and, within each stratum, randomly permuted with a fixed seed (0). Stratified samples were then allocated to the training, tuning, and held-out test sets in a 30/30/40 proportion, ensuring balanced skin-tone representation and complete patient independence across partitions.

2.4 Model Architecture and Training Protocol

We benchmark three architectures chosen to represent successive stages in semantic segmentation design while remaining practical for a single-GPU medical study. U-Net [19] is the canonical encoder–decoder CNN against which most dermatology work is still compared. Our 256×256 implementation (four downsampling stages, two 3×3 convs per block, batch-norm everywhere) contains 31.1 trainable parameters and therefore serves as a strong, yet widely recognizable, baseline. Residual U-Net [27] keeps the same overall topology and feature widths but replaces each plain block with a pre-activation residual pair plus a squeeze-and-excite (SE) channel attention gate. These lightweight additions raise the capacity only marginally to 33.1 M parameters, letting us test whether better optimization and local attention alone can reduce skin-tone bias. Finally, a 21M parameter reference implementation of SETR-small [28] swaps the convolutional encoder for a ViT-S/16 backbone (12 transformer layers, 6 heads, 384-D embeddings; positional tokens only) followed by a one-layer up sampling head. Because the encoder is fully self-attentional and translation-equivariant only after training, SETR probes whether long-range context helps fairness on our limited psoriasis corpus. All three networks are trained with identical 256 × 256 inputs, vanilla SGD optimization with 0.9 momentum, learning rates of 0.01 for UNet and ResUNet (0.0004 for SETR for stability), an identical simple flip, rotate, and jitter data augmentation scheme, early-stopping watching the validation bIoU with a patience setting of 15, and an identical 3:1 weighted binary cross entropy + dice loss; thus any performance differences are most likely attributed to (i) architectural choice and (ii) the use of Fitz-specific versus global operating points, rather than to confounding hyper-parameter changes.

2.5 Operating-Point Search

To evaluate threshold sensitivity we swept decision cut-offs $\tau \in [0.001, 0.99]$ in steps of 0.001 on the *tuning* split and computed binary Intersection-over-Union (bIoU) and Dice:

$$\text{Dice}(\tau) = \frac{2\,|\hat{M}(\tau) \cap M|}{|\hat{M}(\tau)| + |M|}, \quad \text{bIoU}(\tau) = \frac{|\hat{M}(\tau) \cap M|}{|\hat{M}(\tau) \cup M|},$$

where M is the ground-truth mask and $\hat{M}(\tau) = \{\,p \geq \tau\,\}$. We recorded:

- Two *overall* optima, $\tau_{\text{all}}^{\text{Dice}}$ and $\tau_{\text{all}}^{\text{bIoU}}$, maximising performance across the entire tuning set.
- Twelve *tone-stratified* optima, $\tau_g^{\text{Dice}}, \tau_g^{\text{bIoU}}$ for $g \in \{\text{I}, \ldots, \text{VI}\}$, each maximising the metric within its Fitzpatrick subgroup.

All operating points were then frozen and evaluated once on the unseen test set to quantify gains from tone-specific calibration.

3 Results

Figure 2 plots validation bIoU and dice versus threshold for each tone. The curves illustrate a consistent left-shift for Fitzpatrick VI, explaining why the universal cut-off under-segments darker skin. The arrows mark the tone-specific optima chosen during calibration; note that lighter tones cluster around the global optimum, whereas tone VI requires substantially lower thresholds to maximize Dice (Table 2).

Figure 3 illustrates example Fitz VI images that visually illustrate how the lower Fitz VI optimized operating points captures significantly more of the diseased skin than the globally optimized operating point which is dominated by lighter skin tones.

Quantitative Improvements of Fitzpatrick Thresholding. In Table ?? we can see applying a single global threshold already yields reasonable performance for all three networks, but re-tuning the operating point for each Fitzpatrick subgroup uncovers systematic gains that disproportionately benefit the darkest

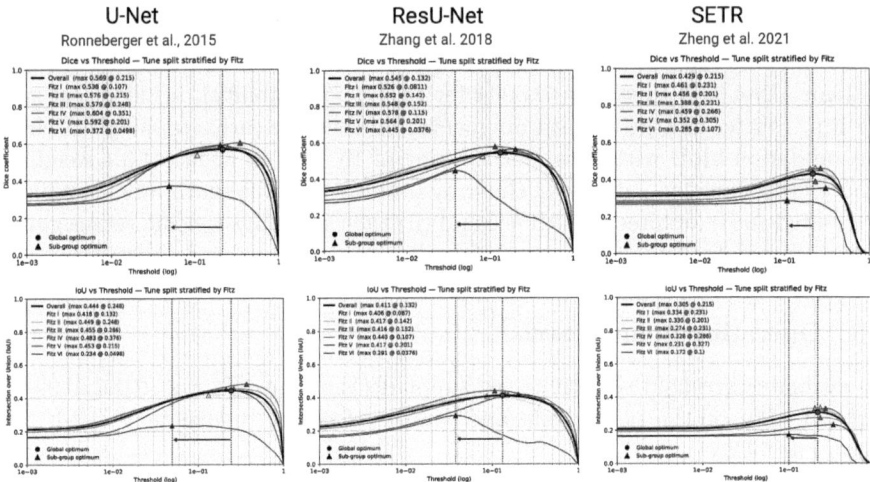

Fig. 2. Data plotted from the validation set. Arrows highlight that the optimal operating points for Fitz VI is consistently and significantly lower than for other Fitzpatrick tones. This observation is consistent between architectures: from all-conv UNet to all-attention SETR, as well as between metrics Dice (top row) and bIoU (bottom row). Fitz tones I-V have optimal operating points around the aggregate overall optimum which is shown in black.

Table 2. Segmentation performance by skin-tone subset. τ_g: global threshold; τ_F: Fitz-specific threshold.

Metric	Subset	U-Net			ResU-Net			SETR-small		
		τ_g	τ_F	Δ (%)	τ_g	τ_F	Δ (%)	τ_g	τ_F	Δ (%)
Dice	Overall	0.682	—	—	0.647	—	—	0.510	—	—
	Fitz I	0.569	0.575	+0.97	0.543	0.556	+2.41	0.472	0.470	−0.54
	Fitz II	0.584	0.584	0.00	0.587	0.585	−0.36	0.512	0.516	+0.66
	Fitz III	0.649	0.650	+0.05	0.619	0.622	+0.49	0.474	0.475	+0.26
	Fitz IV	0.691	0.657	−4.94	0.723	0.730	+1.03	0.597	0.575	−3.71
	Fitz V	0.557	0.563	+1.16	0.593	0.561	−5.26	0.449	0.442	−1.52
	Fitz VI	0.475	0.590	(+24.13)	0.556	0.656	(+18.01)	0.535	0.594	(+11.04)
bIoU	Overall	0.558	—	—	0.514	—	—	0.371	—	—
	Fitz I	0.424	0.434	+2.42	0.398	0.411	+3.24	0.338	0.336	−0.55
	Fitz II	0.457	0.457	0.00	0.454	0.452	−0.42	0.373	0.376	+0.92
	Fitz III	0.514	0.514	+0.01	0.478	0.480	+0.45	0.335	0.338	+0.72
	Fitz IV	0.564	0.530	−6.06	0.600	0.613	+2.31	0.456	0.438	−4.05
	Fitz V	0.414	0.424	+2.37	0.455	0.428	−6.00	0.311	0.306	−1.74
	Fitz VI	0.353	0.464	(+31.46)	0.423	0.527	(+24.63)	0.395	0.463	(+17.14)

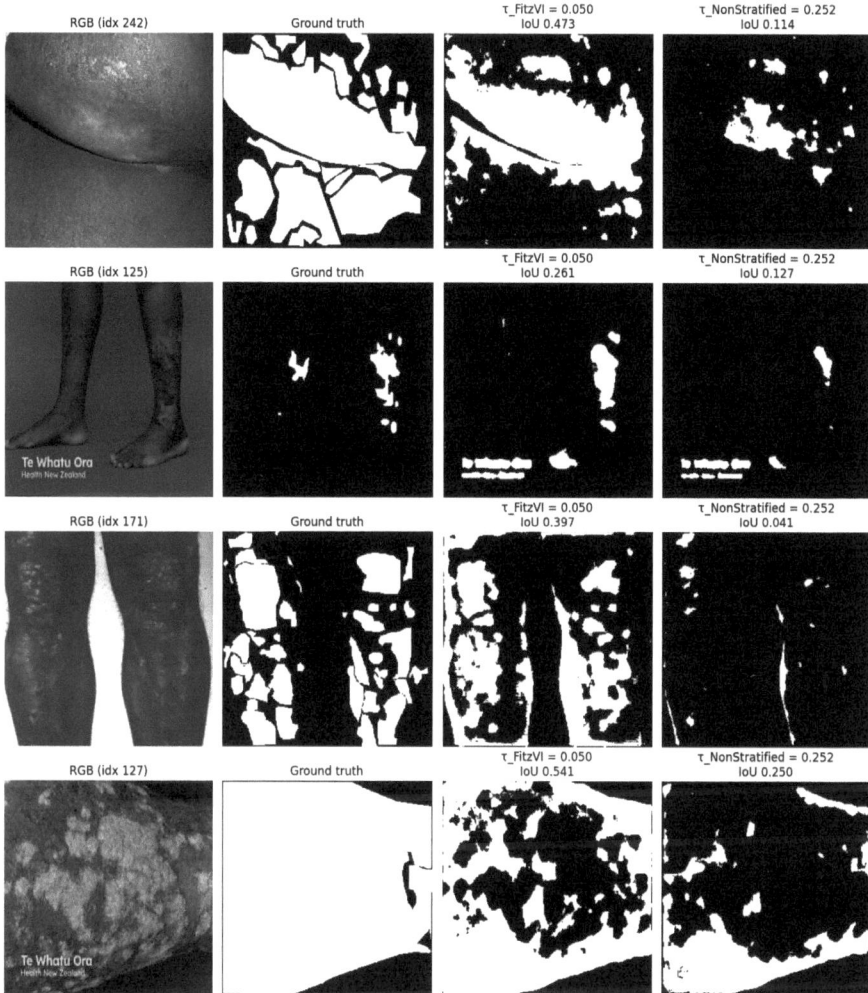

Fig. 3. The lower Fitz-VI optimized threshold (column 3) captures much more of the diseased skin than the global optimized operating point (column 4). Inference examples from U-Net.

skin tones. Because the Fitzpatrick specific operating points are only exercised within its own subgroup, the macro-average for both dice and bIoU across all tones moves minimally for every architecture.

4 Discussion

Labor Intensive Skin-Tone Annotation to Verify Equitable Stratified Performance Is No Longer a Bottleneck. Historically, per-image Fitzpatrick labels required labour-intensive, subjective grading by board-certified dermatologists—prohibitive for million-image repositories. The advent of high-accuracy tone classifiers trained on Fitzpatrick-17k that reach > 95% balanced accuracy in external validation across a broad cross section of dermatology diseases [11]. In practice, a lightweight classifier adds minimal inference time and can be applied retrospectively to every archive or even prospectively on-device.

A Practical Addition to the Fairness Toolbox. Per-group threshold calibration is an immediately deployable fairness lever—orthogonal to, and composable with, data balancing, representation alignment, FairAdaBN [25], or FairPrune [24]. We therefore recommend that future skin-segmentation studies:

1. Define in the metadata the skin tone of images in the pre-processing pipeline via an automated method such as a Fitzpatrick17k classifier.
2. Tune g on a validation split, or ideally on the set of predictions from a cross-fold validation.
3. Report both overall and tone-stratified metrics at those thresholds.

Either the stratified performance with the global threshold is equitable across skin tones, or it may not be, in which case Fitzpatrick thresholding provides a lever to lower the under performance as demonstrated here in psoriasis segmentation. Doing so requires no architectural change, no re-training, and negligible runtime overhead, yet—as shown here—can significantly increase performance on the darkest skin tones. Given its simplicity and efficacy, Fitzpatrick-specific thresholding could become a standard baseline for ISIC fairness tracks and for any clinical deployment of dermatology segmentation models.

Acknowledgments. No sponsoring company was involved in the production of this work.

Disclosure of Interests. The authors have no competing interests to declare that are relevant to the content of this article.

References

1. Benčević, M., Ljubić, A., Horvat, M., Zanchi, M.: Understanding skin colour bias in deep learning-based skin lesion segmentation. Comput. Methods Programs Biomed. **233**, 107593 (2024). https://doi.org/10.1016/j.cmpb.2024.107593
2. Bożek, A., Reich, A.: The reliability of three psoriasis assessment tools: psoriasis area and severity index, body surface area and physician global assessment. Adv. Clin. Exp. Med. **26**(5), 851–856 (2017). https://doi.org/10.17219/acem/69804
3. Centers for Disease Control and Prevention: NAMCS/NHAMCS — web tables. https://www.cdc.gov/nchs/ahcd/web_tables.htm
4. Daneshjou, R., et al.: Disparities in dermatology AI performance on a diverse, curated clinical image set. Sci. Adv. **8**(32), eabq6147 (2022). https://doi.org/10.1126/sciadv.abq6147
5. Daneshjou, R., et al.: Disparities in dermatology AI performance on a diverse, curated clinical image set. Science **376**(6594), 413–419 (2022). https://doi.org/10.1126/science.abj2097

6. of Dermatology, H.S., Venereology: Hellenic dermatological atlas. https://www.hellenicdermatlas.com/ (2025), online Greek atlas with 2 600+ annotated images. Accessed 8 Jul 2025
7. Department of Dermatology, U.o.E., of Heidelberg, U.: Dermis/dermatology information system. http://www.dermis.net/ (2025), dermatology Online Atlas (DOIA) with multilingual diagnostic database. Accessed 8 Jul 2025
8. Diao, J.A., Adamson, A.S.: Representation and misdiagnosis of dark skin in a large-scale visual diagnostic challenge. J. Am. Acad. Dermatol. **86**(4), 950–951 (2022). https://doi.org/10.1016/j.jaad.2021.03.088
9. Dutta, A., Zisserman, A.: The VIA annotation software for images, audio and video. In: Proceedings of the 27th ACM International Conference on Multimedia (MM '19). pp. 2276–2279. Association for Computing Machinery (2019). https://doi.org/10.1145/3343031.3350535, software https://www.robots.ox.ac.uk/~vgg/software/via/
10. George, Y., Aldeen, M., Garnavi, R.: Automatic psoriasis lesion segmentation in two-dimensional skin images using multiscale superpixel clustering. Journal of Medical Imaging 4(4), 044004 (2017). https://doi.org/10.1117/1.JMI.4.4.044004, https://doi.org/10.1117/1.JMI.4.4.044004, [PMC free article] [PubMed]
11. Groh, M., et al.: Evaluating deep neural networks trained on clinical images in dermatology with the fitzpatrick 17k dataset. In: IEEE/CVF Conference on Computer Vision and Pattern Recognition Workshops (CVPR W) 2021 – ISIC, pp. 364–373. IEEE (2021). https://doi.org/10.1109/CVPRW53098.2021.00041
12. Hardt, M., Price, E., Srebro, N.: Equality of opportunity in supervised learning. In: Advances in Neural Information Processing Systems (NeurIPS), vol. 29, pp. 3315–3323 (2016)
13. Kinyanjui, N.M., et al.: Fairness of classifiers across skin tones in dermatology. In: Martel, A.L., et al. (eds.) MICCAI 2020. LNCS, vol. 12266, pp. 320–329. Springer, Cham (2020). https://doi.org/10.1007/978-3-030-59725-2_31
14. Kleinberg, J., Mullainathan, S., Raghavan, M.: Inherent trade-offs in the fair determination of risk scores. In: Proceedings of the 8th Innovations in Theoretical Computer Science Conference (ITCS). pp. 43:1–43:23 (2017). https://doi.org/10.4230/LIPIcs.ITCS.2017.43
15. Li, H., Chen, G., Zhang, L., Xu, C., Wen, J.: A review of psoriasis image analysis based on machine learning. Frontiers in Medicine 11, 1414582 (2024). https://doi.org/10.3389/fmed.2024.1414582, https://doi.org/10.3389/fmed.2024.1414582
16. Mogawer, R.M., Mostafa, W.Z., Elmasry, M.F.: Comparative analysis of the body surface area calculation method used in vitiligo extent score vs the hand unit method used in vitiligo area severity index. J. Cosmet. Dermatol. **19**(10), 2679–2683 (2020). https://doi.org/10.1111/jocd.13311
17. Pakzad, M., Kawesh, O., Lohweg, V., Nazari, M.: CIRCLe: color invariant representation learning for unbiased classification of skin lesions. In: Computer Vision – ECCV 2022 Workshops (Skin Image Analysis) (2022). arXiv:2208.13528
18. Pleiss, G., Raghavan, M., Wu, F., Kleinberg, J., Weinberger, K.Q.: On fairness and calibration. In: Advances in Neural Information Processing Systems 30 (NeurIPS), pp. 5680–5689 (2017)
19. Ronneberger, O., Fischer, P., Brox, T.: U-Net: convolutional networks for biomedical image segmentation. In: Navab, N., Hornegger, J., Wells, W.M., Frangi, A.F. (eds.) MICCAI 2015. LNCS, vol. 9351, pp. 234–241. Springer, Cham (2015). https://doi.org/10.1007/978-3-319-24574-4_28

20. Silva, S.F.D.: Dermatology atlas brazil (atlas dermatológico) (2024). https://www.atlasdermatologico.com.br/. online atlas of 12 000+ clinical photographs. Accessed 8 Jul 2025
21. Silverberg, J.I., Lei, D., Yousaf, M., et al.: Measurement properties of the product of investigator's global assessment and body surface area in children and adults with atopic dermatitis. J. Eur. Acad. Dermatol. Venereol. **35**(1), 180–187 (2021). https://doi.org/10.1111/jdv.16846
22. Trust, D.N.Z.: Dermnet nz—the world's leading free dermatology resource (2025). https://dermnetnz.org/. over 25 000 high-resolution images and accompanying clinical topics. Accessed 8 Jul 2025
23. Usatine, R.P., Madden, B.D.: Interactive dermatology atlas. https://www.dermatlas.net/ (2025), 1 000+ photos cross-referenced by lesion attributes. Accessed 8 Jul 2025
24. Wu, Q., Li, J., Yu, B.W., Zhang, Y., Zhang, H., Xu, C.: Fairprune: achieving fairness through pruning for dermatological disease diagnosis. arXiv preprint arXiv:2203.02110 (2023)
25. Xu, C., Song, L., Zhang, X., Li, Q., Chen, C., Yan, S.: FairadaBN: mitigating unfairness with adaptive batch normalization in dermatological disease classification. In: Medical Image Computing and Computer Assisted Intervention – MICCAI 2023 (2023). arXiv:2303.08325
26. Yoo, K.H., Jeong, G.J., Park, J.H., Park, S.H., Li, K.S.: Estimation error of the body surface area in psoriasis: a comparative study of physician and computer-assisted image analysis (imagej). Clin. Exp. Dermatol. **47**(7), 1298–1306 (2022). https://doi.org/10.1111/ced.15148
27. Zhang, Z., Liu, Q., Wang, Y.: Road extraction by deep residual U-net. IEEE Geosci. Remote Sens. Lett. **15**(5), 749–753 (2018). https://doi.org/10.1109/LGRS.2018.2802944
28. Zheng, S., et al.: Rethinking semantic segmentation from a sequence-to-sequence perspective with transformers. In: Proceedings of the IEEE/CVF Conference on Computer Vision and Pattern Recognition (CVPR), pp. 6877–6886. IEEE (2021). https://doi.org/10.1109/CVPR46437.2021.00681

What Can We Learn from Inter-Annotator Variability in Skin Lesion Segmentation?

Kumar Abhishek[1]($\boxtimes$), Jeremy Kawahara[2], and Ghassan Hamarneh[1]

[1] School of Computing Science, Simon Fraser University, Burnaby, Canada
{kabhishe,hamarneh}@sfu.ca
[2] AIP Labs, Budapest, Hungary
jeremy@aip.ai

Abstract. Medical image segmentation exhibits intra- and inter-annotator variability due to ambiguous object boundaries, annotator preferences, expertise, and tools, among other factors. Lesions with ambiguous boundaries, e.g., spiculated or infiltrative nodules, or irregular borders per the ABCD rule, are particularly prone to disagreement and are often associated with malignancy. In this work, we curate IMA++, the largest multi-annotator skin lesion segmentation dataset, on which we conduct an in-depth study of variability due to annotator, malignancy, tool, and skill factors. We find a statistically significant ($p < 0.001$) association between inter-annotator agreement (IAA), measured using Dice, and the malignancy of skin lesions. We further show that IAA can be accurately predicted directly from dermoscopic images, achieving a mean absolute error of 0.108. Finally, we leverage this association by utilizing IAA as a "soft" clinical feature within a multi-task learning objective, yielding a 4.2% improvement in balanced accuracy averaged across multiple model architectures and across IMA++ and four public dermoscopic datasets. The code is available at https://github.com/sfu-mial/skin-IAV.

Keywords: dermatology · skin lesion segmentation · inter-rater variability · multi-task learning

1 Introduction

Medical image segmentation is a foundational task in modern healthcare, enabling precise quantitative analysis, the development of downstream diagnostic or prognostic models, and treatment planning [4]. However, the process of delineating structures in medical images, whether performed manually or semi-automatically, is prone to variability, leading to intra- and inter-annotator differences. The sources of this variability are multifactorial, including, but not limited to, ambiguous boundaries, varying interpretations of imaging characteristics, discrepancies in annotation protocols, and differences in annotator experience or skill levels. In clinical practice, lesions that lack well-defined boundaries and are therefore often difficult to segment, such as spiculated or infiltrative nodules, are often strongly associated with malignancy [16,37], suggesting that poorly-defined boundaries may be associated with the underlying disease severity.

Specific to skin image analysis, skin lesion segmentation (SLS) [7,18,30] can play an important role in computing segmentation-based clinical features (e.g., irregular borders in the ABCD [22] rule), where the presence of certain clinical features can be used to distinguish melanoma from benign lesions and enhance the interpretability of deep learning-based diagnosis methods [26,31]. However, reliably computing clinical features derived from lesion segmentations can be challenging due to annotator segmentation variability. For example, irregular borders or psuedopods, which are clinical features strongly associated with melanoma [21,44], can be difficult to delineate and may contribute to annotator variability. Thus, in this work, we hypothesize that the level of annotator (dis)agreement in SLS may itself be related to malignancy. Despite numerous works on modeling annotation styles [2,41,47], segmentation selection or aggregation [29,35,42], and studying variability in expert segmentations [13,24,34] and non-expert annotations of clinical features [9,33], no prior research has formally investigated if an association exists between the quantitative level of inter-annotator segmentation agreement (IAA) and lesion malignancy.

Addressing this gap, we first formally examine whether a systematic relationship exists between IAA levels and lesion malignancy. Using a newly curated dataset, IMA++, we demonstrate a significant association: malignant lesions exhibit systematically lower levels of IAA compared to benign lesions. Based on this observation, we treat the IAA as a type of clinical feature that quantifies how ambiguous a lesion is to annotate, which may serve as a proxy for existing clinical features (e.g., irregular border, pseudopods). Driven by this association, our next contribution seeks to predict per-image IAA scores directly from the dermoscopic image using deep regression models, avoiding the segmentation step and allowing us to leverage this signal without requiring multiple annotations during inference. Finally, motivated by multi-task learning's ability to enhance individual task performance [28,48], and following works that simultaneously predict diagnosis and associated clinical features, like the 7-point criteria to improve diagnostic accuracy and interpretability [20,26,31], our approach views IAA as a "soft" clinical feature. Unlike traditional multi-task methods that jointly predict the diagnosis with segmentation [38,45] or related clinical features such as ABCD [33] (which can be ambiguous due to inter-annotator differences), we hypothesize that training a model to learn the variability in human interpretation implicitly captures complex morphological characteristics indicative of malignancy, such as border irregularity and asymmetry, which are often difficult to formalize or are influenced by annotator subjectivity.

To summarize, we make the following contributions: **(1)** We curate, to our knowledge, the largest SLS dataset, IMA++, comprising 5111 masks from 15 unique annotators, and present the largest-scale study of intra- and inter-annotator variability in this context. **(2)** We empirically demonstrate, using rigorous statistical methods, that inter-annotator agreement (IAA) is significantly associated with lesion malignancy in IMA++. **(3)** We show that IAA

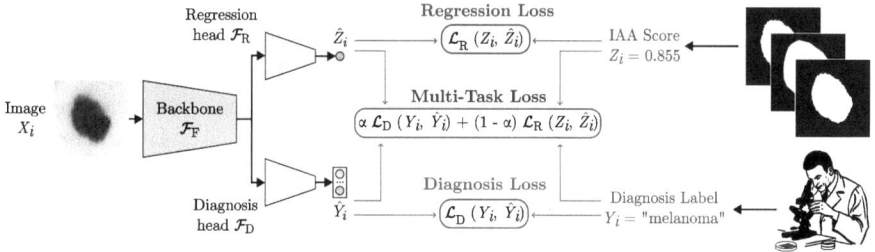

Fig. 1. Regression ($\mathcal{M}_1$), diagnosis-only ($\mathcal{M}_2$), and multi-task ($\mathcal{M}_{MT}$) models.

scores can be predicted, with reasonably low error, directly from image content alone, without requiring any segmentations at inference time. (4) We demonstrate, through extensive evaluation on multiple datasets, that multi-task models jointly predicting diagnosis and IAA outperform diagnosis-only models.

2 Methods

2.1 Agreement Distribution Shift Across Disease Classes

Let $(\mathcal{X}, \mathcal{Y}, \mathcal{S})$ denote a dataset of N images $\{X_i\}_{i=1}^N$, corresponding N diagnoses $\{Y_i\}_{i=1}^N$, and N sets of multiple segmentation masks $\mathcal{S} = \{\{S_{ik}\}_{k=1}^{K_i}\}_{i=1}^N$, where $K_i \geq 2$ is the number of masks for X_i. Let $\mathcal{Z} = \{Z_i\}_{i=1}^N$ be the set of corresponding inter-annotator agreement (IAA) scores, where $Z_i = g(\{S_{ik}\}) \in \mathbb{R}$ is computed per image based on the multiple segmentations, where $g(\cdot)$ uses either overlap-based (e.g., Dice similarity coefficient) or boundary-based (e.g., Hausdorff distance) metrics.

First, we wish to rigorously evaluate if there exists a systematic difference between the IAA scores for benign and malignant lesions. In particular, we examine the relationship between the probability of sampling a certain value from the IAA distribution of benign versus malignant lesions. To this end, we apply first-order stochastic dominance (FOSD) testing: a distribution $f_A(x)$ is said to first-order stochastically dominate a distribution $f_B(x)$, if $F_A(x) \leq F_B(x) \forall x$, with a strict inequality for some x, where $F_A(x)$ and $F_B(x)$ are the cumulative distribution functions (CDFs) of $f_A(x)$ and $f_b(x)$, respectively; loosely put, $f_A(x)$ is more likely to generate higher values of x than $f_B(x)$. This first-order stochastic dominance is denoted as $F_A \succeq_1 F_B$.

We define Z_{ben} and Z_{mal} as the subsets of IAA scores $\mathcal{Z}$ corresponding to benign and malignant lesions, respectively. We conduct two separate one-sided tests of FOSD [6]: (1) testing whether malignant Dice scores stochastically dominate benign scores, with the hypothesis $H_{\text{mal} \succeq_1 \text{ben}} : F_{\text{mal}}(x) \leq F_{\text{ben}}(x) \; \forall x$, and vice versa (2) testing whether benign scores stochastically dominate malignant, with the hypothesis $H_{\text{ben} \succeq_1 \text{mal}} : F_{\text{ben}}(x) \leq F_{\text{mal}}(x) \; \forall x$. As a complementary analysis, we also compare the two distributions using a Mann–Whitney U test [27].

2.2 Image-Based Prediction of Inter-annotator Agreement

Next, we examine the ability to predict the IAA score for an image based on the image content alone and without access to the corresponding segmentations during inference. Given an image X_i, we predict the target $\hat{Z}_i = \mathcal{M}_1(X_i; \Theta_F, \Theta_R)$, where $\mathcal{M}_1 = \mathcal{F}_R \circ \mathcal{F}_F$, $\circ$ denotes function composition, and $\mathcal{F}_F$ and $\mathcal{F}_R$ are the feature-extracting backbone and the regression head, parameterized by Θ_F and Θ_R, respectively (Fig. 1). The regression model $\mathcal{M}_1$ is trained by minimizing a regression loss $\mathcal{L}_R$:

$$\Theta_F^*, \Theta_R^* = \arg\min_{\Theta_F, \Theta_R} \sum_{i=1}^{N} \mathcal{L}_R(Z_i, \hat{Z}_i). \tag{1}$$

2.3 Integrating Inter-annotator Agreement and Diagnosis Prediction

Given an image X_i, a typical image-based diagnosis model $\mathcal{M}_2$ predicts $\hat{Y}_i = \mathcal{M}_2(X_i; \Theta_F, \Theta_D)$, where $\mathcal{M}_2 = \mathcal{F}_D \circ \mathcal{F}_F$, and $\mathcal{F}_D$ is the diagnosis head parameterized by Θ_D. The diagnosis model is optimized by minimizing a diagnosis (classification) loss $\mathcal{L}_D$:

$$\Theta_F^*, \Theta_D^* = \arg\min_{\Theta_F, \Theta_D} \sum_{i=1}^{N} \mathcal{L}_D(Y_i, \hat{Y}_i). \tag{2}$$

Finally, inspired by previous works on multi-task learning in medical imaging [48] and skin images in particular [1,20,33,38,45,46], we investigate whether simultaneous prediction of IAA and diagnosis improves the accuracy of the latter. To this end, we train $\mathcal{M}_{MT}$ to simultaneously predict $\hat{Y}_i$ and $\hat{Z}_i$ such that $(\hat{Y}_i, \hat{Z}_i) = \mathcal{M}_{MT}(X_i; \Theta_F, \Theta_D, \Theta_R)$, where $\mathcal{M}_{MT} = (\mathcal{F}_R \circ \mathcal{F}_F, \mathcal{F}_D \circ \mathcal{F}_F)$ is a multi-task prediction model with prediction heads for diagnosis (classification) and IAA score (regression) that share the same backbone (Fig. 1). $\mathcal{M}_{MT}$ is trained by minimizing a (weighted) sum of the two tasks' objectives:

$$\Theta_F^*, \Theta_D^*, \Theta_R^* = \arg\min_{\Theta_F, \Theta_D, \Theta_R} \sum_{i=1}^{N} \left[\alpha \cdot \mathcal{L}_D(Y_i, \hat{Y}_i) + (1 - \alpha) \cdot \mathcal{L}_R(Z_i, \hat{Z}_i) \right], \tag{3}$$

where α is a loss-weighting hyperparameter. Note that $\alpha = 0$ and $\alpha = 1$ are equivalent to regression-only ($\mathcal{M}_1$) and diagnosis-only ($\mathcal{M}_2$) models, respectively. More details about exact model architectures, losses (Eqs. 1, 2, 3), datasets, training, and evaluation are discussed in the next section.

3 Results and Discussion

3.1 Datasets and Analysis

A New Curated Dataset: Prior work on multi-annotator skin lesion segmentation has produced either **(a)** large datasets without annotator-level information

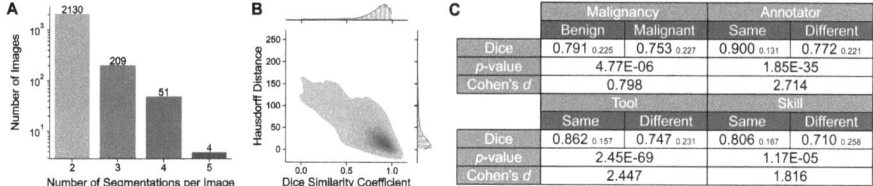

Fig. 2. IMA++ dataset statistics: (A) number of segmentations per image, (B) pairwise agreement metrics (Dice and Hausdoff distance), (C) intra- and inter-factor agreement (mean_{std. dev.} of Dice) with p-value and Cohen's d.

(e.g., Ribeiro et al. [34,35], Mirikharaji et al. [29]: 2223 images, 4647 total segmentations) or, (b) small datasets with annotator or style metadata (e.g., Zepf et al. [47]: 100 images, 300 total segmentations, 3 styles; Abhishek et al. [2]: 454 images, 1058 total segmentations, 10 unique annotators). In this work, we curate and publicly release a new dataset from the ISIC Archive, called **ISIC MultiAnnot++** (**IMA++** hereafter). It contains 2394 dermoscopic images segmented by 15 unique annotators, where 2130 images have 2 masks, 209 images have 3 masks, 51 images have 4 masks, and 4 images have 5 masks, resulting in a total of 5111 segmentation masks (Fig. 2). To the best of our knowledge, IMA++ is the largest public multi-annotator skin lesion segmentation dataset in terms of both mask and annotator counts.

Each mask contains information about the tool used: (T1) manual polygon tracing by a human expert, (T2) semi-automated flood-fill with expert-defined parameters, or (T3) a fully-automated segmentation reviewed and accepted by a human expert; and the skill level of the manual reviewer: (S1) expert or (S2) novice. We partition the images in IMA++ into training, validation, and testing splits in the ratio of 70:15:15, stratified by malignancy, number of segmentations per image, and Dice score range: low (< 0.5), medium, and high (> 0.8).

Calculation of IAA Scores: All images and binary segmentations are resized to 256×256. For each image X_i, we compute the Dice and Hausdorff distance between all $\binom{K_i}{2}$ unique pairs of segmentation masks (Fig. 2B shows the full distribution of pairwise scores). Although previous IAA studies have used Cohen's kappa [35] and Fleiss' kappa [2], these metrics measure categorical agreement and fail to capture spatial overlap between annotations; thus, we adopt the Dice metric, which is standard in IAA studies in medical imaging [3,17,36]. For each image, we average the pairwise Dice scores to obtain a single IAA score. Although most lesions tend to exhibit high agreement between annotators ([344, 818] out of 2394 images have Dice above [0.95, 0.90]), a notable subset shows poor agreement (23 images have 0 Dice), highlighting the wide range of inter-annotator agreement, and in line with the previous study by Ribeiro et al. [34].

Is Malignancy Associated with IAA? Figure 2C reveals a notable difference in IAA scores between benign and malignant lesions: benign lesions tend to exhibit higher Dice scores (0.791 ± 0.215 vs. 0.753 ± 0.227). However, a com-

Model	Params (M)	MACs (G)	MAE Benign	MAE Malignant	MAE Overall	MSE Benign	MSE Malignant	MSE Overall	p-value
VGG-16	14.72	15.36	0.118$_{0.166}$	0.134$_{0.188}$	0.121$_{0.171}$	0.027$_{0.059}$	0.035$_{0.077}$	0.029$_{0.064}$	1.54E-05
ResNet-18[†]	11.31	1.81	0.103$_{0.158}$	0.127$_{0.178}$	0.108$_{0.162}$	0.025$_{0.055}$	0.032$_{0.062}$	0.026$_{0.064}$	1.15E-08
ResNet-50	24.03	4.09	0.124$_{0.175}$	0.143$_{0.195}$	0.128$_{0.180}$	0.031$_{0.074}$	0.038$_{0.081}$	0.032$_{0.075}$	1.41E-37
MobileNetV2[†]	2.55	0.30	0.103$_{0.157}$	0.129$_{0.188}$	0.109$_{0.169}$	0.025$_{0.057}$	0.033$_{0.070}$	0.026$_{0.068}$	3.15E-15
MobileNetV3L	3.22	0.21	0.106$_{0.159}$	0.131$_{0.183}$	0.111$_{0.168}$	0.024$_{0.062}$	0.033$_{0.070}$	0.026$_{0.068}$	6.53E-09
DenseNet-121	7.22	2.83	0.131$_{0.188}$	0.141$_{0.191}$	0.133$_{0.184}$	0.033$_{0.074}$	0.037$_{0.080}$	0.034$_{0.076}$	5.21E-32
EfficientNet-B0	4.34	0.38	0.110$_{0.164}$	0.138$_{0.176}$	0.116$_{0.170}$	0.027$_{0.058}$	0.036$_{0.070}$	0.029$_{0.070}$	1.01E-15
EfficientNet-B1[†]	6.84	0.57	0.107$_{0.165}$	0.121$_{0.177}$	0.110$_{0.167}$	0.027$_{0.074}$	0.032$_{0.068}$	0.028$_{0.077}$	1.63E-07
ConvNeXt-T	28.02	4.47	0.130$_{0.195}$	0.155$_{0.207}$	0.135$_{0.199}$	0.039$_{0.105}$	0.048$_{0.100}$	0.041$_{0.108}$	2.62E-28
Swin-T	27.72	4.50	0.131$_{0.188}$	0.152$_{0.203}$	0.135$_{0.189}$	0.035$_{0.089}$	0.043$_{0.098}$	0.037$_{0.090}$	3.70E-37
SwinV2-T	27.78	5.96	0.127$_{0.188}$	0.155$_{0.207}$	0.133$_{0.198}$	0.039$_{0.105}$	0.048$_{0.102}$	0.041$_{0.104}$	6.02E-19
ViT-B/16	86.00	16.86	0.122$_{0.179}$	0.149$_{0.208}$	0.128$_{0.186}$	0.032$_{0.088}$	0.044$_{0.102}$	0.035$_{0.098}$	3.35E-22
ViT-B/32	87.65	4.37	0.129$_{0.181}$	0.149$_{0.202}$	0.133$_{0.188}$	0.033$_{0.080}$	0.041$_{0.091}$	0.035$_{0.085}$	15.94E-44

(a)   (b)

Fig. 3. Predicting inter-annotator agreement (Dice) on the proposed IMA++ dataset. (a) Quantitative results (mean$_{std.dev.}$ of MAE and MSE, and p-values for 13 model architectures ($\mathcal{M}_1$). [†] denotes top 3 models by overall MAE. (b) GradCAM++ saliency heatmaps from $\mathcal{M}_1$ (ResNet-18). Each image X_i shows corresponding overlaid segmentations $\{S_{ik}\}_{k=1}^{K_i}$ and (ground truth IAA Z_i, predicted IAA $\hat{Z}_i$) below the ISIC image ID.

parison of means alone can be misleading if the underlying distributions differ in shape or variance. To address this, we compared the full distributions of IAA scores for benign and malignant lesions using the Mann-Whitney U test, which confirmed that agreement is significantly higher for benign lesions ($p < 0.01$), suggesting greater annotator consensus in those cases.

Our FOSD tests (Sect. 2.1), conducted using PySDTest [23], reinforce this conclusion. Using 1,000 bootstrap resampling iterations at significance level $\alpha = 0.001$, we rejected the hypothesis that malignant lesions stochastically dominate benign ones ($H_{\text{mal} \succeq_1 \text{ben}}$, $p < 0.001$), while the reverse hypothesis ($H_{\text{ben} \succeq_1 \text{mal}}$) was not rejected ($p = 0.923$). Together, these results support that the distribution of inter-annotator agreement for benign lesions first-order stochastically dominates that for malignant lesions, indicating higher segmentation consensus for benign cases. This is likely due to benign lesions often exhibiting more well-defined, homogeneous boundaries, making them easier to segment consistently. In contrast, malignant lesions tend to be more heterogeneous in appearance and morphology, which likely contributes to higher annotation variability.

Impact of Other Annotation Factors on IAA: In addition to malignancy, Fig. 2C summarizes intra- and inter-factor-dependent IAA scores, along with corresponding Mann–Whitney U test p-values and Cohen's d [12] effect sizes. As expected, and consistent with findings in other medical imaging modalities [14,17], intra-annotator agreement is significantly higher than inter-annotator agreement. We also observe that segmentations performed using the same annotation tool tend to show higher agreement. Similarly, annotators with the same skill level exhibit greater consistency, particularly in the case of malignant lesions. To our knowledge, this represents the largest study of annotator variability in skin lesion segmentation to date in terms of dataset size, substantially exceeding the scale of prior work [13,24,32,34,35,40].

Table 1. Comparing the diagnostic performance of $\mathcal{M}_2$ to $\mathcal{M}_{\mathrm{MT}}$ on IMA++ for different values of α (Eq. 3). $\alpha = 0.9$ performs the best across all architectures.

		ResNet-18		MobileNetV2		EfficientNet-B1	
		Bal. Acc.	AUROC	Bal. Acc.	AUROC	Bal. Acc.	AUROC
Diagnosis Only ($\mathcal{M}_2$)		$0.746_{0.008}$	$0.835_{0.003}$	$0.757_{0.009}$	$0.843_{0.004}$	$0.746_{0.009}$	$0.827_{0.001}$
Multi-Task Learning ($\mathcal{M}_{\mathrm{MT}}$)	$\alpha = 0.1$	$0.711_{0.009}$	$0.785_{0.001}$	$0.748_{0.003}$	$0.859_{0.001}$	$0.744_{0.016}$	$0.826_{0.018}$
	$\alpha = 0.2$	$0.723_{0.009}$	$0.822_{0.002}$	$0.740_{0.007}$	$0.857_{0.035}$	$0.750_{0.000}$	$0.853_{0.002}$
	$\alpha = 0.5$	$0.750_{0.004}$	$0.852_{0.006}$	$0.785_{0.006}$	$0.869_{0.006}$	$0.738_{0.010}$	$0.869_{0.003}$
	$\alpha = 0.8$	$0.757_{0.004}$	$0.852_{0.001}$	$0.797_{0.011}$	$0.879_{0.002}$	$0.767_{0.007}$	$0.873_{0.001}$
	$\alpha = 0.9$	$0.765_{0.002}$	$0.869_{0.002}$	$0.805_{0.004}$	$0.882_{0.001}$	$0.772_{0.009}$	$0.878_{0.003}$

Other Datasets: In addition to IMA++, we also conduct experiments on 4 other dermoscopic image datasets: PH^2 [5], derm7pt [20], ISIC 2018 [10,39], ISIC 2019 [11,19,39]. We use the standardized partitions for ISIC 2018, 2019, and split PH^2 and derm7pt into train:valid:test in 70:15:15 ratio stratified by diagnosis.

All models were trained on an Ubuntu 20.04 workstation with AMD Ryzen 9 5950X, 32 GB RAM, NVIDIA RTX 3090 with Python 3.10.18 and PyTorch 2.7.1. All reported metrics are mean$_{std.\ dev.}$ over 3 runs with different seeds. All trained models and code are available at https://github.com/sfu-mial/skin-IAV.

3.2 Image-Based Prediction of Inter-annotator Agreement

To directly predict IAA scores from images (Sect. 2.2), we evaluate 13 architectures spanning CNNs and Transformers, covering a wide range of capacities in terms of parameters and multiply-accumulate operations (MACs). Each model uses the backbone as a feature extractor with a regression head: `Linear(256)` → `BatchNorm1D` → `ReLU` → `Dropout(0.5)` → `Linear(1)`. All models were trained for 50 epochs using SGD (momentum = 0.9, weight decay = 1e-4, batch size = 32, learning rate = 1e-2 decayed ×0.1 every 10 epochs). We use Smooth-L_1 loss [15] as $\mathcal{L}_\mathrm{R}$, selecting the model with the lowest validation MAE. Results are reported in terms of MAE, MSE, and Mann–Whitney U test p-values (Fig. 3a).

All models achieve good predictive performance (MAE $\in [0.10, 0.135]$), suggesting that IAA scores can be inferred from image content alone. Grad-CAM++ [8] visualizations (Fig. 3b) for the best model (ResNet-18) confirm saliency focused on the lesions and their boundaries. Notably, the third malignant example shows the model correctly localizing the lesion and predicting a plausible IAA (0.635), despite the "true" IAA being 0.0, highlighting label noise rather than prediction error. For all subsequent analyses, we use the top 3 performing architectures: ResNet-18, MobileNetV2, and EfficientNet-B1.

Table 2. Evaluating generalization performance on four other dermoscopic image datasets with 3 model architectures ($\mathcal{M}_{\text{MT}}$ with α set to 0.9 based on Table 1).

		ResNet-18		MobileNetV2		EfficientNet-B1	
		Bal. Acc.	AUROC	Bal. Acc.	AUROC	Bal. Acc.	AUROC
PH^2	Diag. Only ($\mathcal{M}_2$)	$0.938_{0.000}$	$0.988_{0.000}$	$0.943_{0.033}$	$0.988_{0.007}$	$0.870_{0.009}$	$0.979_{0.002}$
	Multi-Task ($\mathcal{M}_{\text{MT}}$)	$0.979_{0.009}$	$0.992_{0.000}$	$0.979_{0.009}$	$0.999_{0.002}$	$0.964_{0.009}$	$0.984_{0.004}$
derm7pt	Diag. Only ($\mathcal{M}_2$)	$0.734_{0.009}$	$0.836_{0.009}$	$0.654_{0.007}$	$0.800_{0.003}$	$0.756_{0.037}$	$0.862_{0.015}$
	Multi-Task ($\mathcal{M}_{\text{MT}}$)	$0.748_{0.005}$	$0.846_{0.001}$	$0.792_{0.012}$	$0.887_{0.002}$	$0.774_{0.011}$	$0.861_{0.003}$
ISIC 2018	Diag. Only ($\mathcal{M}_2$)	$0.744_{0.005}$	$0.893_{0.002}$	$0.727_{0.007}$	$0.872_{0.000}$	$0.713_{0.066}$	$0.868_{0.002}$
	Multi-Task ($\mathcal{M}_{\text{MT}}$)	$0.752_{0.003}$	$0.898_{0.001}$	$0.745_{0.007}$	$0.903_{0.003}$	$0.753_{0.012}$	$0.885_{0.047}$
ISIC 2019	Diag. Only ($\mathcal{M}_2$)	$0.670_{0.004}$	$0.853_{0.002}$	$0.623_{0.004}$	$0.849_{0.001}$	$0.657_{0.009}$	$0.869_{0.003}$
	Multi-Task ($\mathcal{M}_{\text{MT}}$)	$0.698_{0.003}$	$0.881_{0.001}$	$0.716_{0.023}$	$0.890_{0.002}$	$0.667_{0.006}$	$0.873_{0.001}$

3.3 Integrating Inter-annotator Agreement and Diagnosis Prediction

Finally, we leverage this link between malignancy and inter-annotator agreement and investigate whether jointly learning to predict IAA improves diagnostic performance (Sect. 2.3) by comparing diagnosis-only models ($\mathcal{M}_2$) with multi-task models ($\mathcal{M}_{\text{MT}}$). As before, we use Smooth-L_1 loss for $\mathcal{L}_{\text{R}}$ and focal loss [25] for $\mathcal{L}_{\text{D}}$. The multi-task architecture shares a common backbone and employs two heads: a regression head (as in Sect. 3.2) and a classification head (Linear(256) → BatchNorm1D → ReLU → Dropout(0.5) → Linear(n_{classes})). To study the impact of loss weighting, we vary α in Eq. 3, assigning lower ($\alpha \in \{0.1, 0.2\}$), equal ($\alpha = 0.5$), and higher ($\alpha \in \{0.8, 0.9\}$) emphasis on the diagnosis loss $\mathcal{L}_{\text{D}}$. All models are trained under the same setup as Sect. 3.2, except we select the model with the highest balanced accuracy on the validation set. We report balanced accuracy and AUROC in Table 1. Across all architectures, we find that $\alpha = 0.9$ yields the best diagnostic performance. Moreover, multi-task models ($\mathcal{M}_{\text{MT}}$) with equal or greater emphasis on $\mathcal{L}_{\text{D}}$ ($\alpha \geq 0.5$) consistently outperform diagnosis-only models ($\mathcal{M}_2$), confirming our hypothesis that inter-annotator agreement prediction serves as a beneficial auxiliary task for diagnosis.

To assess generalizability, we fine-tune the $\mathcal{M}_2$ and $\mathcal{M}_{\text{MT}}$ models (trained on IMA++ with $\alpha = 0.9$ for $\mathcal{M}_{\text{MT}}$) on external datasets: PH^2, derm7pt, ISIC 2018, and ISIC 2019. Since these datasets lack multiple annotations and thus have no IAA labels, we freeze the regression head of $\mathcal{M}_{\text{MT}}$ before fine-tuning. Fine-tuning is conducted for 15 epochs using SGD (momentum = 0.9, weight decay = 1e-4, batch size = 32, learning rate = 1e-3 with ×0.1 decay every 3 epochs). Results in Table 2 show that $\mathcal{M}_{\text{MT}}$ outperforms $\mathcal{M}_2$ across all datasets and architectures, suggesting that the performance gains from learning to predict IAA on IMA++ may be transferable to new datasets.

4 Conclusion

We studied the problem of inter-annotator agreement (IAA) for skin lesion segmentation, and demonstrated, through agreement metrics and statistical tests, a clear relationship between IAA and malignancy. We showed that IAA can be predicted from image content alone. Across five dermoscopic datasets, we further showed that incorporating IAA prediction as an auxiliary task in a multi-task diagnosis model improves performance over diagnosis-only models. To support this study, we curated IMA++, the largest publicly available multi-annotator skin lesion segmentation dataset, in terms of both the number of segmentations and unique annotators. To our knowledge, this is the most extensive IAA study in skin image analysis. Future work would assess how to test for null of non-dominance against dominance [43], evaluate other boundary-based metrics such as Hausdorff distance and boundary-F1 score, explore groupwise IAA measures instead of the pairwise measures: Dice and Hausdorff distance, and examine how inter-annotator variability impacts the ABCD score.

Acknowledgments. The authors are grateful for the computational resources provided by NVIDIA Corporation and Digital Research Alliance of Canada (formerly Compute Canada). Partial funding for this project was provided by the Natural Sciences and Engineering Research Council of Canada (NSERC RGPIN/06752-2020).

Disclosure of Interests. The authors have no competing interests to declare.

References

1. Abhishek, K., et al.: Predicting the clinical management of skin lesions using deep learning. Sci. Rep. (2021)
2. Abhishek, K., et al.: Segmentation style discovery: Application to skin lesion images. In: MICCAI ISIC (2024). https://doi.org/10.1007/978-3-031-77610-6_3
3. Ahamed, S., et al.: Comprehensive evaluation and insights into the use of deep neural networks to detect and quantify lymphoma lesions in PET/CT images. arXiv preprint arXiv:2311.09614 (2023)
4. Asgari Taghanaki, S., et al.: Deep semantic segmentation of natural and medical images: a review. Artif. Intell. Rev. (2021)
5. Ballerini, L., et al.: A color and texture based hierarchical K-NN approach to the classification of non-melanoma skin lesions. In: Color Medical Image Analysis (2013)
6. Barrett, G.F., et al.: Consistent tests for stochastic dominance. Econometrica (2003)
7. Celebi, M.E., et al.: A state-of-the-art survey on lesion border detection in dermoscopy images. Dermoscopy Image Analis (2015)
8. Chattopadhay, A., et al.: Grad-CAM++: Generalized gradient-based visual explanations for deep convolutional networks. In: WACV (2018)
9. Cheplygina, V., Pluim, J.P.W.: Crowd disagreement about medical images is informative. In: Stoyanov, D., et al. (eds.) LABELS/CVII/STENT -2018. LNCS, vol. 11043, pp. 105–111. Springer, Cham (2018). https://doi.org/10.1007/978-3-030-01364-6_12

10. Codella, N., et al.: Skin lesion analysis toward melanoma detection 2018: A challenge hosted by the international skin imaging collaboration (ISIC). arXiv preprint arXiv:1902.03368 (2019)
11. Codella, N.C., et al.: Skin lesion analysis toward melanoma detection: a challenge at the 2017 international symposium on biomedical imaging (ISBI), hosted by the international skin imaging collaboration (ISIC). In: ISBI (2018)
12. Cohen, J.: Statistical Power Analysis for the Behavioral Sciences. Routledge (2013)
13. Fortina, A.B., et al.: Where's the Naevus? Inter-operator variability in the localization of melanocytic lesion border. Skin Res. Technol. (2012)
14. Fu, M.C., et al.: Interrater and intrarater agreements of magnetic resonance imaging findings in the lumbar spine: significant variability across degenerative conditions. Spine J. (2014)
15. Girshick, R.: Fast R-CNN. In: ICCV (2015)
16. Griff, S.K., et al.: Chapter 16 - breast cancer. In: Bragg, D.G., et al. (eds.) Oncologic Imaging (2002). https://doi.org/10.1016/B0-72-167494-1/50019-0
17. Gut, D., et al.: Use of superpixels for improvement of inter-rater and intra-rater reliability during annotation of medical images. Med Image Anal (2024)
18. Hasan, M.K., et al.: A survey, review, and future trends of skin lesion segmentation and classification. Comput. Biol. Med. (2023)
19. Hernández-Pérez, C., et al.: BCN20000: dermoscopic lesions in the wild. Sci. Data (2024)
20. Kawahara, J., et al.: Seven-point checklist and skin lesion classification using multitask multimodal neural nets. IEEE J. Biomed. Health Inform. (2018)
21. Kaya, S., et al.: Abrupt skin lesion border cutoff measurement for malignancy detection in dermoscopy images. BMC Bioinform. (2016)
22. Korotkov, K., et al.: Computerized analysis of pigmented skin lesions: a review. Artif. Intell. Med. (2012)
23. Lee, K., et al.: PySDTest: a Python/Stata package for stochastic dominance tests. arXiv preprint arXiv:2307.10694 (2023)
24. Li, X., et al.: Estimating the ground truth from multiple individual segmentations with application to skin lesion segmentation. In: MIUA (2010)
25. Lin, T.Y., et al.: Focal loss for dense object detection. In: ICCV (2017)
26. Lucieri, A., et al.: ExAID: a multimodal explanation framework for computer-aided diagnosis of skin lesions. Comput. Methods Programs Biomed. (2022)
27. Mann, H.B., et al.: On a test of whether one of two random variables is stochastically larger than the other. Ann. Math. Stat. (1947)
28. Maurer, A., et al.: The benefit of multitask representation learning. J. Mach. Learn. Res. (2016)
29. Mirikharaji, Z., et al.: D-LEMA: deep learning ensembles from multiple annotations-application to skin lesion segmentation. In: CVPR ISIC (2021)
30. Mirikharaji, Z., et al.: A survey on deep learning for skin lesion segmentation. Med, Image Anal. (2023)
31. Patrício, C., et al.: Coherent concept-based explanations in medical image and its application to skin lesion diagnosis. In: CVPR SAIAD (2023)
32. Peruch, F., et al.: Simpler, faster, more accurate melanocytic lesion segmentation through MEDS. IEEE Trans. Biomed. Eng. (2013)
33. Raumanns, R., et al.: ENHANCE (enriching health data by annotations of crowd and experts): a case study for skin lesion classification. Mach. Learn. Biomed. Imaging (2021)
34. Ribeiro, V., et al.: Handling inter-annotator agreement for automated skin lesion segmentation. arXiv preprint arXiv:1906.02415 (2019)

35. Ribeiro, V., et al.: Less is more: sample selection and label conditioning improve skin lesion segmentation. In: CVPR ISIC (2020)
36. Sampat, M.P., et al.: Measuring intra-and inter-observer agreement in identifying and localizing structures in medical images. In: ICIP (2006)
37. Sohns, C., et al.: Value of the BI-RADS classification in MR-mammography for diagnosis of benign and malignant breast tumors. Eur. Radiol. (2011)
38. Song, L., et al.: An end-to-end multi-task deep learning framework for skin lesion analysis. IEEE J. Biomed. Health Inform. (2020)
39. Tschandl, P., et al.: The HAM10000 dataset, a large collection of multi-source dermatoscopic images of common pigmented skin lesions. Sci. Data (2018)
40. Tschandl, P., et al.: Domain-specific classification-pretrained fully convolutional network encoders for skin lesion segmentation. Comput. Biol. Med. (2019)
41. Wang, J., et al.: Contour-aware multi-expert model for ambiguous medical image segmentation. IEEE Trans. Med. Imaging (2025)
42. Wang, S., et al.: MSE-Nets: multi-annotated semi-supervised ensemble networks for improving segmentation of medical image with ambiguous boundaries. arXiv preprint arXiv:2311.10380 (2023)
43. Whang, Y.J.: Econometric analysis of stochastic dominance: concepts, methods, tools, and applications (2019)
44. Williams, N.M., et al.: Assessment of diagnostic accuracy of dermoscopic structures and patterns used in melanoma detection: a systematic review and meta-analysis. JAMA Dermatol. (2021)
45. Xie, Y., et al.: A mutual bootstrapping model for automated skin lesion segmentation and classification. IEEE Trans. Med. Imaging (2020)
46. Yang, X., et al.: A novel multi-task deep learning model for skin lesion segmentation and classification. arXiv preprint arXiv:1703.01025 (2017)
47. Zepf, K., et al.: That label's got style: handling label style bias for uncertain image segmentation. arXiv preprint arXiv:2303.15850 (2023)
48. Zhao, Y., et al.: Multi-task deep learning for medical image computing and analysis: a review. Comput. Biol. Med. (2023)

Topology-Aware Deep Models for Skin Lesion Classification

Sayoni Chakraborty, Philmore Koung, and Baris Coskunuzer[✉]

Department of Mathematical Sciences, University of Texas at Dallas, Richardson, TX 75080, USA
{sayoni.chakraborty,philmore.koung,coskunuz}@utdallas.edu

Abstract. Skin cancer is among the most prevalent and potentially deadly cancers worldwide, with early detection essential for effective treatment, particularly for aggressive types such as melanoma. Deep learning (DL) models have shown strong performance in skin lesion classification tasks, yet they often struggle to capture the complex geometric and topological structures present in dermoscopic images. In this study, we propose a hybrid classification framework that combines topological descriptors with CNNs and Vision Transformers to improve diagnostic performance across multiple categories of skin lesions. By extracting topological signatures, we quantify shape and connectivity patterns that are often overlooked by standard convolutional neural networks. Our experiments in multiple publicly available dermatology datasets demonstrate that topological models perform competitively on their own, and their integration with DL models consistently improves classification metrics. These results establish topological features as a valuable complement to deep learning in the diagnosis of skin cancer.

Keywords: Topological data analysis · Cubical Persistence · Skin cancer detection · Dermoscopic image analysis · CNNs · Vision Transformers

1 Introduction

Skin cancer is one of the most common and potentially lethal malignancies worldwide, making early and accurate detection crucial for reducing morbidity and mortality. Clinical decision support systems (CDSS) powered by machine learning (ML) have shown great promise in automating the analysis of dermoscopic images, with deep learning (DL) models achieving dermatologist-level performance in various lesion classification tasks [15,35]. However, these conventional DL approaches are based primarily on pixel-level features and often do not fully capture the complex shape and boundary patterns that distinguish malignant from benign lesions [15].

S. Chakraborty and P. Koung—Equal contribution.

Topological data analysis (TDA) offers a complementary perspective by extracting robust scale-invariant descriptors of the geometric and connectivity structure of an image [5]. Persistent homology, in particular, encodes how features such as connected components and holes evolve across intensity thresholds, producing high-dimensional topological signatures that are insensitive to changes in noise and illumination. Recent work has demonstrated the utility of TDA in medical imaging contexts such as tumor margin delineation and histopathology analysis [16].

In this paper, we bring together the strengths of TDA and DL in a unified CDSS for skin cancer detection. We extract persistence-based features from dermoscopic images of multiple types of lesion, including melanoma, basal cell carcinoma, squamous cell carcinoma, and benign nevi, and evaluate both standalone topological classifiers and their integration with state-of-the-art convolutional and transformer-based architectures. By encoding the persistence diagrams as sequential inputs to a transformer, we leverage its capacity to model long-range dependencies among topological events.

Our contributions can be summarized as follows:

- We present the first comprehensive evaluation of topological data analysis for automated skin lesion classification across multiple cancerous and benign categories.
- We propose a novel fusion strategy that encodes persistence outputs as sequences and integrates them with transformers to capture global topological interactions.
- We show that topological models rival conventional DL methods and that combining them with CNNs and ViTs consistently improves classification performance.
- Our results highlight the potential of topological features to enhance the accuracy and robustness of deep learning-based CDSS for skin cancer detection.

2 Related Work

Machine Learning Methods in Skin Cancer Detection. Machine learning and deep learning have revolutionized automated skin lesion analysis. Esteva et al. trained a CNN on over 100 000 clinical and dermoscopic images to match expert performance across more than a dozen lesion categories [13]. Subsequent work fine-tuned ImageNet-pretrained ResNets for marked accuracy gains [27], confirmed cross-cohort robustness [3], and leveraged large benchmarks like HAM10000 alongside ensemble methods to boost generalization [15,36]. Despite these advances, challenges persist in data heterogeneity, interpretability, and clinical integration [28]. Recent strategies include fusing dermoscopy with patient metadata for better risk stratification [20] and adopting transformer-based models to capture global context [38]. Yet most approaches remain pixel-centric, and the use of topological data analysis to encode shape and connectivity is still largely unexplored in skin cancer diagnostics.

Topological Machine Learning in Medical Image Analysis. Persistent homology (PH) offers robust, shape-based descriptors that are resilient to noise and photometric variation, making it a powerful tool in medical imaging. PH-based features have been applied in diverse biomedical contexts, including modeling cell development [24], delineating tumor margins [29], analyzing brain connectivity [30], and extracting multiscale genomic signatures [22]. For a broader overview, see Skaf et al. [33]. Recently, *topological deep learning* has emerged as a paradigm for integrating persistence features into neural networks. Architectures by [1,16] embed persistence summaries to improve segmentation [19,32] and classification [6,18]. We extend this framework to skin cancer detection, extracting PH from dermoscopic images and evaluating both standalone and hybrid models combining PH with CNNs and ViTs. Although prior studies have applied TDA to melanoma detection [8,23], this work presents the first comprehensive evaluation of topological descriptors for skin lesion classification, demonstrating both competitive standalone performance and consistent enhancement of deep learningâĂŞbased diagnostics.

3 Methodology

Our methodology involves two key steps. First, we extract topological feature vectors from dermascopic images. Then, we evaluate their standalone performance in ML models and integrate them with the latest DL models to assess their impact on improving SOTA performance.

3.1 Topological Feature Vectors for Dermascopic Images

PH is a powerful mathematical tool in TDA for analyzing complex data structures. It identifies hidden patterns at multiple resolutions and effectively extracts features from various data formats, including point clouds and networks [9]. This paper focuses on its application in image analysis, specifically *cubical persistence*, a variant of PH. While we provide an accessible overview, deeper insights can be found in [11]. PH follows a three-step procedure:

- **Filtration**: Inducing a sequence of nested topological spaces from the data.
- **Persistence Diagrams**: Recording the topological changes within this sequence.
- **Vectorization**: Converting these diagrams into vectors to be utilized in ML models.

Step 1 - Constructing Filtrations. Since PH essentially functions as a mechanism for monitoring the progression of topological characteristics within a sequence of simplicial complexes, constructing this sequence stands out as a crucial step. In image analysis, the common approach is to generate a nested sequence of binary images, also known as *cubical complexes*. To achieve this from a given color (or grayscale) image $\mathcal{X}$ (with dimensions $r \times s$), one needs to select a specific color

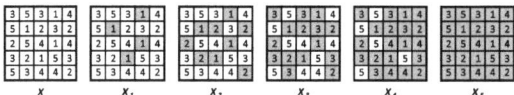

Fig. 1. For the 5×5 image $\mathcal{X}$ with the given pixel values, **the sublevel filtration** is the sequence of binary images $\mathcal{X}_1 \subset \mathcal{X}_2 \subset \cdots \subset \mathcal{X}_5$.

channel (e.g., red, blue, green, or grayscale). The color values γ_{ij} of individual pixels $\Delta_{ij} \subset \mathcal{X}$ are then utilized. Specifically, for a sequence of color values $(0 = t_1 < t_2 < \cdots < t_N = 255)$,
a nested sequence of binary images $\mathcal{X}_1 \subset \mathcal{X}_2 \subset \cdots \subset \mathcal{X}_N$ is obtained, where $\mathcal{X}_n = \{\Delta_{ij} \subset \mathcal{X} \mid \gamma_{ij} \leq t_n\}$ (See Fig. 1). In particular, this involves starting with a blank $r \times s$ image and progressively activating (coloring black) pixels as their grayscale values reach the specified threshold t_n. This process, known as *sublevel filtration*, is conducted on $\mathcal{X}$ relative to a designated function (in this instance, grayscale).

Step 2 - Persistence Diagrams. PH traces the development of topological characteristics across the filtration sequence $\{\mathcal{X}_n\}$ and presents it through a *persistence diagram* (PD). Specifically, if a topological feature σ emerges in $\mathcal{X}_m$ and disappears in $\mathcal{X}_n$ with $1 \leq m < n \leq N$, the thresholds t_m and t_n are denoted as the *birth time* b_σ and *death time* d_σ of σ, respectively ($b_\sigma = t_m$ and $d_\sigma = t_n$). Therefore, PD contains all such 2-tuples $\text{PD}_k(\mathcal{X}) = \{(b_\sigma, d_\sigma)\}$ where k represents the dimension of the topological features. The interval $d_\sigma - b_\sigma$ is termed as the *lifespan* of σ. Formally, the kth persistence diagram can be defined as $\text{PD}_k(\mathcal{X}) = \{(b_\sigma, d_\sigma) \mid \sigma \in H_k(\mathcal{X}_n) \text{ for } b_\sigma \leq t_n < d_\sigma\}$, where $H_k(\mathcal{X}_n)$ denotes the kth homology group of the cubical complex $\mathcal{X}_n$. Thus, $\text{PD}_k(\mathcal{X})$ contains 2-tuples indicating the birth and death times of k-dimensional voids $\{\sigma\}$ (such as connected components, holes, and cavities) in the filtration sequence $\{\mathcal{X}_n\}$. For instance, for $\mathcal{X}$ in Fig. 1, $\text{PD}_0(\mathcal{X}) = \{(1, \infty), (1, 3), (1, 3), (2, 3)\}$ represents the connected components, while $\text{PD}_1(\mathcal{X}) = \{(2, 5), (2, 3), (4, 5)\}$ illustrates the holes in the corresponding binary images in Fig. 1.

Step 3 - Vectorization. Persistence Diagrams (PDs), consisting of collections of 2-tuples, are impractical for ML tools. A common alternative is *vectorization* [2], which converts PD information into vectors or functions. One widely used method is the *Betti vector*, which tracks the number of *alive* topological features at each threshold. It is a step function where $\beta_0(t_n)$ counts connected components in the binary image $\mathcal{X}_n$, and $\beta_1(t_n)$ counts holes (loops). In ML, Betti functions are typically represented as vectors $\vec{\beta_k} = [\beta_k(t_1) \ldots \beta_k(t_N)]$. For example, in Fig. 1, $\vec{\beta_0}(\mathcal{X}) = [3\ 2\ 1\ 1\ 1]$ shows the connected components, while $\vec{\beta_1}(\mathcal{X}) = [0\ 2\ 1\ 2\ 0]$ represents the holes.

Other PD vectorization methods include persistence images [1], landscapes [4], silhouettes [7], and kernel methods [2]. However, in this work, we primarily use Betti vectors due to their computational efficiency, interpretability, and flexibility to be represented as sequences rather than just vectors, making them well-suited for SOTA ML approaches such as transformers.

3.2 ML and DL Models

We employ topological vectors in two distinct approaches to thoroughly evaluate their effectiveness in skin image analysis.

Basic ML Model. In our basic model, we evaluate the standalone performance of topological vectors by directly feeding them into ML classifiers. Using the procedure outlined in Sect. 3.1, we extract topological feature vectors from each image via sublevel filtration applied to each color channel. Since our vectorization approach employs Betti vectors, these representations can be treated both as static feature vectors and sequential data. To leverage this dual nature, we integrate them into state-of-the-art ML models: a multi-layer perceptron for topological embeddings (PH+MLP) and a Transformer-based sequential classifier for structured sequence modeling (PH+TR). This setup enables us to assess the optimal utilization of topological features across different ML architectures.

Hybrid Deep Learning Models. In our hybrid models, we evaluate the improvements topological vectors bring to SOTA DL models. In order to test this direction, we used pre-trained CNN models, and Vision Transformers (Fig. 2).

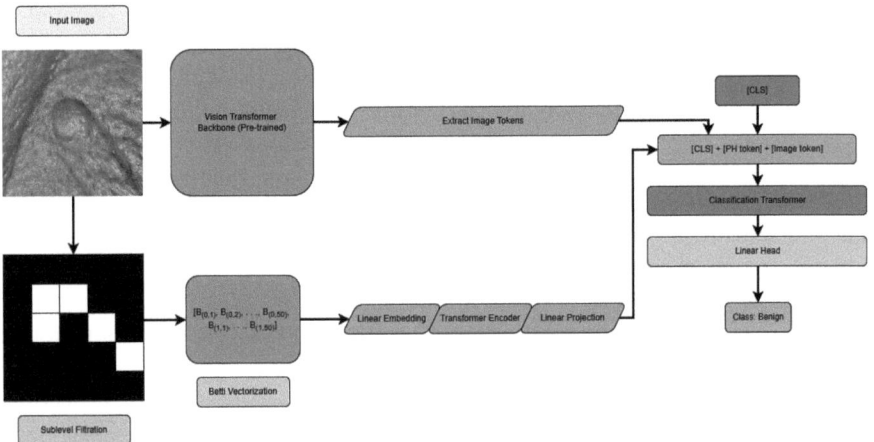

Fig. 2. Top-Layer ViT Model. Hybrid DL framework integrating topological features with Vision Transformers. PH extracts topological feature vectors from dermascopic images, which are concatenated with deep feature embeddings extracted via hierarchical self-attention mechanisms in vision Transformer blocks.

Topo-ViT Model. We propose a dual-branch Transformer architecture, **Topo-ViT**, that integrates TDA with vision-based representation learning for skin lesion classification. The model consists of two parallel encoders: one for dermoscopic images and a second for PH features.

The image branch uses a Vision Transformer backbone (e.g., DaViT-Tiny) to convert a 224×224 RGB image into a sequence of patch tokens, each embedded into a vector of dimension d, capturing spatial and textural patterns.

The topology branch processes a 400-dimensional PH vector computed from sublevel filtrations across color channels. This vector is reshaped into a sequence of smaller tokens each linearly projected and passed through a shallow transformer encoder. These PH tokens are then up-projected to match the embedding dimension of the image tokens.

A learnable [CLS] token is prepended to the combined sequence:

$$[\text{CLS}] + [\text{image tokens}] + [\text{PH tokens}]$$

This fused token sequence is passed through a shared classifier transformer composed of multiple layers of self-attention. By allowing all tokens to attend to each other, the [CLS] token aggregates joint information from both visual and topological modalities.

The final output of the [CLS] token is passed through a linear classification head to generate logits for skin disease prediction. By combining complementary cues—texture from images and structure from topology—**Topo-ViT** improves generalization, robustness to noise, and interpretability in melanoma and basal cell carcinoma detection tasks.

4 Experiments

4.1 Experimental Setup

Datasets. We evaluated our models using four publicly available skin image datasets that vary in size, class granularity (Table 1). Our primary dataset, *ISIC2018*, used in the ISIC 2018 Challenge [15], originally derived from the HAM10000 dataset [36] and a benchmark task in the MedMNIST v2 collection [37]. It comprises 10K dermoscopic RGB images across seven diagnostic classes. We used the dataset for both 7-class multiclass classification and binary classification, where all malignant lesions were grouped and contrasted against benign cases.

To evaluate performance of our models on smaller datasets, we used the PH^2 dataset [26], which includes 200 dermoscopic images labeled as *Common Nevus*, *Atypical Nevus*, or *Melanoma*. We also used the *MedNode* dataset [14], containing 170 macroscopic images categorized as *Benign Nevus* or *Melanoma*, and the *Diverse Dermatology Images (DDI)* dataset [10], which includes 656 clinical images across two classes: *Benign* and *Malignant*. All images were resized to 224 × 224 pixels for consistency across models.

Topological Vectors. As described in Sect. 3.1, we apply sublevel filtration to each color

Table 1. Summary of dermatoscopic datasets used in this study.

Dataset	Class	# Images
ISIC2018	Melanocytic Nevus	6,705
	Melanoma	1,113
	Basal Cell Carcinoma	514
	Actinic Keratoses	327
	Benign Keratosis	1,099
	Dermatofibroma	115
	Vascular Lesions	142
PH^2	Common Nevus	80
	Atypical Nevus	80
	Melanoma	40
MedNode	Benign Nevus	100
	Melanoma	70
DDI	Benign	485
	Malignant	171

channel (R, G, B, and an additional G) using 50 threshold levels per channel. This process generates 50-dimensional $\vec{\beta_0}$ and $\vec{\beta_1}$ vectors for each channel. By concatenating these vectors across all channels, we construct a 400-dimensional topological vector $\widehat{\beta}(\mathcal{X})$ for each image $\mathcal{X}$. Notably, since $\widehat{\beta}(\mathcal{X})$ is directly induced by the filtration process, it can also be interpreted as a sequential representation.

Evaluation. For the ISIC2018 dataset, which includes predefined training (7,007), validation (1,003), and test (2,005) splits [37], we used these official partitions without modification to ensure consistency and reproducibility. For all smaller datasets (PH^2, MedNode, and DDI), we employed an 80:20 stratified split to preserve class distribution between training and testing sets. Final metrics included AUC, accuracy, recall, specificity, precision, and F1 (Table 4).

Table 2. AUC results across all datasets. T-CNN and T-ViT denote the corresponding CNN and ViT architectures augmented with topological vectors via attention. The final column shows the mean AUC improvement of each topological model over its vanilla counterpart.

Model	ISIC (7)	ISIC (2)	DDI (2)	PH^2 (3)	MedNode (2)	Av. Imp
PH+MLP	87.90	83.06	66.03	81.21	74.29	
PH+TR	87.42	81.60	66.63	83.42	87.50	2.82
Inception v3 [34]	93.17	85.30	60.02	71.18	74.28	
T-Inception v3	89.03	84.64	73.58	75.69	80.00	3.80
DenseNet121 [17]	92.92	85.52	61.10	66.84	81.43	
T-DenseNet121	91.47	89.28	71.78	82.81	74.28	4.36
MobileNet v2 [31]	61.28	79.01	50.78	66.84	77.14	
T-MobileNet v2	89.28	87.89	73.10	80.38	57.14	10.55
MobileViT [25]	94.09	93.78	69.06	82.81	90.71	
T-MobileViT	95.25	92.06	70.80	89.41	92.14	1.84
Swin v2 [21]	97.95	94.95	78.24	87.57	88.93	
T-Swin v2	**98.01**	95.48	79.62	87.76	94.29	1.50
DaViT [12]	94.93	95.57	76.32	83.46	91.43	
T-DaViT	95.55	**95.73**	**83.33**	**89.50**	**94.64**	3.41

Hyperparameters. For ISIC2018, Topo-CNNs were trained on 224×224 images with batch size 64 for up to 50 epochs, using early stopping (patience 5) and

LR scheduling. The ImageNet-pretrained CNN backbone was frozen; its global-average-pooled features were concatenated with 400-D Betti vectors and fed through two FC layers (256, 128 units) with batch norm and dropout (0.3, 0.2). We optimized with Adam (LR=1e-3), using sparse categorical cross-entropy for the 7-class task and binary cross-entropy (threshold 0.35) for the binary task.

Our default Topo-ViT reshapes each 400-D PH vector into 25 tokens of 16 D, projects them to 128 D, and encodes with a 4-head transformer. The resulting topological embeddings are linearly mapped to the ViT's feature width (768 D, or 512 D for MobileViT) and concatenated with image patch tokens plus a learnable class token. A 6-layer transformer decoder (width 768, 8 heads) fuses these tokens, with uniform dropout (0.3) across all embedding layers, transformer blocks, and the classification head. Our code is available at the following link:[1].

4.2 Results and Discussion

Tables 2 and 4 report the performances for baseline and topologically-enhanced models across five skin-lesion datasets. Across the large ISIC2018 benchmark, topological augmentation yields modest gains (+1–4 pts), while CNNs and ViTs augmented with persistence features consistently outperform their vanilla counterparts. For example, T-DenseNet121 and T-Inception v3 improve by +4.36 and +3.80 AUC points on average, and even the lightweight MobileNetV2 backbone jumps by +10.55 pts when fused with Betti vectors. Standalone topological classifiers remain competitive (Table 2).

Table 3. MedMNIST baselines for ISIC 2018 (7) [37].

Model	AUC	ACC
ResNet-18 (28)	91.7	73.5
ResNet-18 (224)	92.0	75.4
ResNet-50 (28)	91.3	73.5
ResNet-50 (224)	91.2	73.1
auto-sklearn	90.2	71.9
AutoKeras	91.5	74.9
Google AutoML Vision	91.4	76.8
T-Swin	98.0	88.2

Notably, the benefits of topological vectors are more pronounced on smaller datasets (DDI, PH^2, and MedNode), where deep models often struggle to generalize. In these low-data regimes, persistence-based features provide robust, scale-invariant signals that help guide learning. As a result, AUC gains often exceed 10 points—for example, +10.68 for T-DenseNet121 on DDI and +15.97 on PH^2—while improvements on the larger ISIC dataset remain modest. T-DaViT achieves the highest AUCs across all three small datasets (83.33, 89.50, and 94.64), highlighting the value of topological augmentation in data-scarce settings. Compared to MedMNIST baselines on DermaMNIST (ISIC2018 (7)) [37], our Topo-ViT models also achieve superior performance (Table 3).

---

[1] Code link: https://anonymous.4open.science/r/TopoDerma-28EB/.

Table 4. Performance comparison of models across all datasets. T-CNN and T-ViT models denote the corresponding CNN and ViT architectures augmented with topological vectors.

Model	ISIC2018 (7-class)					ISIC2018 (Binary)				
	AUC	Acc	Sens	Spec	F-1	AUC	Acc	Sens	Spec	F-1
PH+MLP	87.90	71.67	71.67	91.27	68.56	83.06	80.30	64.80	84.07	56.26
PH+TR	87.42	70.97	36.52	91.93	39.48	81.60	80.00	65.17	65.17	44.38
Inception v3	93.17	75.81	57.44	93.01	50.90	85.30	82.29	17.60	98.02	27.99
T-Inception v3	89.03	72.91	33.23	65.38	36.19	84.64	81.64	60.20	86.85	56.19
DenseNet121	92.92	69.58	27.83	87.11	31.83	85.52	82.49	52.81	79.79	45.92
T-DenseNet121	91.47	75.52	45.48	85.71	48.52	89.28	83.04	68.62	86.54	61.27
MobileNetV2	61.28	64.39	17.61	85.75	33.38	79.01	58.2	91.33	50.15	46.07
T-MobileNetV2	89.28	74.36	36.83	34.21	39.80	87.89	83.59	67.61	87.47	61.69
MobileViT	94.09	87.23	70.87	96.60	72.32	93.78	88.98	82.63	82.63	82.53
T-MobileViT	95.25	82.54	56.15	95.13	60.93	92.06	86.13	80.67	80.67	66.90
DaViT	94.93	89.38	76.13	97.21	78.79	95.57	91.67	85.46	85.46	86.40
T-DaViT	95.55	85.69	70.88	96.44	71.00	95.73	91.32	85.24	85.24	77.23
Swin v2	97.95	87.38	75.95	96.61	77.81	94.95	89.68	86.63	86.63	84.51
T-Swin v2	98.01	88.18	74.60	96.76	78.09	95.48	90.92	84.51	84.51	76.12

Model	DDI (Binary)					PH² (3-class)					MedNode (Binary)				
	AUC	Acc	Sens	Spec	F1	AUC	Acc	Sens	Spec	F1	AUC	Acc	Sens	Spec	F1
PH+MLP	66.03	74.24	47.06	83.67	48.48	81.21	70.00	70.00	84.38	69.94	74.29	67.65	78.57	60.00	66.67
PH+TR	66.63	75.76	35.29	89.80	42.86	83.42	72.50	70.83	85.42	71.47	87.50	79.41	78.57	80.00	75.86
DenseNet121	61.10	77.27	11.76	95.91	19.04	66.84	45.00	45.83	70.14	47.19	81.43	76.47	100.00	42.85	83.33
T-DenseNet121	71.78	66.67	58.82	69.38	47.62	82.81	55.00	58.33	77.08	49.62	74.28	70.58	85.71	60.00	70.58
InceptionV3	60.02	66.67	41.17	75.51	38.89	71.18	55.00	54.16	75.00	56.50	74.28	58.82	80.00	58.57	69.56
T-InceptionV3	73.58	74.24	76.47	73.47	60.46	75.69	50.05	54.16	75.00	48.90	80.00	76.47	85.71	70.00	75.00
MobileNetV2	50.78	75.75	17.64	95.91	27.27	66.84	55.00	58.33	75.69	56.11	77.14	70.58	60.00	85.71	70.58
T-MobileNetV2	73.10	69.69	64.71	71.43	52.38	80.38	65.00	62.50	80.56	63.59	57.14	47.06	85.71	50.00	66.67
MobileViT	69.06	72.73	61.46	61.46	41.94	82.81	67.50	70.83	82.99	68.54	90.71	82.35	82.86	82.86	80.00
T-MobileViT	70.80	75.76	75.76	65.43	48.39	89.41	75.00	79.17	87.15	76.17	92.14	79.41	77.14	77.14	72.00
DaViT	76.32	73.48	62.94	62.94	44.44	83.46	70.00	72.92	83.68	72.92	91.43	79.41	81.43	81.43	78.79
T-DaViT	83.33	72.50	75.00	85.42	73.92	89.50	77.50	79.17	87.50	80.32	94.64	94.12	92.86	92.86	92.31
Swin v2	78.24	80.30	68.49	68.49	53.57	87.57	70.00	72.92	84.03	71.74	88.93	73.53	74.29	74.29	70.97
T-Swin v2	79.62	81.06	70.92	70.92	57.63	87.76	72.50	72.92	85.07	73.89	94.29	91.18	89.29	89.29	88.00

5 Conclusion

We presented a topological deep learning framework for skin cancer detection, combining persistent homology-based features with convolutional and transformer architectures. Our experiments demonstrate that topological signatures alone are competitive, and their integration with deep models consistently improves classification accuracy across diverse skin lesion types. By capturing global shape and connectivity information, topological features enhance both robustness and interpretability, key limitations of conventional deep learning. In future work, we plan to extend our framework to multimodal data by incorporating patient metadata and clinical images, explore end-to-end differentiable topological layers, and validate our approach through prospective clinical studies. This study highlights the potential of TDA to improve diagnostic performance and interpretability in dermatological AI systems.

Acknowledgements. This work was partially supported by National Science Foundation under grants DMS-2220613, and DMS-2229417.

References

1. Adams, H., et al.: Persistence images: a stable vector representation of persistent homology. J. Mach. Learn. Res. **18**(8), 1–35 (2017)
2. Ali, D., et al.: A survey of vectorization methods in topological data analysis. IEEE Trans. Pattern Anal. Mach. Intell. (2023)
3. Brinker, T.J., et al.: CNN outperforms dermatologists in melanoma classification: a prospective, multicenter, noninferiority study. JAMA Dermatol. **155**(11), 922–926 (2019)
4. Bubenik, P., Dłotko, P.: A persistence landscapes toolbox for topological statistics. J. Symb. Comput. **78**, 91–114 (2017)
5. Carlsson, G.: Topology and data. Bull. Am. Math. Soc. **46**(2), 255–308 (2009)
6. Chachólski, W., Hiraoka, Y., Obayashi, I.: Topological data analysis for complex medical imaging. IEEE Trans. Med. Imaging **38**(6), 1389–1398 (2019)
7. Chazal, F., Fasy, B.T., Lecci, F., Rinaldo, A., Wasserman, L.: Stochastic convergence of persistence landscapes and silhouettes. In: SoCG, pp. 474–483 (2014)
8. Chung, Y.M., Hu, C.S., Lawson, A., Smyth, C.: Topological approaches to skin disease image analysis. In: 2018 IEEE International Conference on Big Data (Big Data), pp. 100–105. IEEE (2018)
9. Coskunuzer, B., Akçora, C.G.: Topological methods in machine learning: A tutorial for practitioners. arXiv preprint arXiv:2409.02901 (2024)
10. Daneshjou, R., et al.: Disparities in dermatology ai performance on a diverse, curated clinical image set. Sci. Adv. **8**(6), eabj7790 (2022)
11. Dey, T.K., Wang, Y.: Computational topology for data analysis. Cambridge University Press (2022)
12. Ding, M., et al.: Davit: Dual attention vision transformers. In: ECCV, pp. 74–92. Springer (2022)
13. Esteva, A., et al.: Dermatologist-level classification of skin cancer with deep neural networks. Nature **542**(7639), 115–118 (2017)

14. Giotis, I., Molders, N., Land, S., Biehl, M., Jonkman, M.F., Petkov, N.: Med-node: a computer-assisted melanoma diagnosis system using non-dermoscopic images. Expert Syst. Appl. **42**(19), 6578–6585 (2015)
15. Gutman, D.A., et al.: Skin lesion analysis toward melanoma detection: a challenge at the 2016 International Symposium on Biomedical Imaging (isbi). In: ISBI, pp. 168–172 (2016)
16. Hofer, C., Kwitt, R., Niethammer, M., Uhl, A.: Deep learning with topological signatures. In: Advances in Neural Information Processing Systems, vol. 30 (2017)
17. Huang, G., Liu, Z., Van Der Maaten, L., Weinberger, K.Q.: Densely connected convolutional networks. In: CVPR, pp. 4700–4708 (2017)
18. Johnson, K., Söderkvist, J., Hansson, P.: Application of persistent homology in histopathological grading. Comput. Biol. Med. **145**, 105379 (2022)
19. Kahle, R., Rieck, B., Moor, M., Horn, M.: Topological regularization for deep image segmentation. In: Proceedings of the IEEE International Symposium on Biomedical Imaging, pp. 235–239 (2021)
20. Li, Y., Shen, L.: Integrating dermoscopic images and patient metadata for enhanced melanoma detection using deep learning. Comput. Biol. Med. **123**, 103900 (2020). https://doi.org/10.1016/j.compbiomed.2020.103900
21. Liu, Z., et al.: Swin transformer v2: Scaling up capacity and resolution. In: Proceedings of the IEEE/CVF Conference on Computer Vision and Pattern Recognition, pp. 12009–12019 (2022)
22. Lum, P., et al.: Extracting insights from the shape of complex data using topology. Sci. Rep. **3**, 1236 (2013)
23. Maurya, A., et al.: Hybrid topological data analysis and deep learning for basal cell carcinoma diagnosis. J. Imaging Inf. Med. **37**(1), 92–106 (2024)
24. McGuirl, M.R., Volkening, A., Sandstede, B.: Topological data analysis of zebrafish patterns. PNAS **117**(10), 5113–5124 (2020)
25. Mehta, S., Rastegari, M.: Mobilevit: Light-weight, general-purpose, and mobile-friendly vision transformer. In: ICLR (2022)
26. Mendonça, T., Ferreira, P.M., Marques, J.S., Marcal, A., Rozeira, J.: Ph^2: a dermoscopic image database for research and benchmarking. In: 2013 35th Annual International Conference of the IEEE Engineering in Medicine and Biology Society (EMBC), pp. 5437–5440 (2013)
27. Menegola, A., Tavares, J.M.R.S., Fornaciali, M., Li, L., Avila, S., Valle, E.: Knowledge transfer for melanoma screening with deep learning. arXiv preprint arXiv:1703.02223 (2017)
28. Patel, S., et al.: Artificial intelligence in dermatology: a systematic review of applications and challenges. J. Am. Med. Inform. Assoc. **28**(8), 1842–1857 (2021)
29. Qaiser, T., et al.: Fast and accurate tumor segmentation of histology images using persistent homology and deep convolutional features. Med. Image Anal. **55**, 1–14 (2019)
30. Saggar, M., et al.: Towards a new approach to reveal dynamical organization of the brain using topological data analysis. Nat. Commun. **9**(1), 1399 (2018)
31. Sandler, M., et al.: MobileNetV2: Inverted residuals and linear bottlenecks. In: CVPR, pp. 4510–4520, June 2018. https://doi.org/10.1109/CVPR.2018.00474
32. Santhirasekaram, A., Winkler, M., Rockall, A., Glocker, B.: Topology preserving compositionality for robust medical image segmentation. In: Proceedings of the IEEE/CVF Computer Vision and Pattern Recognition Workshops (CVPRW), pp. 999–1008 (2023)
33. Skaf, Y., Laubenbacher, R.C.: Topological data analysis in biomedicine: a review. J. Biomed. Inform. **130**, 104082 (2022). https://doi.org/10.1016/j.jbi.2022.104082

34. Szegedy, C., Ioffe, S., Vanhoucke, V., Alemi, A.: Inception-v4, inception-resnet and the impact of residual connections on learning. In: Proceedings of the AAAI Conference on Artificial Intelligence, vol. 31 (2017)
35. Tang, P., Li, X., He, J., Zheng, Y.: Automated melanoma detection using deep learning based on multiple image modalities. IEEE J. Biomed. Health Inform. **24**(7), 1922–1931 (2020)
36. Tschandl, P., Rosendahl, C., Kittler, H.: The ham10000 dataset, a large collection of multisource dermatoscopic images of common pigmented skin lesions. Sci. Data **5**(1), 180161 (2018)
37. Yang, J., et al.: Medmnist v2-a large-scale lightweight benchmark for 2d and 3d biomedical image classification. Sci. Data **10**(1), 41 (2023), https://medmnist.com
38. Yuan, L., et al.: Tokens-to-token vision transformer: training vision transformers from scratch on imagenet. In: Proceedings of the IEEE/CVF International Conference on Computer Vision (ICCV), pp. 558–567, October 2021

Retrieval-Augmented VLMs for Multimodal Melanoma Diagnosis

Jihyun Moon[iD] and Charmgil Hong[✉][iD]

Handong Global University, Pohang, Republic of Korea
{jhmoon,charmgil}@handong.ac.kr

Abstract. Accurate and early diagnosis of malignant melanoma is critical for improving patient outcomes. While convolutional neural networks (CNNs) have shown promise in dermoscopic image analysis, they often neglect clinical metadata and require extensive preprocessing. Vision-language models (VLMs) offer a multimodal alternative but struggle to capture clinical specificity when trained on general-domain data. To address this, we propose a retrieval-augmented VLM framework that incorporates semantically similar patient cases into the diagnostic prompt. Our method enables informed predictions without fine-tuning and significantly improves classification accuracy and error correction over conventional baselines. These results demonstrate that retrieval-augmented prompting provides a robust strategy for clinical decision support.

Keywords: Vision-Language Model · Retrieval-Augmented Generation · Melanoma Diagnosis · Classification Task

1 Introduction

Malignant melanoma is the most common and deadliest form of skin cancer, with 100,640 new cases and 8,290 deaths reported in the United States in 2024 [16]. Early detection significantly improves survival, which emphasizes the need for accurate and timely diagnosis. Automated diagnostic tools can assist clinicians in detecting malignant lesions at an earlier stage. This can lead to improved prognosis and make timely intervention more achievable. While convolutional neural network (CNN)-based methods have shown promise [10,11], most rely solely on dermoscopic images and often require preprocessing steps such as region of interest (ROI) segmentation, which limits their utility in clinical practice.

To address these limitations, recent efforts have explored multimodal frameworks that incorporate both images and clinical metadata have gained attention for improving diagnostic accuracy and personalization. Vision-language models (VLMs) [2,13] have emerged as strong candidates for such tasks, as they jointly process visual and textual data without the need for handcrafted preprocessing. However, off-the-shelf VLMs that are trained on general-purpose data often fail to capture domain-specific complexities [5]. Although fine-tuning with clinical data can mitigate this issue, it requires curated datasets and significant computational resources. As a result, this approach is often infeasible due to privacy constraints and institutional variability.

As an alternative, retrieval-augmented generation (RAG) [12] provides external knowledge-based inference by retrieving similar patient cases and incorporating them into prompts. This approach is particularly appealing for clinical applications, since it enables reasoning without modifying model weights. Previous studies in content-based image retrieval (CBIR) have shown that case-based reasoning can support dermatological diagnosis by referencing visually similar lesions [3,19]. Building on this idea, our work extends case-based reasoning to a multimodal context by integrating retrieved image–text pairs into VLM prompts. This design supports clinical reasoning by reflecting the way how physicians interpret new cases through analogical comparison with prior patient examples.

More specifically, this study proposes a multimodal diagnostic framework that integrates RAG into a VLM to support more accurate and clinically relevant melanoma classification. We investigate whether retrieved examples improve diagnostic decisions, particularly in correcting false positives and false negatives. Through comprehensive experiments, we show that our method consistently outperforms conventional classification models in both accuracy and error correction. Our main contributions are as follows:

- We propose a retrieval-augmented VLM-based diagnostic framework for melanoma classification by incorporating image–metadata–label examples into prompts to improve decision accuracy.
- We evaluate the effects of different metadata serialization strategies and image encoders on retrieval effectiveness and diagnostic performance.
- We show that the proposed method consistently outperforms conventional image-based, text-based, and early-fusion baselines across multiple metrics and architectures, without requiring fine-tuning.

2 Proposed Approach

This section presents a multimodal diagnostic framework that combines a VLM with RAG to classify melanoma using both dermoscopic images and clinical metadata. In clinical practice, diagnosis often involves comparing a case with prior cases that share similar visual features or clinical attributes. This case-based reasoning improves diagnostic accuracy by using past experience.

Our framework incorporates a retrieval module that searches a database of dermoscopic images and metadata to find semantically similar cases. These examples serve as clinical references and provide contextual support for the prediction of the model. By embedding the retrieved cases into the VLM input prompt, the system emulates the comparative reasoning process used in human diagnosis. This design addresses the limitations of general-purpose VLMs and

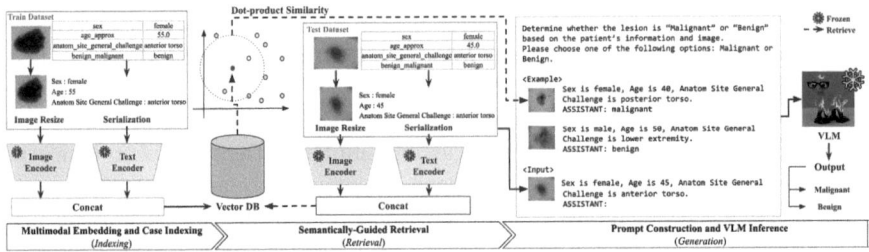

Fig. 1. Overview of the proposed retrieval-augmented classification framework incorporating attribute-value pair-based prompting.

better aligns the model with the specific demands of melanoma classification. An overview of the architecture is shown in Fig. 1.

Multimodal Embedding and Case Indexing. Each training sample includes a dermoscopic image and associated metadata (*e.g.*, age, sex, and lesion location). To process these modalities, we use modality-specific encoders: CNN-based backbones (*e.g.*, ResNeXt-50 [22], EfficientNet-V2-M [17]) for images and BERT [8] for text. Metadata is serialized into natural language using template-based sentence transformations (see below) to improve compatibility with language models. The resulting image and text embeddings are concatenated into a single multimodal vector and stored in a FAISS [9] vector database for efficient approximate nearest neighbor search. This setup enables scalable indexing of large dermatological datasets and allows seamless updates as new data is added.

Template-Based Sentence Transformations. To make structured metadata compatible with VLMs, we convert patient records into natural language using predefined templates. We apply three serialization strategies:

- **Sentence format**: Expresses each field as a simple sentence (*e.g.*, Age is 45, Sex is female.), matching the VLM's training style.
- **Attribute-value pair**: Uses compact key-value pairs (*e.g.*, Age: 45, Sex: Female) to reduce prompt length and improve parsing.
- **HTML format**: Encodes tabular structure with tags like <table>, <tr>, <th>, and <td> to retain column semantics.

Semantically-Guided Retrieval. At inference time, the query sample (image and metadata) is encoded with the same modality-specific encoders used to index the database. We compute dot-product similarity between the query and database embeddings to retrieve the top-K most similar cases. These examples, selected based on both visual and clinical similarity, provide contextual support for VLM prompting. This retrieval introduces domain-specific knowledge without updating model weights and enables adaptation to the target domain. We found that $K = 2$ offers the best balance between contextual relevance and noise.

Prompt Construction and VLM Inference. To adapt general-purpose VLMs for binary melanoma classification, we design structured prompts con-

Table 1. Comparison of image(I)-based, metadata(M)-based, early-fusion, zero-shot VLM, and our proposed framework (bold: the highest performance).

	I M	Model	Serialization	Accuracy	Balanced Accuracy	Precision	Sensitivity	F1-score	TN	TP	FN	FP
Single Modality	✓ -	ResNeXt-50 [22]	-	0.7380	0.5054	0.2022	0.1316	0.1594	6402	223	1472	880
	✓ -	EfficientNet-V2-M [17]	-	0.6954	0.5061	0.1985	0.2018	0.2001	5901	342	1353	1381
	- ✓	RF [4]	-	0.8156	0.5209	0.6667	0.0472	0.0882	7242	80	1615	40
	- ✓	Vicuna 7B v1.5 [23]	HTML	0.6547	0.4873	0.1725	0.2183	0.1927	5507	370	1325	1775
	- ✓	Vicuna 7B v1.5	Attribute-value pair	0.737	0.5263	0.2294	0.2413	0.2352	5908	409	1286	1374
	- ✓	Vicuna 7B v1.5	Sentence	0.6063	0.5152	0.2023	0.3687	0.2613	4818	625	1070	2464
Early-Fusion with RF	✓ ✓	BERT [8]+ResNeXt-50	HTML	0.8607	0.6557	0.8366	0.3263	0.4694	7174	553	1142	108
	✓ ✓	BERT+ResNeXt-50	Attribute-value pair	0.8623	0.6568	0.8536	0.3268	0.4277	7187	554	1141	95
	✓ ✓	BERT+ResNeXt-50	Sentence	0.8622	0.6589	0.8428	0.3322	0.4765	7177	563	1132	105
	✓ ✓	BERT+EfficientNet-V2-M	HTML	0.8501	0.6208	0.8442	0.2525	0.3887	7203	428	1267	79
	✓ ✓	BERT+EfficientNet-V2-M	Attribute-value pair	0.8501	0.6220	0.8375	0.2555	0.3915	7198	433	1262	84
	✓ ✓	BERT+EfficientNet-V2-M	Sentence	0.8514	0.6232	**0.8546**	0.2566	0.3947	7208	435	1260	74
Early-Fusion with FNN	✓ ✓	BERT [8]+ResNeXt-50	HTML	0.6819	0.5079	0.2000	0.2283	0.2132	5734	387	1308	1548
	✓ ✓	BERT+ResNeXt-50	Attribute-value pair	0.7040	0.5089	0.2038	0.1953	0.1995	5989	331	1364	1293
	✓ ✓	BERT+ResNeXt-50	Sentence	0.7029	0.5009	0.1904	0.1764	0.1832	6011	299	1396	1271
	✓ ✓	BERT+EfficientNet-V2-M	HTML	0.7024	0.4967	0.1830	0.1664	0.1743	6023	282	1413	1259
	✓ ✓	BERT+EfficientNet-V2-M	Attribute-value pair	0.7084	0.5063	0.2001	0.1817	0.1905	6051	308	1387	1231
	✓ ✓	BERT+EfficientNet-V2-M	Sentence	0.7108	0.5090	0.2050	0.1847	0.1943	6068	313	1382	1214
Zero-Shot VLM	✓ ✓	LLaVA 7B v1.5 hf [13]	HTML	0.5845	0.6113	0.2608	0.6543	0.3729	4138	1109	586	3144
	✓ ✓	LLaVA 7B v1.5 hf	Attribute-value pair	0.7126	0.6128	0.3171	0.4525	0.3729	5630	767	928	1652
	✓ ✓	LLaVA 7B v1.5 hf	Sentence	0.5610	0.5658	0.2320	0.5735	0.3303	4064	972	723	3218
Ours ($K = 2$)	✓ ✓	BERT+ResNext-50	HTML	0.7396	0.7202	0.3921	**0.6891**	0.4998	5471	1168	527	1811
	✓ ✓	BERT+ResNext-50	Attribute-value pair	**0.8876**	**0.7970**	0.7254	0.6513	**0.6864**	6864	1104	591	418
	✓ ✓	BERT+ResNext-50	Sentence	0.8810	0.7891	0.7027	0.6413	0.6706	6822	1087	608	460
	✓ ✓	BERT+EfficientNet-V2-M	HTML	0.7123	0.6746	0.3505	0.6142	0.4463	5353	1041	654	1929
	✓ ✓	BERT+EfficientNet-V2-M	Attribute-value pair	0.8491	0.7345	0.6114	0.5504	0.5793	6689	933	762	593
	✓ ✓	BERT+EfficientNet-V2-M	Sentence	0.8459	0.7294	0.6022	0.4322	0.5706	6675	919	776	607

sists of: (1) instruction specifying the task; (2) K retrieved examples as image–metadata–label triplets; and (3) the query sample with a classification request.

The frozen VLM processes the prompt and generates a textual response indicating the predicted class. This few-shot design mirrors clinical reasoning by analogy and leads to better contextual understanding and more reliable predictions. Unlike early-fusion [18] or naive multimodal concatenation [14], our method maintains modality alignment and exploits the ability of the VLM to perform implicit multimodal reasoning.

3 Experiment

Dataset. We use the SIIM-ISIC 2019 Challenge dataset [6,7,20], which includes 29,923 dermoscopic images with clinical metadata. Among them, 5,608 cases are histopathologically confirmed melanomas. We treat this as a binary classification task: malignant vs. benign. Each sample includes an image and metadata (*age*, *sex*, and *anatomical site*). Images are provided in JPEG format and resized to 224×224 RGB. We apply two-stage stratified sampling to preserve class balance: 70% of the data is used for training and 30% for testing. The training set is further split 80:20 for validation during hyperparameter tuning.

Table 2. Comparison of baseline models and the proposed approach (Ours, $K = 2$), showing the number of corrected errors (FN/FP corrected as TP/TN) and the corresponding recovery rate (%). Recovery is defined as the proportion of corrected errors relative to the total baseline errors (I: Image, M: Metadata).

(a) Performance Comparison Across Different Experimental Settings.

	I	M	Model	Serialization		Ours ($K=2$)	Recovery (%)
Single Modality	-	✓	RF [4]	-	FP	34	85.00
	-	✓	RF	-	FN	1035	64.09
	-	✓	Vicuna 7B v1.5 [23]	Attribute-value pair	FP	1258	70.87
	-	✓	Vicuna 7B v1.5	Attribute-value pair	FN	827	64.31
Early-Fusion with RF	✓	✓	BERT [8]+ResNeXt-50 [22]	Attribute-value pair	FP	71	74.74
	✓	✓	BERT+ResNeXt-50	Attribute-value pair	FN	604	52.94
Zero-Shot VLM	✓	✓	LLaVA 7B v1.5 hf [13]	Attribute-value pair	FP	1507	91.22
	✓	✓	LLaVA 7B v1.5 hf	Attribute-value pair	FN	571	61.53

(b) Performance Comparison Across Different Serialization Methods.

	I	M	Model	Serialization		Attribute-value pair	Recovery (%)
Ours ($K=2$)	✓	✓	BERT [8]+ResNeXt-50 [22]	HTML	FP	1513	83.55
	✓	✓	BERT+ResNeXt-50	HTML	FN	116	22.01
Ours ($K=2$)	✓	✓	BERT+ResNeXt-50	Sentence	FP	113	24.57
	✓	✓	BERT+ResNeXt-50	Sentence	FN	43	7.07

(c) Performance Comparison Across Different Image Encoder.

	I	M	Model	Serialization		BERT [8]+ResNeXt-50 [22]	Recovery (%)
Ours ($K=2$)	✓	✓	BERT+EfficientNet-V2-M [17]	Attribute-value pair	FP	487	82.12
	✓	✓	BERT+EfficientNet-V2-M	Attribute-value pair	FN	325	42.65

Experimental Setup. We evaluate performance under five settings: image-based, text-based, multimodal early-fusion, zero-shot VLM, and our retrieval-augmented VLM framework. For image-based models, we fine-tune ResNeXt-50 [22] and EfficientNet-V2-M [17], both initialized with ImageNet weights. Training uses the Adam optimizer with binary cross-entropy loss, and hyperparameters are tuned via Optuna [1]. For text-based classification, we use Random Forest (RF) [4] and 4-bit quantized Vicuna 7B v1.5 [23], implemented with Scikit-learn [15] and Hugging Face Transformers [21]. In the early-fusion baseline, we extract image features from the final CNN layer and use the [CLS] token from the 11th layer of BERT, following the approach in [8]. The two representations are concatenated and classified using either an RF or a ReLU-activated feedforward neural network (FNN). Hyperparameters are tuned via Grid Search [15] or Optuna [1]. For VLM-based experiments, we use the 4-bit quantized version of LLaVA v1.5 [13]. In the RAG configuration, we construct a FAISS [9] index containing 16,756 image–text pairs from the training set. For each query, the top two nearest neighbors ($K = 2$) are retrieved and inserted into the model prompt. We empirically evaluate different values of K ($K = 1, 2, 3, 4$) and find that $K = 2$ offers the best trade-off between contextual relevance and noise.

3.1 Quantitative Evaluation

Table 1 summarizes the classification results. We report accuracy, balanced accuracy, precision, sensitivity, F1-score, and confusion matrix components. Given the class imbalance and the clinical importance of minimizing both false negative (FN) and false positive (FP), we adopt F1-score as the primary metric.

Single-Modality Models. Models using only dermoscopic images or clinical metadata show limited diagnostic performance. Among image-based methods, EfficientNet-V2-M achieves the best results, though its performance is affected by visual noise due to the absence of preprocessing. In text-based models, Vicuna 7B v1.5 outperforms RF, likely benefiting from general-domain pretraining. The RF model struggles to capture patterns effectively due to the limited number of metadata features. These results suggest that single-modality approaches are inadequate for accurate melanoma diagnosis and highlight the importance of multimodal integration.

Multimodal Fusion and Zero-Shot VLM. Zero-shot VLM outperforms early-fusion with FNN due to its use of attention-based mechanisms that capture cross-modal interactions. In contrast, FNN relies on simple feature concatenation, which limits its ability to represent semantic relationships. Interestingly, early-fusion with RF achieves better results than zero-shot VLM, indicating that pretrained VLMs do not fully capture clinical signals. These observations point to the need for strategies that incorporate domain knowledge and task-specific examples to improve VLM-based classification.

Proposed RAG Framework. Our RAG-based VLM framework achieves the highest performance across all settings. Using BERT, ResNeXt-50, and attribute-value pair serialization, it reaches an F1-score of 0.6864, improving by 0.2099 over the best early-fusion model and by 0.3135 over zero-shot VLM. Sensitivity increases to 0.6513, more than doubling that of early-fusion, while precision reaches 0.7254. These results demonstrate that retrieval-augmented prompting provides consistent gains in both accuracy and clinical error correction, while maintaining a strong balance between precision and recall.

3.2 Qualitative Evaluation

The quantitative results show that the RAG-based VLM framework outperforms image-based, text-based, early-fusion, and zero-shot VLM models. To better understand this performance, we qualitatively examine how retrieved examples contribute to correcting FP and FN that baseline methods fail to resolve.

Error Analysis of Baseline Predictions. Each baseline model uses the best-performing architecture for its modality. Our framework ($K = 2$) applies BERT with ResNeXt-50 and attribute–value pair serialization. Table 2a presents recovery rates, defined as the proportion of FP and FN errors that our method correctly reclassifies. Zero-shot VLM achieves recovery rates of 91.22% for FP and

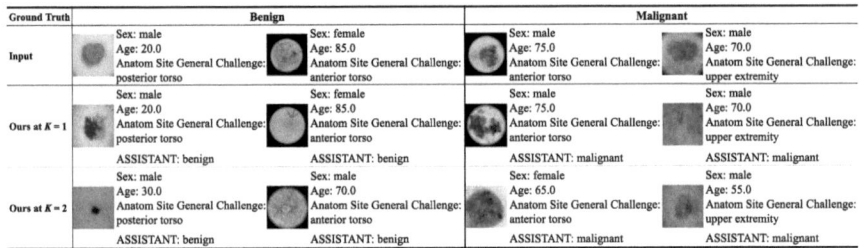

(a) Misclassified case by all baselines (LLM, early-fusion, zero-shot VLM) correctly classified by our method ($K = 2$).

(b) Comparison of HTML and attribute–value formats within RAG framework ($K = 2$), showing better results with attribute–value input.

(c) Comparison of sentence and attribute–value formats, showing improved classification with attribute–value input.

(d) Impact of image encoder choice (EfficientNet-V2-M vs. ResNeXt-50) using attribute–value format in RAG framework.

Fig. 2. Error cases corrected by our framework with retrieved cases.

61.53% for FN. In contrast, early-fusion with RF shows substantially lower recovery, likely due to limited capacity to model semantic interactions across modalities. Figure 2a shows representative cases. In the left column, baseline models misclassify benign lesions as malignant. In the right, malignant lesions are predicted as benign. Our method retrieves clinically similar examples based on *sex*, *age*, and *anatomical site*, and inserts them into the prompt. For instance, two retrieved benign cases from the same *anatomical site* (posterior torso) help correct a prior false positive. This context influences the model's decision and leads to more accurate predictions.

Overall, these results suggest that retrieval-based prompting addresses key limitations of conventional models and supports more reliable clinical reasoning.

Effect of Input Serialization Format. To evaluate the impact of input serialization, we compare three formats: HTML, attribute–value pair, and sentence, using the same configuration (BERT + ResNeXt-50, $K = 2$). Table 2b shows recovery rates where FP and FN errors under HTML and sentence formats are corrected to true positive (TP) and true negative (TN) by switching to attribute–value format.

For HTML input, 83.55% of FP and 22.01% of FN errors are corrected. In contrast, conversion from sentence format yields 24.57% for FP and 7.07% for FN. These results suggest that attribute–value input encodes clinical variables more explicitly. Although HTML preserves the same content, its tag-based structure may obscure important features during embedding. While sentence format aligns with VLM training data, its classification performance remains lower than attribute–value format. Figure 2b and 2c show representative examples. In Fig. 2b, the HTML-based model yields a false positive for a benign lesion. The attribute–value format retrieves benign cases with matching *sex* and *age* and enables correct classification. For the malignant example, the HTML input produces false negatives, whereas attribute–value input retrieves similar malignant lesions and supports accurate prediction. Figure 2c presents a false positive under sentence format that is corrected by attribute–value input, which retrieves benign cases with matching *sex* and *anatomical site*. Its more explicit structure strengthens contextual alignment and improves classification.

In summary, these results show that structured input formats, especially attribute–value pairs, better support retrieval-based reasoning by clarifying the semantic role of each variable.

Effect of Image Encoder Configuration. To assess the influence of image encoder on diagnostic performance, we compare ResNeXt-50 and EfficientNet-V2-M, using the same text encoder (BERT), input format (attribute-value pair), and retrieval setting ($K = 2$). Table 2c shows recovery rates where predictions by the EfficientNet-V2-M model are corrected by the ResNeXt-50 model. The recovery rate for FPs reaches 82.12%, and for FNs 42.65%, indicating that ResNeXt-50 is more effective at correcting errors. Figure 2d presents examples where the two models produce different outcomes for the same inputs. In the benign case, EfficientNet-V2-M misclassifies the lesion as malignant. In contrast, ResNeXt-50 retrieves benign cases with similar *anatomical site* and *sex*, which results in correct classification. These retrieved cases show strong alignment with the query in both spatial and demographic attributes. EfficientNet-V2-M, by comparison, retrieves cases with lower consistency, which may reduce contextual reliability. A similar difference appears in the malignant case. EfficientNet-V2-M predicts FN, whereas ResNeXt-50 retrieves two malignant cases with similar color and lesion spread, resulting in correct classification. These examples provide clearer visual evidence that supports the decision of the model.

Altogether, the results suggest that ResNeXt-50 captures visual features relevant to melanoma classification more effectively and provides stronger contextual alignment in retrieval-based inference.

4 Conclusion

We presented a retrieval-augmented diagnostic framework that integrates VLMs with case-based prompting for melanoma classification. The framework improves diagnostic performance without fine-tuning by retrieving semantically similar examples and inserting them into the input prompt. Quantitative and qualitative results show improved contextual reasoning and fewer classification errors. Comparisons across serialization formats and encoders confirm the benefit of structured input and ResNeXt-50 visual features. These findings support retrieval-augmented prompting as a robust and generalizable strategy for clinical decision support using pretrained multimodal models. Although the framework shows promising results, its reliance on a single VLM may limit generalizability across diverse diagnostic tasks. Future work may expand this approach to multi-class skin lesion classification and other domains that require multimodal reasoning and greater model flexibility.

Acknowledgments. This research was supported (1) by the MSIT (Ministry of Science and ICT), Korea, under the Global Research Support Program in the Digital Field (RS-2024-00431394), supervised by the IITP (Institute for Information & Communications Technology Planning & Evaluation); (2) by the MSIT and NIPA (National IT Industry Promotion Agency), Korea, under the Development of AI Precision Medical Solution project (Dr. Answer 2.0, S0252-21-1001); and (3) under the High Performance Computing Support project.

References

1. Akiba, T., Sano, S., Yanase, T., Ohta, T., Koyama, M.: Optuna: a next-generation hyperparameter optimization framework. In: Proceedings of the 25th ACM SIGKDD International Conference on Knowledge Discovery & Data Mining, pp. 2623–2631 (2019)
2. Akrout, M., Cirone, K.D., Vender, R.: Evaluation of vision llms gtp-4v and llava for the recognition of features characteristic of melanoma. J. Cutan. Med. Surg. **28**(1), 98–99 (2024)

3. Allegretti, S., Bolelli, F., Pollastri, F., Longhitano, S., Pellacani, G., Grana, C.: Supporting skin lesion diagnosis with content-based image retrieval. In: 2020 25th International Conference on Pattern Recognition (ICPR), pp. 8053–8060. IEEE (2021)
4. Breiman, L.: Random forests. Mach. Learn. **45**, 5–32 (2001)
5. Chen, J., Jiang, Y., Yang, D., Li, M., Wei, J., Qian, Z., Zhang, L.: Can llms' tuning methods work in medical multimodal domain? In: International Conference on Medical Image Computing and Computer-Assisted Intervention, pp. 112–122. Springer (2024)
6. Codella, N.C., et al.: Skin lesion analysis toward melanoma detection: a challenge at the 2017 international symposium on biomedical imaging (isbi), hosted by the international skin imaging collaboration (isic). In: 2018 IEEE 15th international symposium on biomedical imaging (ISBI 2018), pp. 168–172. IEEE (2018)
7. Combalia, M., et al.: Bcn20000: dermoscopic lesions in the wild. arXiv preprint arXiv:1908.02288 (2019)
8. Devlin, J., Chang, M.W., Lee, K., Toutanova, K.: Bert: pre-training of deep bidirectional transformers for language understanding. In: Proceedings of the 2019 Conference of the North American chapter of the Association for Computational Linguistics: Human Language Technologies, volume 1 (long and short papers), pp. 4171–4186 (2019)
9. Douze, M., et al.: The faiss library. arXiv preprint arXiv:2401.08281 (2024)
10. Esteva, A., Kuprel, B., Novoa, R.A., Ko, J., Swetter, S.M., Blau, H.M., Thrun, S.: Dermatologist-level classification of skin cancer with deep neural networks. Nature **542**(7639), 115–118 (2017)
11. Han, S.S., Kim, M.S., Lim, W., Park, G.H., Park, I., Chang, S.E.: Classification of the clinical images for benign and malignant cutaneous tumors using a deep learning algorithm. J. Investig. Dermatol. **138**(7), 1529–1538 (2018)
12. Lewis, P., et al.: Retrieval-augmented generation for knowledge-intensive nlp tasks. Adv. Neural. Inf. Process. Syst. **33**, 9459–9474 (2020)
13. Liu, H., Li, C., Wu, Q., Lee, Y.J.: Visual instruction tuning. Adv. Neural. Inf. Process. Syst. **36**, 34892–34916 (2023)
14. Liu, K., Li, Y., Xu, N., Natarajan, P.: Learn to combine modalities in multimodal deep learning. arXiv preprint arXiv:1805.11730 (2018)
15. Pedregosa, F., et al.: Scikit-learn: Machine learning in python. J. Mach. Learn. Res. **12**, 2825–2830 (2011)
16. Siegel, R.L., Giaquinto, A.N., Jemal, A.: Cancer statistics, 2024. CA: a cancer journal for clinicians **74**(1), 12–49 (2024)
17. Tan, M., Le, Q.: Efficientnet: rethinking model scaling for convolutional neural networks. In: International Conference on Machine Learning, pp. 6105–6114. PMLR (2019)
18. Team, C.: Chameleon: mixed-modal early-fusion foundation models. arXiv preprint arXiv:2405.09818 (2024)
19. Tschandl, P., Argenziano, G., Razmara, M., Yap, J.: Diagnostic accuracy of content-based dermatoscopic image retrieval with deep classification features. Br. J. Dermatol. **181**(1), 155–165 (2019)
20. Tschandl, P., Rosendahl, C., Kittler, H.: The ham10000 dataset, a large collection of multi-source dermatoscopic images of common pigmented skin lesions. Scientific data **5**(1), 1–9 (2018)
21. Wolf, T., et al.: Transformers: state-of-the-art natural language processing. In: Proceedings of the 2020 Conference on Empirical Methods in Natural Language Processing: System Demonstrations, pp. 38–45 (2020)

22. Xie, S., Girshick, R., Dollár, P., Tu, Z., He, K.: Aggregated residual transformations for deep neural networks. In: Proceedings of the IEEE Conference on Computer Vision and Pattern Recognition, pp. 1492–1500 (2017)
23. Zheng, L., et al.: Judging llm-as-a-judge with mt-bench and chatbot arena. Adv. Neural. Inf. Process. Syst. **36**, 46595–46623 (2023)

Lightweight Dual-Task Framework for Semi-supervised Lesion Segmentation with Knowledge Distillation from SAM

Xuan-Loc Huynh[1](✉), Huy-Thach Pham[2], Anh Mai Vu[3], Thanh-Minh Nguyen[4], Tran Quang Khai Bui[5], Tat-Bach Nguyen[6], Quan Nguyen[7], Minh Huu Nhat Le[8], and Phat K. Huynh[2](✉)

[1] Boston University, Boston, MA, USA
xlhuynh@bu.edu
[2] PASSIO Lab, North Carolina A&T State University, Greensboro, NC, USA
pkhuynh@ncat.edu
[3] University of Houston, Houston, TX, USA
[4] Ho Chi Minh City University of Medicine and Pharmacy,
Ho Chi Minh City, Vietnam
[5] University of Science, Viet Nam National University, Ho Chi Minh City, Vietnam
[6] Iowa State University, Ames, IA, USA
[7] Posts and Telecommunications Institute of Technology, Hanoi, Vietnam
[8] Interventional Cardiology Department, Methodist Hospital, Houston, TX, USA

Abstract. In real-world clinical settings, deploying medical AI applications requires lightweight models that can operate under limited computational resources. For skin lesion segmentation, a crucial step in the early detection of skin cancer, the key challenge is to develop models that are not only efficient but also perform reliably with minimal annotated data. To address this, we propose a lightweight and efficient semi-supervised segmentation framework that combines multi-task consistency learning with the representational power of foundation models. Our method is built on three key components: (1) a dual-network co-training framework combining a lightweight MobileNet with a strong ViT-based teacher to balance efficiency and representation power, (2) a fused mask prompt inspired by multi-task consistency, which combines coarse segmentation masks with boundary-aware Signed Distance Function (SDF) maps to guide SAM, and (3) a SAM-guided knowledge distillation strategy, where refined outputs from SAM are used as high-quality pseudo-labels to train the Main Network on unlabeled data. Extensive experiments demonstrate that our approach achieves competitive segmentation performance with significantly reduced annotation effort, offering a practical solution for semi-supervised medical image segmentation in real-world applications.

Keywords: Medical image segmentation · Semi-supervised learning · Segment Anything Model (SAM) · Lightweight models

1 Introduction

Medical image segmentation is a critical component of many clinical applications, but acquiring high-quality annotations remains both expensive and time-consuming as highlighted by Antonelli et al. [1]. Within this domain, skin lesion segmentation is particularly important for the early diagnosis of skin cancer, as it helps extract key visual features like lesion shape and boundary, as demonstrated in Li et al. [9]. To overcome the challenge of limited labeled data, numerous semi-supervised methods for skin lesion segmentation have been proposed, demonstrating strong performance by effectively leveraging both labeled and unlabeled images as reported in Nguyen et al. [13].

One of the core ideas in semi-supervised learning (SSL) is consistency regularization, which encourages models to produce similar predictions when the same input is perturbed. These methods promote smooth decision boundaries in low-density regions of the data space. Data augmentation-based methods include FixMatch [18], which applies weak augmentations to generate pseudo-labels that supervise predictions on strongly augmented versions of the same image, conditioned on a confidence threshold. Many self-training works by Luu et al., Nguyen et al. and Yang et al. [10,12,25] build on this by adding sharpening techniques and temporal ensembling to make the pseudo-labels more reliable over time. Other methods, proposed by Pham et al. [16] and Yu et al. [26], also rely on input perturbations with specialized mechanisms, including transformation consistency, uncertainty weighting, or attention-based confidence, to refine how consistency regularization is applied.

Beyond perturbation-based consistency, multi-branch models enforce consistency across complementary task-specific outputs. For example, the method proposed by Li et al. [8] enforces agreement between pixel-wise segmentation and a shape-aware branch to enhance boundary accuracy. Similar multi-branch strategies have been explored in fully supervised settings as well Wan et al. [20], Nguyen et al. [14], where combining pixel-level and structure-level cues has been shown to enhance segmentation quality. Additionally, in semi-supervised domain adaptation, approaches like Ngo et al. [11] extend this idea by promoting consistency across domains to improve generalization under distribution shifts. Besides, Pseudo-labeling frameworks play a major role in SSL segmentation. PseudoSeg [28], CCT [15], CPS [3], and GTA-Seg [7] implement dual-branch co-training or teacher-student setups to improve pseudo-label stability. Unimatch [24] aligns predictions under different augmentation strengths. In the medical domain, DME-FD [13] addresses noise via dual-mask ensemble and feature discrepancy co-training.

Knowledge distillation (KD), first introduced by Hinton et al. [5], is a training approach where a student model learns from the predictions of a stronger teacher model. It has been widely adopted in semi-supervised medical image segmentation to transfer knowledge from well-trained models to weaker ones using unlabeled data. Recent extensions include collaborative teacher teams by Wang et al. [21] and mutual distillation between student networks by Xie et al. [23]. A growing trend is to distill knowledge from powerful foundation models. For instance, Zhang et al. [27] explores using the Segment Anything Model (SAM) for semi-supervised segmentation by guiding SAM with domain-specific prompts and leveraging its outputs as pseudo-labels for training. Similarly, Huang et al. [6] proposes a Multi-view Co-training framework with a Learnable Prompt Strategy (LPS) and SAM-induced Knowledge Distillation (SKD), enabling sub-networks to adapt and learn from SAM's predictions while reducing noise from incorrect pseudo-labels.

While recent SSL methods have shown strong performance, many rely on large, complex models or struggle to produce accurate boundaries both of which are important for skin lesion segmentation. Newer approaches that use foundation models like SAM are promising, but they often miss the opportunity to guide SAM using rich multi-task cues such as coarse masks and boundary details. To address these challenges, we propose a lightweight co-training framework designed for clinical use. Our method combines a fused mask prompt with SAM to improve boundary accuracy and distills SAM's refined output into a more efficient main network.

In this work, we propose a semi-supervised skin lesion segmentation framework that integrates a lightweight Main Network with a foundation model (SAM) for enhanced supervision. Our main contributions are summarized as follows:

- **Lightweight Co-Training Framework:** We propose a dual-network training setup that pairs a lightweight Main Network (MobileNet) with a more powerful Teacher Network (ViT). This design enables the Main Network to run efficiently during inference, while still receiving strong supervision during training. It makes our framework practical for real-world deployment, particularly in resource-limited clinical settings.
- **Fused Mask Prompt for Boundary-Aware Guidance:** Inspired by consistency regularization across multi-task branches, we design a fused prompt that combines coarse semantic predictions with fine-grained boundary information. Specifically, we fuse the Main Network's initial segmentation mask and its corresponding Signed Distance Function (SDF) map into a single *mask prompt*. This unified representation captures both region-level confidence and structural contour cues, offering SAM a more holistic input for downstream refinement.
- **SAM-Guided Knowledge Distillation:** Leveraging the fused mask prompt, we introduce a SAM-guided distillation strategy. The task-aware prompt is passed into SAM, which produces a refined segmentation output. This output acts as a high-quality pseudo-label for training the Main Network on unlabeled data. By incorporating SAM's structured knowledge, the Main Network learns to generate more accurate and boundary-aligned predictions.

2 Methodology

Overview. We adopt a semi-supervised learning framework for lesion segmentation, where the dataset is divided into two subsets: a labeled set $\mathcal{D}_l =$

$\{(x_i, y_i)\}_{i=1}^{N_l}$, in which each image x_i is annotated with a corresponding segmentation mask y_i; and an unlabeled set $\mathcal{D}_u = \{x_j\}_{j=1}^{N_u}$, which contains only raw input images without annotations.

Our architecture consists of three main components: (1) a lightweight **Main Network** based on MobileNet for efficient segmentation; (2) a powerful **Teacher Network**, built upon a ViT backbone and augmented with SAM, to generate high-quality pseudo-labels; and (3) a structured training pipeline that enables interaction between the two. As shown in Fig. 1, the Main Network performs dual-task segmentation by predicting both binary masks and Signed Distance Function (SDF) maps. These outputs are fused to create task-aware prompts that guide the SAM module. SAM then refines the predictions and provides supervision signals back to the Main Network.

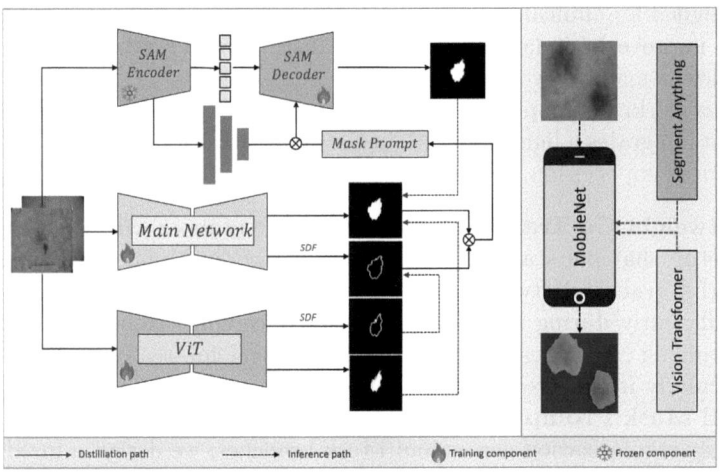

Fig. 1. Overview of our proposed semi-supervised segmentation framework. The Main Network (MobileNet) jointly predicts segmentation masks and Signed Distance Function (SDF) maps. These are fused into a mask prompt that guides the SAM decoder. SAM refines the predictions and provides high-quality pseudo-labels via knowledge distillation to train the Main Network. The Teacher Network (ViT) offers additional supervision, while only the Main Network is used at inference time for lightweight deployment.

2.1 Dual-Output Semi-Supervised Framework

Dual-Output Head with SDF Representation. Following [2], both the Main and Teacher networks employ a dual-output prediction head. For each input image, they output: (1) a binary segmentation mask for identifying semantic regions, (2) a Signed Distance Function (SDF) map for capturing fine-grained boundary geometry.

The SDF representation encodes the distance of each pixel to the nearest object boundary. Given a binary mask Y, the SDF at each pixel x is defined as:

$$\phi_Y(x) = \begin{cases} -\min_{y \in \partial V_Y} \|x-y\|, & \text{if } x \in V_Y^{\text{in}}, \\ 0, & \text{if } x \in \partial V_Y, \\ +\min_{y \in \partial V_Y} \|x-y\|, & \text{if } x \in V_Y^{\text{out}}, \end{cases}$$

where ∂V_Y, V_Y^{in}, and V_Y^{out} denote the boundary, interior, and exterior of the segmentation region, respectively. This continuous representation enables the network to model object contours more accurately and reason about spatial structure.

Dual-Task Consistency and Knowledge Distillation. To jointly learn semantic and geometric cues, the Main Network is trained with a dual-task objective: it predicts both a segmentation mask and an SDF map. This enforces consistency between region classification and boundary localization, encouraging the network to align its outputs both spatially and structurally. For unlabeled data, both the Main and Teacher networks process the same input image. The Teacher generates high-quality pseudo-labels consisting of a binary mask and an SDF map, which serve as supervision targets for the Main Network. This knowledge distillation process enables the Main Network to mimic the Teacher's predictions, benefiting from both region-based and geometry-aware guidance.

Fused Mask Prompt Generation. Once the Main Network produces its segmentation mask and SDF map, these two outputs are fused into a single *mask prompt*. The binary mask provides region-level confidence, while the SDF introduces detailed boundary information. This fused prompt forms a task-specific, enriched input used to guide the SAM decoder more effectively.

2.2 Learnable Prompt for SAM Using Fused Mask

Following Huang et al. [6] and Zhang et al. [27], the SAM decoder generates segmentation masks conditioned on prompts (e.g., points, boxes, masks) and image features. To enhance this process, we introduce a lightweight decoder $\psi(\cdot)$ that transforms the SAM encoder feature map $Z \in \mathbb{R}^{B \times D \times H \times W}$ into dense learnable prompts: $\mathbf{P}_b = \psi(Z; \Theta_m)$, where Θ_m are the decoder parameters and $\mathbf{P}_b \in \mathbb{R}^{B \times N_b \times L}$ represents the output prompt tokens.

To construct the final prompt for SAM, we fuse the Main Network's predicted binary mask and Signed Distance Function (SDF) map. This fused signal, together with $\mathbf{P}_b$, is fed to the SAM decoder: $\hat{Y}_s = \mathcal{F}_s(\mathbf{P}_b, \hat{Y}_f; \Theta_s)$, where $\hat{Y}_f$ is the prior prediction and Θ_s denotes the decoder parameters.

To support this prompting strategy, we integrate an adapter module from [22] for decoder fine-tuning. The segmentation loss is defined as:

$$\mathcal{L}_{\text{sam}} = \mathcal{L}_{\text{SEG}}(\hat{Y}_s, Y^l). \tag{1}$$

2.3 SAM-Guided Knowledge Distillation

Inspired by [6], we adopt the knowledge distillation framework from [5] to transfer supervision from SAM to the Main Network. Specifically, we use a temperature-scaled softmax to obtain softened probability maps:

$$\hat{Y}_T^c = \frac{\exp(\hat{q}_c/T)}{\sum_c \exp(\hat{q}_c/T)}, \quad (2)$$

where $\hat{q}_c$ is the SAM logit for class c, and T is a temperature parameter that controls the distribution's smoothness.

Soft predictions from both SAM (teacher) and the Main Network (student) are computed, and the distillation loss is defined via KL divergence:

$$\mathcal{L}_{\text{kd}} = KL(\hat{Y}_T, \hat{Y}_T^{\text{main}}), \quad (3)$$

where $\hat{Y}_T$ and $\hat{Y}_T^{\text{main}}$ are the temperature-softened outputs from SAM and the Main Network, respectively. The SAM model remains frozen, and gradients are only applied to the Main Network.

In summary, our method leverages semantic and geometric cues under a semi-supervised setup. The Main Network jointly predicts binary masks and SDF maps, supervised by pseudo-labels from the SAM-enhanced Teacher. The fused outputs form a prompt that guides SAM refinement, creating a feedback loop that improves learning efficiency. This design supports accurate segmentation with limited labels, while remaining lightweight and deployment-friendly.

3 Experiment

3.1 Dataset

We evaluated our framework on two widely used skin lesion segmentation datasets ISIC-2018 and HAM10000 under a semi-supervised learning setup. To simulate low-annotation scenarios, only 2%, 4%, or 8% of the training data was labeled, with the remainder treated as unlabeled. All experiments followed a 5-fold cross-validation protocol. The ISIC-2018 dataset [4] consists of 3,694 dermoscopic images, of which 2,955 were used for training and 739 for validation. The HAM10000 dataset [19] includes 10,015 images, split into 8,012 training and 2,003 validation samples.

3.2 Methods Under Comparison

To evaluate the effectiveness of our proposed lightweight SAM-assisted segmentation framework, we compare it against six representative state-of-the-art semi-supervised segmentation methods: PseudoSeg [28], CCT [15], CPS [3], GTA-Seg [7], Unimatch [24], and DME-FD [13]. In addition, we include comparisons with methods that incorporate SAM for semi-supervised segmentation, such as SemiSAM [27].

3.3 Evaluation Metrics

We evaluate segmentation performance using Dice, IoU, Sensitivity, and Specificity. Dice and IoU measure the overlap between predicted and ground truth masks. Sensitivity assesses how well lesion areas are detected, while Specificity indicates how well non-lesion areas are excluded.

4 Results

Table 1. Segmentation performance on ISIC-2018 under 2% and 4% labeled data settings. The SupOnly row reports results using fully supervised training.

Method	Data (%)		Metrics			
	Label	Unlabel	Dice (%) ↑	IoU (%) ↑	Sensitivity (%) ↑	Specificity (%) ↑
SupOnly	2%	0%	74.65 ± 2.92	60.81 ± 2.99	76.16 ± 2.44	93.38 ± 3.01
	4%	0%	77.23 ± 0.48	65.35 ± 0.56	79.53 ± 1.37	95.10 ± 0.59
	8%	0%	82.28 ± 0.61	70.66 ± 0.85	81.35 ± 0.42	96.12 ± 0.21
	100%	0%	87.66 ± 0.93	78.49 ± 1.38	87.11 ± 1.05	96.90 ± 0.35
PseudoSeg	2%	98%	79.76 ± 2.11	67.16 ± 2.77	76.65 ± 3.72	96.26 ± 0.83
CCT			78.66 ± 2.02	65.80 ± 2.63	77.17 ± 4.15	95.56 ± 0.69
CPS			79.61 ± 1.66	67.04 ± 2.28	78.43 ± 4.64	95.52 ± 1.04
GTA-Seg			77.33 ± 2.20	64.21 ± 2.59	80.04 ± 3.87	93.37 ± 2.00
Unimatch			80.03 ± 2.04	67.55 ± 2.71	78.46 ± 4.74	95.84 ± 1.50
DME-FD			80.07 ± 1.75	67.62 ± 2.37	78.97 ± 3.51	95.69 ± 0.58
Ours			**83.44 ± 1.91**	**68.97 ± 2.50**	**80.67 ± 3.79**	**97.01 ± 0.72**
PseudoSeg	4%	96%	81.77 ± 0.66	71.18 ± 1.03	81.98 ± 3.13	96.37 ± 0.85
CCT			80.96 ± 1.11	68.95 ± 1.41	79.75 ± 1.68	95.93 ± 0.28
CPS			80.89 ± 0.91	70.31 ± 1.07	82.08 ± 2.35	95.67 ± 0.96
GTA-Seg			80.83 ± 0.80	70.03 ± 1.07	82.54 ± 2.35	94.64 ± 1.46
Unimatch			81.41 ± 1.22	69.46 ± 1.58	79.50 ± 1.76	96.34 ± 0.56
DME-FD			82.06 ± 0.69	71.54 ± 1.04	82.87 ± 1.58	96.23 ± 0.36
Ours			**85.33 ± 0.72**	**73.61 ± 0.98**	**84.01 ± 1.21**	**96.91 ± 0.60**

Quantitative Results on ISIC-2018: Table 1 shows that our method achieves the highest Dice (83.44%, 85.33%) and IoU (68.97%, 73.61%) scores under both 2% and 4% labeled settings, outperforming all semi-supervised. It also leads in sensitivity and specificity, notably surpassing the fully supervised model trained with 8% labels, demonstrating its strength in low-label regimes.

Quantitative Results on HAM10000: As shown in Table 2, our method consistently outperforms semi-supervised baselines across both 2% and 4% label settings, achieving Dice scores of 91.02% and 91.56%, and IoU scores of 83.02% and

Table 2. Segmentation performance on HAM10000 under 2% and 4% labeled data settings. The SupOnly row reports results using fully supervised training.

Method	Data (%)		Metrics			
	Label	Unlabel	Dice (%) ↑	IoU (%) ↑	Sensitivity (%) ↑	Specificity (%) ↑
SupOnly	2%	0%	88.15 ±0.21	78.90 ±0.31	88.37 ±0.72	95.72 ±0.27
	4%	0%	89.59 ±0.07	81.24 ±0.12	88.58 ±0.97	96.80 ±0.40
	8%	0%	91.46 ±0.22	84.33 ±0.37	91.01 ±0.29	97.17 ±0.06
	100%	0%	93.54 ±0.25	87.92 ±0.42	93.30 ±0.07	97.80 ±0.22
PseudoSeg	2%	98%	90.02 ±0.17	81.94 ±0.28	88.18 ±1.32	97.29 ±0.51
CCT			89.93 ±0.10	81.79 ±0.15	88.54 ±0.86	97.09 ±0.30
CPS			89.94 ±0.14	81.81 ±0.23	87.95 ±0.48	97.35 ±0.28
GTA-Seg			89.55 ±0.32	81.17 ±0.54	88.89 ±0.70	96.60 ±0.09
Unimatch			89.66 ±0.15	81.35 ±0.26	87.89 ±0.38	97.15 ±0.31
DME-FD			90.45 ±0.17	82.65 ±0.27	88.74 ±0.83	97.39 ±0.44
Ours			**91.02 ±0.21**	**83.02 ±0.32**	**89.00 ±0.67**	**97.91 ±0.35**
PseudoSeg	4%	96%	90.97 ±0.39	83.21 ±0.64	89.11 ±0.77	97.49 ±0.45
CCT			90.64 ±0.53	82.97 ±0.86	89.08 ±0.94	97.39 ±0.15
CPS			90.76 ±0.51	83.17 ±0.84	89.20 ±0.54	97.44 ±0.19
GTA-Seg			90.86 ±0.19	83.34 ±0.31	89.74 ±0.69	97.24 ±0.32
Unimatch			90.32 ±0.44	82.43 ±0.73	88.93 ±1.29	97.20 ±0.61
DME-FD			91.13 ±0.30	83.79 ±0.50	**90.05 ±0.43**	97.33 ±0.08
Ours			**91.56 ±0.37**	**83.81 ±0.52**	90.02 ±0.60	**97.82 ±0.12**

Table 3. Comparison with SemiSAM methods on ISIC-2018, where SemiSAM denotes approaches that incorporate SAM for semi-supervised segmentation.

Method	Data (%)		Metrics		Params (M)	Speed (s)
	Label	Unlabel	Dice ↑	IoU ↑		
Unet (SupOnly)	100%	0%	0.7723 ± 0.0048	0.6535 ± 0.0056	7.8	0.8
DME-FD	4%	96%	0.8206 ± 0.0069	0.7154 ± 0.0104	41.4	1.2
SemiSAM			0.8412 ± 0.0110	0.7213 ± 0.0149	7.8	0.8
Ours			**0.8533 ± 0.0072**	**0.7361 ± 0.0098**	**2.9**	**0.02**

83.81%. It also records the highest sensitivity (90.02%) and specificity (97.82%), outperforming fully supervised baselines with more labeled data. Table 3 presents a broader comparison across three key categories: (1) the supervised baseline using Unet [17] trained on 100% labeled data, (2) the semi-supervised baseline DME-FD [13], and (3) the SAM-enhanced semi-supervised method, SemiSAM [27]. Despite using only 4% labeled data, our method achieves the highest Dice (85.33%) and IoU (73.61%) scores. At the same time, it maintains the smallest model size (2.9M parameters) and the fastest inference speed (0.02s). These results highlight that our approach not only delivers strong segmentation accuracy, but also meets the requirements of lightweight, real-time deployment in clinical environments.

5 Conclusion

We present a semi-supervised segmentation framework that integrates lightweight networks with SAM for efficient and accurate lesion segmentation. By jointly predicting masks and SDF maps, the Main Network captures both semantic and boundary cues. These are fused into prompts to guide SAM, enabling a closed-loop distillation process that improves learning under limited labels. The design ensures strong performance while remaining practical for clinical deployment.

Acknowledgement. We would like to thank AI VIETNAM for financial and computational support.

References

1. Antonelli, M., et al.: The medical segmentation decathlon. Nature Commun. **13**(1), 4128 (2022)
2. Bu, Q., Dong, B., Zhu, Z., Ni, J.: Edge enhancement based semi-supervised medical image segmentation method. In: 2025 2nd International Conference on Digital Image Processing and Computer Applications (DIPCA), pp. 39–43. IEEE (2025)
3. Chen, X., Yuan, Y., Zeng, G., Wang, J.: Semi-supervised semantic segmentation with cross pseudo supervision. In: Proceedings of the IEEE/CVF Conference on Computer Vision and Pattern Recognition, pp. 2613–2622 (2021)
4. Codella, N.C., et al.: Skin lesion analysis toward melanoma detection: a challenge at the 2017 international symposium on biomedical imaging (isbi), hosted by the international skin imaging collaboration (isic). In: 2018 IEEE 15th international symposium on biomedical imaging (ISBI 2018), pp. 168–172. IEEE (2018)
5. Hinton, G., Vinyals, O., Dean, J.: Distilling the knowledge in a neural network. arXiv preprint arXiv:1503.02531 (2015)
6. Huang, K., et al.: Learnable prompting sam-induced knowledge distillation for semi-supervised medical image segmentation. IEEE Trans. Med. Imaging (2025)
7. Jin, Y., Wang, J., Lin, D.: Semi-supervised semantic segmentation via gentle teaching assistant. Adv. Neural. Inf. Process. Syst. **35**, 2803–2816 (2022)
8. Li, S., Zhang, C., He, X.: Shape-aware semi-supervised 3d semantic segmentation for medical images. In: Martel, A.L., Abolmaesumi, P., Stoyanov, D., Mateus, D., Zuluaga, M.A., Zhou, S.K., Racoceanu, D., Joskowicz, L. (eds.) MICCAI 2020. LNCS, vol. 12261, pp. 552–561. Springer, Cham (2020). https://doi.org/10.1007/978-3-030-59710-8_54

9. Li, X., Yu, L., Chen, H., Fu, C.W., Heng, P.A.: Semi-supervised skin lesion segmentation via transformation consistent self-ensembling model. arXiv preprint arXiv:1808.03887 (2018)
10. Luu, Q.V., Le, K.D., Nguyen, T.H., Nguyen, T.M., Nguyen, Q., Nguyen, T.T., Dinh, Q.V.: Semi-supervised semantic segmentation using redesigned self-training for white blood cells. In: 2025 IEEE 6th International Conference on Image Processing, Applications and Systems (IPAS), pp. 1–6. IEEE (2025)
11. Ngo, B.H., Lam, B.T., Nguyen, T.H., Dinh, Q.V., Choi, T.J.: Dual dynamic consistency regularization for semi-supervised domain adaptation. IEEE Access **12**, 36267–36279 (2024). https://doi.org/10.1109/ACCESS.2024.3374105
12. Nguyen, T.H., Ngo, T.K.N., Vu, M.A., Tu, T.Y.: Blurry-consistency segmentation framework with selective stacking on differential interference contrast 3d breast cancer spheroid. In: Proceedings of the IEEE/CVF Conference on Computer Vision and Pattern Recognition, pp. 5223–5230 (2024)
13. Nguyen, T.H., Nguyen, T., Nguyen, X.B., Vu, N.L.V., Dinh, V.Q., MERIAUDEAU, F.: Semi-supervised skin lesion segmentation under dual mask ensemble with feature discrepancy co-training. In: Medical Imaging with Deep Learning
14. Nguyen, T.H., Vu, N.L.V., Nguyen, H.T., Dinh, Q.V., Li, X., Xu, M.: Semi-supervised histopathology image segmentation with feature diversified collaborative learning. In: AAAI Bridge Program on AI for Medicine and Healthcare, pp. 165–172. PMLR (2025)
15. Ouali, Y., Hudelot, C., Tami, M.: Semi-supervised semantic segmentation with cross-consistency training. In: Proceedings of the IEEE/CVF Conference on Computer Vision and Pattern Recognition, pp. 12674–12684 (2020)
16. Pham, H.H., et al.: Fetal-bcp: addressing empirical distribution gap in semi-supervised fetal ultrasound segmentation. In: 2025 IEEE 22nd International Symposium on Biomedical Imaging (ISBI), pp. 1–4. IEEE (2025)
17. Ronneberger, O., Fischer, P., Brox, T.: U-net: convolutional networks for biomedical image segmentation. In: Medical image computing and computer-assisted intervention–MICCAI 2015: 18th international conference, Munich, Germany, October 5-9, 2015, proceedings, part III 18, pp. 234–241. Springer (2015)
18. Sohn, K., Berthelot, D., Carlini, N., Zhang, Z., Zhang, H., Raffel, C.A., Cubuk, E.D., Kurakin, A., Li, C.L.: Fixmatch: simplifying semi-supervised learning with consistency and confidence. Adv. Neural. Inf. Process. Syst. **33**, 596–608 (2020)
19. Tschandl, P., Rosendahl, C., Kittler, H.: The ham10000 dataset, a large collection of multi-source dermatoscopic images of common pigmented skin lesions. Sci. Data **5**(1), 1–9 (2018)
20. Wang, Y., et al.: Deep distance transform for tubular structure segmentation in ct scans. In: Proceedings of the IEEE/CVF Conference on Computer Vision and Pattern Recognition, pp. 3833–3842 (2020)
21. Wang, Y., Cao, P., Hou, Q., Lan, L., Yang, J., Liu, X., Zaiane, O.R.: Progressively correcting soft labels via teacher team for knowledge distillation in medical image segmentation. In: International Conference on Medical Image Computing and Computer-Assisted Intervention, pp. 521–530. Springer (2024)
22. Wu, J., Fu, R., Fang, H., Liu, Y., Wang, Z., Xu, Y., Jin, Y., Arbel, T.: Medical sam adapter: Adapting segment anything model for medical image segmentation. arxiv 2023. arXiv preprint arXiv:2304.12620 (2023)
23. Xie, Y., Yin, Y., Li, Q., Wang, Y.: Deep mutual distillation for semi-supervised medical image segmentation. In: International Conference on Medical Image Computing and Computer-Assisted Intervention, pp. 540–550. Springer (2023)

24. Yang, L., Qi, L., Feng, L., Zhang, W., Shi, Y.: Revisiting weak-to-strong consistency in semi-supervised semantic segmentation. In: Proceedings of the IEEE/CVF Conference on Computer Vision and Pattern Recognition, pp. 7236–7246 (2023)
25. Yang, L., Zhuo, W., Qi, L., Shi, Y., Gao, Y.: St++: Make self-training work better for semi-supervised semantic segmentation. In: Proceedings of the IEEE/CVF Conference on Computer Vision and Pattern Recognition, pp. 4268–4277 (2022)
26. Yu, L., Wang, S., Li, X., Fu, C.-W., Heng, P.-A.: Uncertainty-aware self-ensembling model for semi-supervised 3d left atrium segmentation. In: Shen, D., et al. (eds.) MICCAI 2019. LNCS, vol. 11765, pp. 605–613. Springer, Cham (2019). https://doi.org/10.1007/978-3-030-32245-8_67
27. Zhang, Y., Yang, J., Liu, Y., Cheng, Y., Qi, Y.: Semisam: enhancing semi-supervised medical image segmentation via sam-assisted consistency regularization. In: 2024 IEEE International Conference on Bioinformatics and Biomedicine (BIBM), pp. 3982–3986. IEEE (2024)
28. Zou, Y., Zhang, Z., Zhang, H., Li, C.L., Bian, X., Huang, J.B., Pfister, T.: Pseudoseg: designing pseudo labels for semantic segmentation. arXiv preprint arXiv:2010.09713 (2020)

Proceedings of Computer-Aided Pelvic Imaging for Female Health (CAPI)

UteroVAE: A Shape-Informed Variational Autoencoder for Uterine MRI Encoding in Adenomyosis, Fibroids, and Healthy Uteri

Richard Ruppel[1]($\boxtimes$), Maximilian Lindholz[1], Robin Schmidt[1], Yasmin El-Nahry[1], Sylvia Mechsner[1], Sophia Elisabeth Ellen Schulze-Weddige[1], Georg Lukas Baumgärtner[1], Tillmann Arlt[1], Charlie Alexander Hamm[1], Sebastian Arndt[2], Lisa Siegler[2], Leonard Stepansky[2], Jana Hutter[2], Matthias May[2], and Tobias Penzkofer[1]

[1] Charité – Universitätsmedizin Berlin, Berlin, Germany
{richard.ruppel,maximilian.lindholz,robin.schmidt,yasmin.el-nahry,
sylvia.mechsner,sophia.schulze-weddige,georg.baumgaertner,
tillmann.arlt,charlie.hamm,tobias.penzkofer}@charite.de
[2] Universitätsklinikum Erlangen, Erlangen, Germany
{sebastian.arndt,lisa.siegler,matthias.may}@uk-erlangen.de,
{leonard.stepansky,jana.hutter}@fau.de

Abstract. Uterine disorders, such as adenomyosis and fibroids, are major contributors to pelvic pain, abnormal uterine bleeding, and infertility. Morphologic configurations and geometric alterations of the uterine cavity serve as critical imaging biomarkers in clinical diagnosis. One well established example is the question mark sign, a highly specific indicator of adenomyosis, characterized by distinctive uterine contour distortions. However, beyond this singular marker, a broader range of shape variations may hold diagnostic significance.

To systematically capture these morphologic and geometric patterns, we adapted a Variational Autoencoder (VAE) pre-trained on fastMRI datasets. Instead of encoding MRI images alone, we designed the model to jointly incorporate both the segmented uterine cavity and MRI scans. By embedding an anatomy-informed prior, the model is better equipped to characterize structural anatomy relevant to uterine pathology.

Our results indicate that both fine-tuning the VAE and using the hybrid encoding approach produce embeddings that align more closely with clinically relevant disease patterns and improve downstream clustering performance. By refining the joint representation of segmentation and MRI data, our method could enhance the potential of latent diffusion models for extracting imaging biomarkers in female pelvic disorders.

Keywords: Pelvic Imaging · Autoencoder · Phenotyping

1 Introduction

Uterine disorders, such as adenomyosis and fibroids (myomas), significantly contribute to pelvic pain, abnormal uterine bleeding, and infertility. Adenomyosis occurs when endometrial tissue invades the myometrium, causing diffuse enlargement or focal bulges of the uterus, while fibroids are benign smooth muscle tumors that can distort the uterine wall. Accurate diagnosis is complicated by the natural variability of uterine shape, which changes throughout the menstrual cycle and varies by individual anatomy [1–3]. In ultrasound imaging, the "question mark sign"—where the uterus curves like a question mark—has demonstrated high diagnostic sensitivity and specificity. Other shape characteristics, such as a bulky shape, also hold great diagnostic value [4]. Most of these signs rely mainly on ultrasound imaging instead of MRI. Therefore, we aimed to analyze uterine shapes using MRI. To determine whether MRI-based uterine shapes hold clinical significance—and to reduce human bias—we propose a novel framework that segments the uterine cavity and general uterine contour using the state-of-the-art nnU-Net framework, followed by a dual autoencoder that encodes both the raw image and the organ segmentation.

Autoencoder architectures have been successfully utilized in medical imaging for various applications, including classification, clustering, data harmonization, and segmentation tasks [5,6]. Unlike traditional methods that depend on autoencoders to create segmentation masks, we introduce a novel framework where the segmentation masks themselves act as auxiliary inputs to the autoencoder. This approach benefits greatly from the accessibility of advanced segmentation tools like TotalSegmentator, which can be used right away to accurately outline specific anatomical regions—including the face, skin pathologies, vessels, and solid organs—without requiring any additional fine-tuning or training [7,8]. Advances in computational power and large-scale datasets have enabled these tools to provide readily accessible segmentation information. We hypothesize that integrating this information into unsupervised clustering pipelines can improve phenotyping efforts. Inspired by previous work that demonstrated incorporating bone morphology as a point cloud along with MRI images can enhance classification performance by capturing clinically relevant tibial features [9].

Our contributions are summarized as follows: (1) We fine-tuned a VAE for female pelvic MRI and applied unsupervised clustering to analyze shape and imaging features of both healthy uteri and those affected by fibroids or adenomyosis. (2) We introduce a segmentation-informed shared encoder approach that harnesses segmentation prior information to concentrate on specific image regions. (3) In light of recent advancements in large-scale automated segmentation models, our approach acts as a generalizable framework for automated phenotyping. Its modular design, which features interchangeable components, facilitating deployment across various anatomical domains.

2 Dataset

To enable a dual-input embedding framework that analyzes both image sequences and segmentations, we developed a novel dataset labeled as

$$D = \{(X_i, S_i, c_i)\}_{i=1}^{N}, \quad N = 336.$$

Here, X_i represents the input image sequence, S_i denotes the segmentation data corresponding to the images in X_i, and c_i is the label indicating a healthy patient, adenomyosis, or fibroid patient.

The dataset consists of 300 scans from the publicly available "Large-Scale Uterine Myoma MRI Dataset Covering All FIGO Types With Pixel-Level Annotations" (UMD) and 36 scans from Charité University Hospital [10]. Among the Charité University Hospital scans, 18 patients were healthy and 18 had adenomyosis, while the UMD dataset included 300 patients with fibroids. For training the autoencoder, we utilized all 336 imaging volumes. To address the class imbalance for clustering, we randomly selected 36 fibroid cases, resulting in a more balanced clustering dataset of 72 patients (18 healthy, 36 with fibroids, and 18 with adenomyosis). Data from Charité University Hospital were collected as part of the multi-center RACOON Faden project, approved by the ethics committee at University Hospital Erlangen (ID: 24-87_1-B), with notification of the local ethics committee at Charité University Hospital. Refer to Fig. 3 for representative samples from our curated dataset; the samples have been normalized and preprocessed to maintain a uniform appearance (Fig. 1).

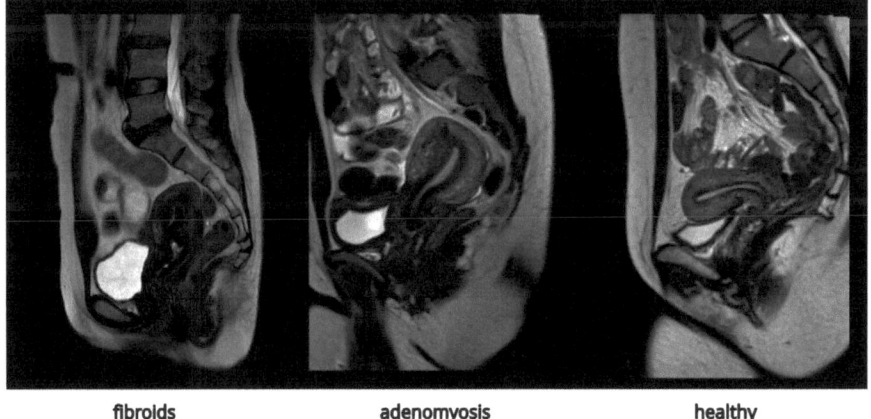

Fig. 1. Sample slices from our dataset: fibroids, adenomyosis, and healthy tissue from left to right.

2.1 3D MRI Image Data

For each case, sagittal T2-weighted imaging (T2WI) sequences were utilized. As the original sagittal MRI sequence varied in resolutions, length, slice spacing, and thickness, they were standardized through preprocessing steps, including z-score normalization of pixel values, as well as resizing to the most common shape. The resulting uniform dataset consists of $24 \times 512 \times 512$ 3D image data, represented as X_i. All scans were manually assessed to capture the female pelvis from cranially at vertebrae L4/5.

2.2 3D Segmentation Data

Building on the segmentations included in the UMD dataset, we trained an nnU-Net model to predict segmentations for all cases in our dataset [11]. Afterward, all segmentation masks were manually refined to ensure accuracy. We then trained a nnU-Net model on the entire dataset to predict segmentations for the uterus and the uterine cavity in the MRI images. These segmentation masks, generated by our trained nnU-Net, were reviewed and approved by medical experts and are denoted as S_i.

2.3 Clinical Imaging Report

The UMD dataset consists of patients diagnosed with fibroids, while the Charité University Hospital dataset includes patients diagnosed with adenomyosis or identified as healthy. Diagnoses were confirmed during the study inclusion process for both healthy and adenomyosis patients. In the case of the UMD dataset, MRIs were verified by 11 experienced radiologists as part of their data curation process [10].

Figure 2 provides visual examples of our pipeline, along with a representative sample of the 3D image data and the corresponding 3D segmentations mask utilized in our study. This dataset forms the foundation for a detailed examination of uterine disorders through a shape-informed autoencoder model.

3 Methodology

We implemented a systematic three-step methodology to investigate whether segmentation-informed auto-encoding better aligns with human judgment compared to traditional auto-encoding methods that lack preprocessing and dual encoding techniques.

1. Segmentation Model Training: We trained a custom nnU-Net model to generate segmentation masks for the uterus and uterine cavity. This model was tailored specifically for our task but remains compatible with other pre-trained segmentation networks, such as the TotalSegmentator.

2. Shared Autoencoder Development: We developed a shared autoencoder that incorporates both raw MRI image data and the associated segmentation masks. This method utilizes the anatomical guidance offered by the segmentation masks, minimizing variability in the autoencoder's latent space.
3. Automated Evaluation Pipeline: We used an automated evaluation pipeline to evaluate the resulting clustering outcomes. This pipeline comprises dimensionality reduction, clustering, and comparison with human-defined disease labels.

Our proposed framework, illustrated in Fig. 2, is based on a custom-trained nnU-Net model specifically designed for uterine and cavity segmentation. While our main approach employs a specialized segmentation model, our framework remains compatible with other pre-trained segmentation networks.

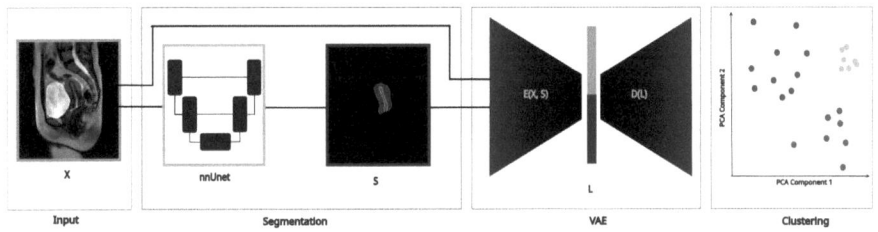

Fig. 2. UteroVAE's pipeline first creates a segmentation, which is then input into the VAE together with the corresponding MRI image. The generated latent vectors are subsequently post-processed and clustered.

3.1 Autoencoder Architecture

Our autoencoder architecture is derived from the Stable Diffusion SDXL VAE model and implemented as an autoencoder with KL divergence loss [15]. The architecture is adapted from the mri-autocncoder-v0.1, which also serves as our baseline approach [12]. The network processes two-channel inputs using the SiLU activation function. Its encoder consists of three sequential DownEncoderBlock2D blocks that output feature maps with 128, 256, and 512 channels, respectively—each block comprises two layers and employs group normalization with 32 groups. The decoder mirrors this structure with three UpDecoderBlock2D blocks, reconstructing the input from a latent space of 4 channels. The network processes images of size 256 with a scaling factor of 0.262.

Originally trained on fast magnetic resonance images from the brain and knee to encode both magnetic resonance and phase shift images, the model was adapted by substituting the phase shift images with segmentation masks and fine-tuning it on our dataset [13]. For comparison, we also used only the MRI images as input, omitting the segmentation masks. In this case, we duplicated the MRI images to create a two-channel input. For our proposed pipeline, we utilized both the MRI and segmentation masks; they are employed as separate channels.

4 Experiments and Results

The experiments are designed to assess the effectiveness of the nnU-Net model for uterine and cavity segmentation, the fine-tuning of the autoencoder to integrate segmentation masks, and the qualitative analysis of the latent space representations. The results demonstrate the capability of our approach to accurately capture and differentiate between healthy and pathological uterine conditions, providing valuable insights for clinical diagnosis and treatment planning.

4.1 nnU-Net Training

The best segmentation results were achieved by the nnU-Net architecture for our task, utilizing full resolution, 3D convolutions, and 5 folds to capture spatial dependencies within the MRI data. The model was trained using a combination of cross-entropy loss and Dice loss to optimize segmentation accuracy. We employed an initial learning rate of 0.01, training the model for 1,000 epochs with a batch size of 2. The model's performance was validated on our train/test split, with an 80:20 ratio, achieving a mean Dice coefficient for the uterus of 0.934 with an Intersection over Union of 0.876, while for the uterine cavity, the Dice coefficient was 0.919 with an Intersection over Union of 0.849.

4.2 Autoencoder Finetuning

After the segmentation process, we fine-tuned the autoencoder to incorporate both raw MRI images and their corresponding segmentation masks. Initially, the autoencoder was trained on the complete dataset of 336 MRI scans, optimizing the representation of the latent space through a combination of reconstruction loss and KL divergence loss. For fine-tuning, we used the dual input of segmentation masks in conjunction with the corresponding MRI images. To enhance the fine-tuning, we applied an 80:20 train/test split and conducted a hyperparameter search on the training set using the Optuna framework [18]. We optimized learning rate, KL weight, batch size, and epochs. The final model used a learning rate of 3.32×10^{-5}, a KL weight of 4.70×10^{-10}, a batch size of 2, and 9 epochs.

Table 1. SSIM Results (Mean ± Standard Deviation). Results are presented for both the MRI image and the segmentation masks.

Config	SSIM (Image)	SSIM (Segmentation)
UteroVAE	**0.536 ± 0.387**	**0.718 ± 0.422**
mri-autoencoder-v0.1	0.089 ± 0.136	0.093 ± 0.096

The model's performance was evaluated using the Structural Similarity Index Measure (SSIM). The results are summarized in Table 1, which presents the mean and standard deviation for both MRI images and segmentation masks. The mean SSIM of 0.536 for MRI images and 0.718 for segmentation masks indicates that the fine-tuned autoencoder captured the essential structural characteristics of the female pelvis reasonably well (cf. Fig. 3). After training and testing, the model was employed on all scans in our dataset to determine the latent vectors for each image or image-segmentation combination. For comparison, this was also done using the microsoft/mri-autoencoder-v0.1 without additional fine-tuning.

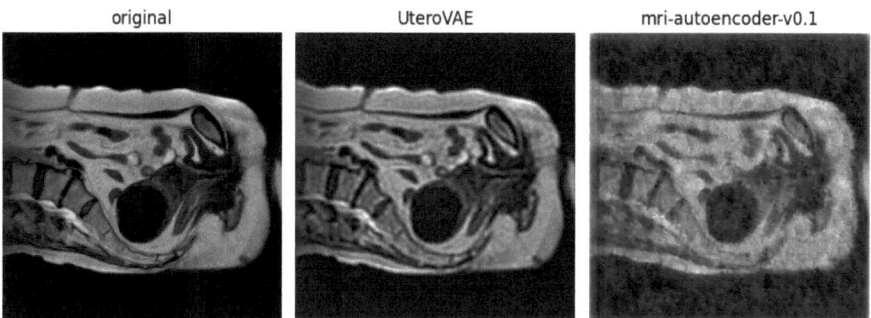

Fig. 3. Sample slice reconstructions from left to right: original image, UteroVAE output, and MRI autoencoder (v0.1) output. The figure illustrates qualitative differences in reconstruction quality across models.

4.3 Clustering Results

To assess clustering performance, we developed an automated pipeline combining dimensionality reduction and clustering. We applied UMAP [19] (with default settings) to project the AutoEncoder's latent representations into a lower-dimensional space, as UMAP preserves both local and global structure and is particularly well suited for visualizing and clustering high-dimensional, non-linear embeddings. MiniBatch K-Means was then used to partition the data into three clusters, reflecting the three known diagnostic categories. This variant of K-Means offers computational efficiency on larger datasets while maintaining similar clustering quality, making it appropriate for repeated analyses and real-time applications.

To address class imbalance, we fixed the number of fibroid cases to 36 (out of 300) and included all available adenomyosis and healthy samples. We ran 30 bootstrap iterations, each with a newly sampled fibroid subset, and computed the mean and standard deviation of clustering metrics to ensure robustness and reduce sensitivity to sampling variability.

Clustering results were compared to human-defined diagnostic labels using two metrics. The V-measure, the harmonic mean of homogeneity and completeness, assesses both cluster purity and label consistency. The Adjusted Mutual Information (AMI) quantifies agreement with ground truth while correcting for chance. Together, these metrics provide a robust evaluation of how well the unsupervised clustering aligns with clinical labels.

Table 2. Clustering results (Mean ± Std) for different configurations using ARI, AMI, and V-measure.

Method	Configuration	AMI	V-measure
UteroVAE	Segmentation + MRI	**0.572 ± 0.087**	**0.584 ± 0.085**
UteroVAE	MRI Only	0.562 ± 0.085	0.575 ± 0.083
mri-autoencoder-v0.1	Segmentation + MRI	0.490 ± 0.092	0.505 ± 0.089
mri-autoencoder-v0.1	MRI Only	0.486 ± 0.108	0.501 ± 0.105

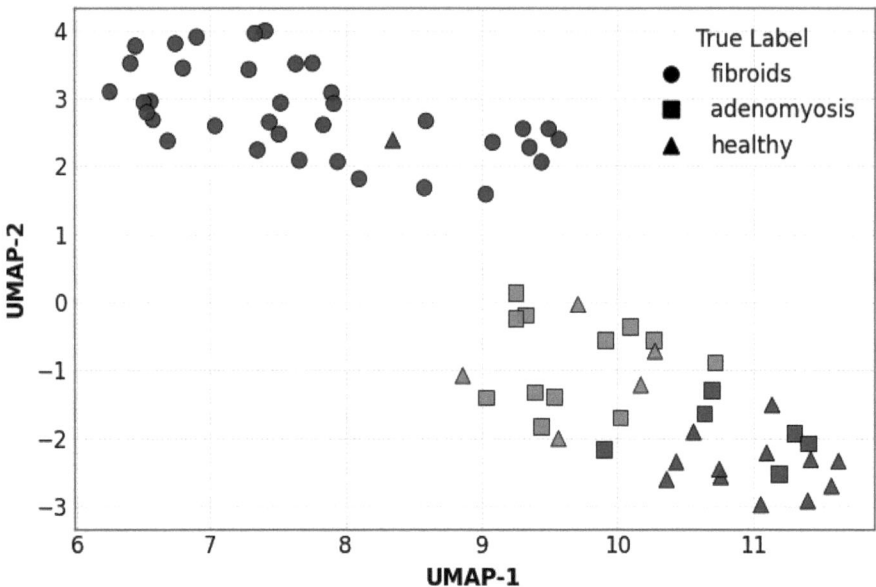

Fig. 4. UMAP projection (Axes 1 and 2) of encoded MRI + Segmentation representations from the UteroVAE model. Colors show cluster assignments (MiniBatch K-Means), while marker shapes represent the original diagnostic labels. The plot displays a sample output using the first random seed from the bootstrapped clustering process. (Color figure online)

Table 2 summarizes the performance of the objective clustering in various configurations. The fine-tuned UteroVAE autoencoder, which leverages a joint representation of segmentation masks and MRI images, achieves the highest performance and exhibits the highest concordance with human feedback. In contrast, models that use only MRI inputs, whether implemented with UteroVAE or mri-autoencoder-v0.1, demonstrate reduced efficacy, with the mri-autoencoder-v0.1 MRI-only configuration yielding the lowest performance metrics. These findings suggest that incorporating segmentation masks provides a modest improvement in clustering outcomes for unsupervised phenotyping, both with and without fine-tuning. Figure 4 shows the first and second UMAP axes for the first bootstrap run involving 30 fibroid patients. A distinct fibroid cluster is visible. While there is some overlap between healthy and adenomyosis patients, one cluster mainly consists of healthy individuals, and another primarily includes adenomyosis cases.

5 Conclusion

In this study, we introduced UteroVAE, a shape-informed variational autoencoder designed for encoding uterine MRI images in cases of adenomyosis, fibroids, and healthy uteri. Our approach leverages segmentation masks as auxiliary inputs to the fine-tuned autoencoder, enhancing the model's ability to capture clinically relevant morphological features. By integrating both raw MRI images and segmentation masks, our method provides a comprehensive representation of uterine anatomy, facilitating improved clustering and classification of uterine conditions.

Our experiments demonstrate the effectiveness of the proposed segmentation-informed autoencoder framework. The nnU-Net model achieved high accuracy in segmenting the uterus and uterine cavity, and the fine-tuned autoencoder generated latent representations that aligned moderately to well with clinical diagnoses. By comparing model output with expert labels, we showed that both fine-tuning and the inclusion of segmentation as auxiliary input improve clustering alignment with human clinical reasoning.

While the results are promising, the absence of established baseline models specifically designed for learning robust latent representations of uterine disease in MRI limits direct comparisons. Furthermore, the interpretability of clustering results could be enhanced through more extensive qualitative analysis and the inclusion of larger, more balanced datasets.

Future work will focus on expanding the imaging dataset to include a broader range of scanners and patient characteristics, as well as investigating disease expression across different phases of the menstrual cycle.

Acknowledgments. This study was funded by "NUM 2.0" (FKZ: 01KX2121).

Disclosure of Interests. M.L. receives funding from the Berlin Institute of Health (Junior Digital Clinician Scientist Grant). C.A.H. receives funding from the Berlin

Institute of Health (Digital Clinician Scientist Grant) and Siemens Healthineers and previously received seed funding from the University Medicine Greifswald and speaker fees from Siemens Healthineers, Bayer AG, Koelis AG, and Bracco Imaging Deutschland outside the submitted work. T.P. also receives funding from the Berlin Institute of Health (Advanced Clinician Scientist Grant, Platform Grant), the Ministry of Education and Research (BMBF, 01KX2121 ("NUM 2.0", RACOON), 68GX21001A, 01ZZ2315D), the German Research Foundation (DFG, SFB 1340/2), and the European Union (H2020, CHAIMELEON: 952172, DIGITAL, EUCAIM:101100633). Furthermore, T.P. declares relationships with the following companies: research agreements (no personal payments) with AGO, Aprea AB, AR-CAGY-GINECO, Astellas Pharma Global Inc. (APGD), Astra Zeneca, Clovis Oncology, Inc., Holaira, Incyte Corporation, Karyopharm, Lion Biotechnologies, Inc., MedImmune, Merck Sharp & Dohme Corp, Millennium Pharmaceuticals, Inc., Morphotec Inc., NovoCure Ltd., PharmaMar S.A. and PharmaMar USA, Inc., Roche, Siemens Healthineers, and TESARO Inc.; fees for a book translation (Elsevier B.V.); and fees for speaking engagements (Bayer Healthcare).

References

1. Bourdon, M., et al.: Adenomyosis: an update regarding its diagnosis and clinical features. J. Gynecol. Obstet. Hum. Reprod. **50**, 102228 (2021)
2. Freytag, D., Günther, V., Maass, N., Alkatout, I.: Uterine fibroids and infertility. Diagnostics **11**, 1455 (2021)
3. Andres, M.P., Borrelli, G.M., Ribeiro, J., Baracat, E.C., Abrão, M.S., Kho, R.M.: Transvaginal ultrasound for the diagnosis of adenomyosis: systematic review and meta-analysis. J. Minim. Invasive Gynecol. **25**, 257–264 (2018)
4. Zannoni, L., et al.: Question mark sign and transvaginal ultrasound uterine tenderness for the diagnosis of adenomyosis: a prospective validation. J. Ultrasound Med. **39**, 1405–1412 (2020)
5. Atlason, H.E., Love, A., Sigurdsson, S., Gudnason, V., Ellingsen, L.M.: SegAE: unsupervised white matter lesion segmentation from brain MRIs using a CNN autoencoder. NeuroImage: Clin. **24**, 102085 (2019)
6. Muhammad, H., et al.: Unsupervised subtyping of cholangiocarcinoma using a deep clustering convolutional autoencoder. In: Shen, D., et al. (eds.) MICCAI 2019. LNCS, vol. 11764, pp. 604–612. Springer, Cham (2019). https://doi.org/10.1007/978-3-030-32239-7_67
7. Wasserthal, J., et al.: TotalSegmentator: robust segmentation of 104 anatomic structures in CT images. Radiol Artif Intell **5**, e230024 (2023)
8. Lindholz, M., et al.: Analyzing the TotalSegmentator for facial feature removal in head CT scans. Radiography **31**, 372–378 (2025)
9. Liu, C., Yu, X., Wang, D., Jiang, T.: ACLNet: a deep learning model for ACL rupture classification combined with bone morphology. In: International Conference on Medical Image Computing and Computer-Assisted Intervention, pp. 57-67. Springer, Cham (2024)
10. Pan, H., et al.: Large-scale uterine myoma MRI dataset covering all FIGO types with pixel-level annotations. Sci. Data **11**, 410 (2024)
11. Isensee, F., Jaeger, P.F., Kohl, S.A., Petersen, J., Maier-Hein, K.H.: nnU-Net: a self-configuring method for deep learning-based biomedical image segmentation. Nat. Methods **18**, 203–211 (2021)

12. Microsoft, MRI Autoencoder v0.1, Hugging Face Model Hub. https://huggingface.co/microsoft/mri-autoencoder-v0.1. Accessed 27 Feb 2025
13. Zbontar, J., et al.: fastMRI: an open dataset and benchmarks for accelerated MRI. arXiv preprint arXiv:1811.08839 (2018)
14. Podell, D., et al.: Sdxl: improving latent diffusion models for high-resolution image synthesis. arXiv preprint arXiv:2307.01952 (2023)
15. Kingma, D.P., Welling, M.: Auto-encoding variational bayes. Banff, Canada (2013)
16. Kingma, D.P., Salimans, T., Welling, M.: Variational dropout and the local reparameterization trick. In: Advances in Neural Information Processing Systems, vol. 28 (2015)
17. Ho, J., Jain, A., Abbeel, P.: Denoising diffusion probabilistic models. Adv. Neural. Inf. Process. Syst. **33**, 6840–6851 (2020)
18. Akiba, T., Sano, S., Yanase, T., Ohta, T., Koyama, M.: Optuna: a next-generation hyperparameter optimization framework. In: Proceedings of the 25th ACM SIGKDD International Conference on Knowledge Discovery & Data Mining, pp. 2623–2631 (2019)
19. McInnes, L., Healy, J., Melville, J.: UMAP: uniform manifold approximation and projection for dimension reduction. arXiv preprint arXiv:1802.03426 (2020)

Delineation Uncertainty from Clinician Ranges in Cervical Cancer Radiotherapy Planning

Omar Todd[1]([✉]), Sooha Kim[2,3], Katherine Mackay[4], Raghav Mehta[1], Fabio De Sousa Ribeiro[1], David Bernstein[2,3], Alexandra Taylor[2,3], and Ben Glocker[1]

[1] Department of Computing, Imperial College London, London, UK
omar.todd16@imperial.ac.uk
[2] The Institute of Cancer Research, London, UK
[3] The Royal Marsden Hospital, London, UK
[4] Imperial College Healthcare NHS Trust, London, UK

Abstract. Accurate contouring of target areas affected by cancer is crucial in radiotherapy planning to provide effective treatment for patients. Beyond producing sufficiently precise contours, it is also important to have a reliable measure of the associated uncertainty of where the true anatomical boundaries may be located. Inter-observer variability arising from multiple experts annotating the boundaries of the target area provides a representation of this uncertainty; however, these annotations are labour-intensive to obtain over a large number of images, often making it infeasible in practice. In this study, we evaluate the clinical relevance of predictive auto-contouring uncertainty from training on clinician-defined ranges - a set of annotations from a single expert representing the delineation uncertainty of the target area, which are far more efficient to produce. This aims to bridge the gap in the performance of uncertainty estimates between training on a single contour and a set of contours from multiple annotators. This is achieved by curating a cervical cancer dataset with uncertainty annotations produced on CT scans from patients undergoing radiotherapy. We demonstrate that the resulting uncertainty from a model trained on these clinician-defined ranges is more meaningful compared with training on single contours without an uncertainty range. We also validated its clinical utility with respect to the inter-observer variation on a small hold-out set.

Keywords: Segmentation Uncertainty · Cervical Health · Radiotherapy

1 Introduction

Cervical cancer is the fourth most common cancer in women around the world, with hundreds of thousands of new cases and deaths reported each year, and the highest rates occurring in low and middle-income countries [1]. Radiotherapy is the primary treatment for patients with bulky cervical cancer or disease that has extended beyond the cervix. The goal is to deliver an adequate radiation dose to the tumour (target volumes) and areas at high risk of microscopic spread, while minimising exposure to surrounding healthy tissues (organs at risk) to reduce treatment-related side effects. These structures are traditionally contoured or delineated by clinical oncologists. Advancements in deep learning (DL) have facilitated the development of auto-contouring models that can accurately delineate target volumes and organs at risk, making the radiotherapy planning workflow faster [3]. However, it is important to consider the uncertainty associated with the contours generated from these models [9], due to the inherent ambiguity in defining the exact boundaries of tumour volumes and organs at risk, known as delineation uncertainty.

Delineation uncertainty is the biggest source of systematic error in modern-day radiotherapy planning processes [4]. This reflects both intra-observer variability, where the same observer may define the structure's boundaries differently at different times; and inter-observer variability (IOV) [8,11], where different observers may produce varying contours. In the context of uncertainty quantification, both of these modes of variation fall under aleatoric uncertainty, which is the irreducible variation present in the data due to factors such as image resolution [22]. A reliable measure of IOV is valuable, as it quantifies the delineation uncertainty around annotated regions of interest [21], enabling this uncertainty to be accounted for in radiotherapy planning. However, incorporating the IOV in the auto-contouring pipeline is challenging due to the substantial cost of collecting annotations on a large number of images from different clinical experts. Given the practical infeasibility of collecting these annotations, in this work, we conduct a study into the clinical relevance of utilising the predictive uncertainty arising from approximating IOV through a clinician-defined uncertainty range (CDR).

Our study makes two key contributions to advancing the discussion on how to efficiently produce clinically meaningful uncertainty in the absence of a large set of multi-observer annotations, which are costly and time-consuming to acquire:

1. Curation of a new cervical cancer dataset where each image is annotated with a CDR, representing expert aleatoric uncertainty.
2. Quantitative and qualitative analysis of an auto-contouring model trained on these CDRs, showing clinical applicability of our model.

2 Clinician-Defined Ranges

2.1 Related Work

IOV is widely regarded as the gold standard for quantifying delineation uncertainty; however, it is subject to unwanted variation due to contouring style and protocol interpretation, even when clear guidelines are provided [19]. Prior studies have shown that the IOV of contours can decrease following peer review

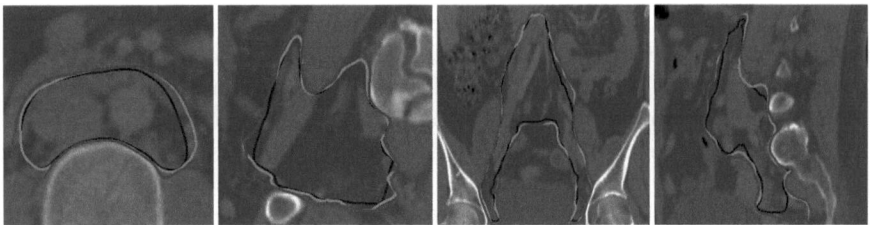

Fig. 1. Visualisations of the CTV uncertainty in the cervical cancer dataset showing the inner (blue), reference (green) and outer (red) contours from different views. (Color figure online)

and collaboration among clinicians [15,17]. The practical challenges of obtaining annotations from multiple observers, along with evidence that IOV may overestimate uncertainty, have led to increased clinical research exploring how to generate meaningful uncertainty from smaller groups or even single annotators. Previous work explored creating measures for delineation uncertainty tailored to individual patients [5]. This involved using two contours representing the tumour uncertainty, produced by a single clinician. These contours were used in conjunction with a suitable probability density function to estimate the true tumour boundary position within the contour bounds. More recent work extended this concept of annotating an uncertainty area to evaluate the performance of an auto-contouring model in relation to a ground truth range. In this study, a single clinician annotated a small number of cases with an inner and outer boundary and measured how closely the predicted contour was contained within this range [13]. This was beneficial in introducing the range-based annotation scheme in an auto-contouring context. However, to enable these models to be used as part of a treatment planning pipeline, they must produce uncertainty estimates to meaningfully aid the clinicians' decisions. This calls for further investigation into whether the uncertainty from these single contour models is sufficient for downstream planning, or if it is necessary to utilise the range information from clinicians more directly during training.

2.2 Cervical Cancer Dataset

This study seeks to explore the efficacy of a range-based labelling strategy to produce clinically relevant uncertainty, which can guide radiotherapy planning for target areas at risk. We curated a new cervical cancer dataset that uses CT scans from patients covering the pelvic region. In this work, we specifically focus on delineation uncertainty associated with nodal clinical target volumes (CTVs), which encompass lymph nodes and surrounding regions at high risk of harbouring cancer cells. To facilitate the experiments, we annotated 55 cases of scans from cervical cancer patients. The label acquisition process consisted of a clinician annotating a reference, inner, and outer CTV contour on each image in the dataset. This was followed by verification with a small number of additional experts to ensure the reliability of the annotations. Throughout the rest of this work, we use the following terms to distinguish between the different types of contours in the labels:

- **Reference**: A typical single contour provided for general segmentation tasks.
- **Inner**: Contour that gives an estimate of the smallest region that would be clinically feasible to contain the area of interest. This marks the area with a high probability of containing the structure of interest.
- **Outer**: Contour that gives an estimate of the largest region that would be clinically feasible to contain the area of interest. This marks the area beyond which the structure of interest is unlikely to be present.

A set of example inner (blue), reference (green), and outer (red) contours from our dataset are shown in Fig. 1, showcasing a high degree of non-uniformity in the uncertainty throughout the target area.

Hold-Out Set. In addition to the main dataset used for model training and validation, a separate hold-out set was also curated for clinical validation. This dataset consists of six cases where ten different clinical experts provided annotations for the CTV, producing IOV. The manner of variation on these cases from the different observers was studied and used to guide the annotation protocol for the CDRs on new images. This ensured that while these clinically defined ranges will naturally have less variation compared with IOV from multiple experts, they still retain the most important uncertainty in the correct regions to make them usable in practice. Furthermore, the time to obtain the IOV annotations on this hold-out set took approximately two years, mainly due to logistical delays from coordinating across a number of centres. In contrast, the ranges for our experimentation were produced at a rate of around fifteen cases per week, demonstrating a substantial increase in labelling efficiency.

3 Method

The experiments for this study were formulated as a segmentation task using different options for the training strategy concerning the ground truth labels. Specifically, we explore three training variations for this work to quantify the effect of the labels on predictive uncertainty:

Single Contour – Reference Only ($SC_{Reference}$): The baseline experiment to determine how much useful uncertainty we can obtain by training on only a single contour. The model was trained on the dataset using only the reference contour as the target for optimization.

Single Contour – Repeated Image ($SC_{Repeated}$): We also investigate the effect of using the same training process as before; however during training the model sees all combinations; the image with each of the inner, outer, and reference labels. This is to determine whether seeing the additional uncertainty

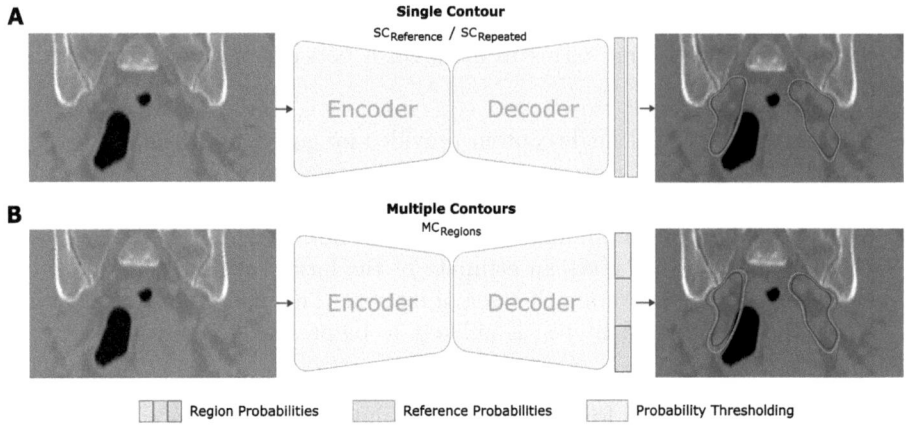

Fig. 2. Overview of different methods used for training the segmentation model on the dataset. **A**: Single contour training with just the reference or image repetition with each contour from the range. Probabilistic thresholding applied on outputs for uncertainty estimates. **B**: Multiple contour training with region-based optimization using a combined label of the inner, outer, and reference contours.

context during single-contour optimization results in more meaningful uncertainty in the output probabilities while not degrading general segmentation performance. We simulate this by repeating the image in our dataset, where each instance contains one of the three contours as the label pair.

Multiple Contours – Region-Based ($MC_{Regions}$): For this experiment, we leverage the inner, outer, and reference contours to train a model to predict the full uncertainty range. In other medical segmentation tasks, such as brain lesions, where the evaluation is performed on regions of aggregated labels rather than each individual label, it has been demonstrated that training on these regions directly can lead to increased performance in the relevant metrics [7,14]. Given the hierarchical structure of our contours, we leverage this mechanism to train a segmentation model in a multi-contour setting, using the combined contour as the label for optimisation. The training regions for the model are defined as the inner voxels, the inner and reference voxels, and the inner, reference, and outer voxels.

A visual representation of the three training strategies is depicted in Fig. 2. Region-based training produces a direct measure of the CTV uncertainty. However, for single-contour training, we estimate this uncertainty region by using thresholding on the probabilities obtained from the logits in the last layer. These probabilities indicate the model's confidence in including each voxel as part of the CTV. The reference contour is obtained by thresholding the output probabilities at 0.5. The inner and outer contour predictions are simulated by thresholding the output probabilities at 0.9 and 0.1, respectively.

4 Experiments

The 55 labelled cases are split into 45 for training and validation and 10 for testing. For each training strategy outlined, evaluation on the test set is performed using an ensemble of 5 segmentation models generated as part of cross-validation.

Table 1. Quantitative results of the three different training methods evaluated using DSC, HD95, and VD ($\times 10^3$ voxels). The MC$_{\text{Regions}}$ method demonstrates the best performance overall. For the single contour methods, SC$_{\text{Repeated}}$ shows slightly better alignment with the clinician range.

Method	DSC ↑			HD95 ↓			VD ↓
	Inner	Ref	Outer	Inner	Ref	Outer	
SC$_{\text{Reference}}$	0.901$_{\pm.01}$	0.906$_{\pm.02}$	0.905$_{\pm.01}$	4.03$_{\pm.67}$	4.63$_{\pm1.15}$	5.59$_{\pm1.38}$	45.56$_{\pm16.40}$
SC$_{\text{Repeated}}$	0.906$_{\pm.01}$	**0.907$_{\pm.02}$**	0.915$_{\pm.01}$	3.80$_{\pm.61}$	**4.58$_{\pm1.05}$**	4.95$_{\pm1.27}$	34.84$_{\pm13.02}$
MC$_{\text{Regions}}$	**0.912$_{\pm.01}$**	0.906$_{\pm.02}$	**0.923$_{\pm.01}$**	**3.67$_{\pm.69}$**	4.75$_{\pm1.07}$	**3.94$_{\pm0.85}$**	**4.33$_{\pm3.141}$**

4.1 Implementation Details

We employ nnU-Net [6,18], a state-of-the-art segmentation framework for medical image segmentation, to train an auto-contouring model. The patch-based training option provided by the framework is used due to the large resolution of the 3D CT images in our dataset. The loss function is a combination of the dice and cross-entropy loss to directly utilise segmentation performance as well as the probabilities in the optimization process. Deep supervision is performed at each layer of the model in the optimization [12]. We use the SGD optimizer with an initial learning rate of 1×10^{-2} and a polynomial learning rate schedule. The standard nnU-Net data augmentation pipeline is applied, containing a rich variety of spatial and intensity operations to aid with generalisability.

4.2 Quantitative Results

To compare the performance of each method, we use two standard segmentation metrics, namely the Dice score (DSC) and the 95-percentile Hausdorff distance (HD95). From Table 1 we observe that the MC$_{\text{Regions}}$ method is the best performing across both metrics. The results also show a slight performance increase using SC$_{\text{Repeated}}$ compared with SC$_{\text{Reference}}$, suggesting a higher degree of label variance was propagated to the underlying uncertainty maps. Given the hierarchical relationship of the three contours, it appears the model is capturing the uncertainty range well, but is marginally worse at correctly placing the reference contour between the bounds. To further highlight the accuracy of the predicted range, we also report the absolute volumetric difference (VD) in thousands of voxels. This is calculated using the difference in number of voxels between the inner and outer contours for both the ground truth and the model predictions.

We then take the difference between these two to measure the volumetric alignment of the two ranges. While the same order of performance is preserved, this metric shows the predictions from $MC_{Regions}$ have significantly better alignment with the ground truth, arising due to the much tighter ranges predicted from SC methods.

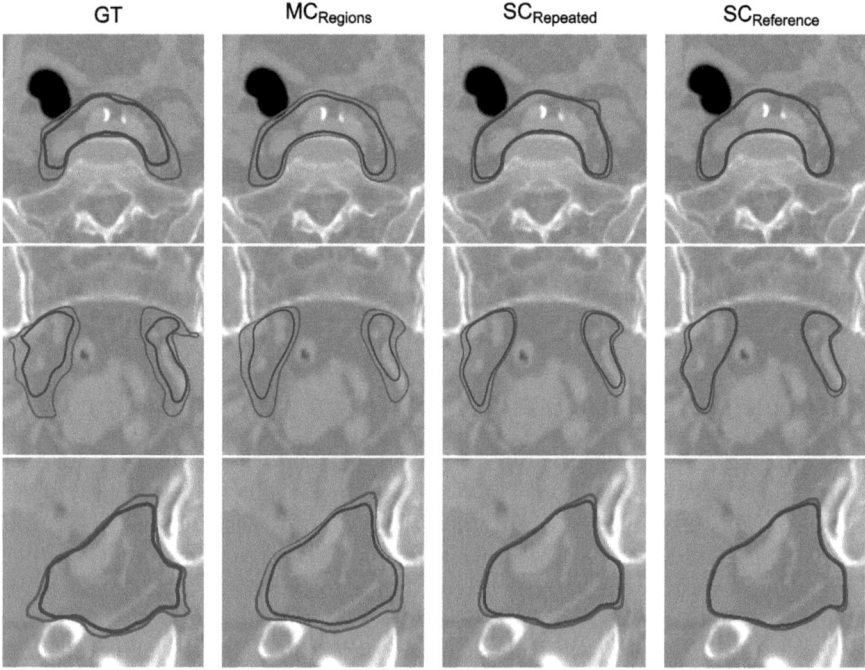

Fig. 3. Qualitative results, from different views, of inner (blue), reference (green) and outer (red) predictions on the test set using the three different training strategies. $MC_{Regions}$ most closely matches the ground truth (GT) uncertainty range with $SC_{Repeated}$ showing more variation than $SC_{Reference}$. (Color figure online)

4.3 Qualitative Results

In Fig. 3, we also present a set of visualisations of the model predictions compared with the ground truth for three different views. With regard to the qualitative analysis, we first observe that the models are able to capture the shapes of the contours sufficiently well; however, some fine-grained details present in the clinical annotations are smoothed out during training. These results also support the findings from the metrics, where the predictions from $MC_{Regions}$ are clearly providing the most variation in the predictive range, while in the SC training methods, the inner and outer contours are predicted much more closely around the reference.

4.4 Clinical Evaluation

The $MC_{Regions}$ model predictions from the six hold-out set images, described in Sect. 2.2, were sent to the clinicians to validate their clinical relevance. The first evaluation consisted of the clinicians measuring the level of alignment between the model predictions and the CDRs for the hold-out set. When comparing the model outputs against the set of CDRs on this data, the average DSC scores were 0.88 and 0.90 for the inner and outer contours respectively. This demonstrates that the model output maintains strong agreement with the CDR from this hold-out set. Crucially, the ranges for this hold-out set were produced by different experts from the one who annotated the training set. This highlights that the annotation protocol is reliable in ensuring that clinically relevant uncertainty is preserved across annotations from different experts. Additionally, to quantify the localisation accuracy of the range in relation to the IOV, the extent to which the consensus contour among the observers was contained within the range was also evaluated. The consensus contour was derived using the STAPLE algorithm [20], to produce a statistical estimate of the most probable contour based on the level of agreement among observers. The ideal result is that the entire consensus contour sits within the inner and outer boundaries of the CDR provided by a single annotator. The error of the consensus falling outside of these boundaries was expressed as a percentage of the consensus contour's volume. Across the six cases, the maximum error of the consensus being outside of the $MC_{Regions}$ outer boundary was 3.6%, and the maximum error for the consensus being inside of the inner boundary was 0.35%. The respective errors for the CDR were 13.0% and 0.45%. To account for sensitivity to outliers, we also report the corresponding median errors which were 0.06% and 2.13% for the $MC_{Regions}$ outer and inner boundaries. The median errors for the CDR outer and inner boundaries were 0.03% and 2.43% A visual depiction of the consensus alignment with respect to

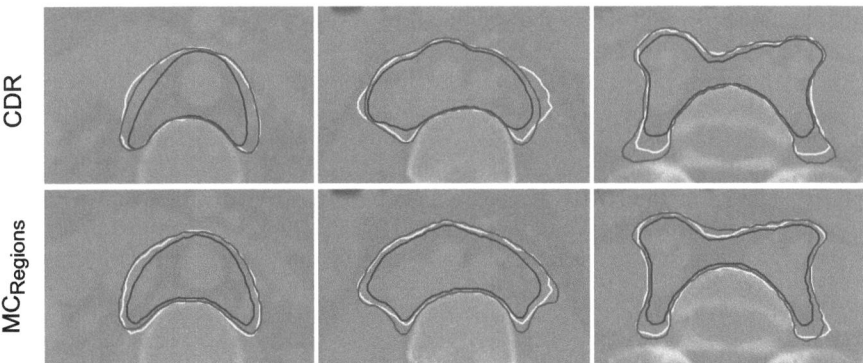

Fig. 4. Consensus contour (yellow) alignment with range contours (inner: blue and outer: red) for the clinician defined range (CDR) and $MC_{Regions}$ predictions on the hold-out set. $MC_{Regions}$ range contours show better alignment with the consensus contours compared to the CDR contours. (Color figure online)

the predictive range and CDR is shown in Fig. 4. These errors for the CDR were validated by the clinicians as being within tolerance for an acceptable level of alignment with the IOV consensus. The model outputs being well aligned with the CDR demonstrates their clinical usefulness and potential for facilitating delineation uncertainty research.

5 Conclusion and Future Work

In this study, we analysed the usefulness of using CDR annotations to facilitate the training of auto-contouring models to produce delineation uncertainty for cervical cancer. The experiments with these ranges are strongly motivated by (i) the practical difficulties of obtaining annotations from a number of different clinicians, and (ii) the need for a more efficient data solution that allows for accurate modelling of uncertainty. Uncertainty arising from multiple annotators (i.e., IOV) will always be difficult to replicate precisely from a single annotator. However, the protocol for constructing the ranges was defined in conjunction with studying the IOV, ensuring the ground truth ranges used for model training were clinically relevant. The quantitative and qualitative results demonstrate strong alignment between the model predictions and the ranges. This indicates that the model is capturing uncertainty in the right regions, and preserving alignment with protocol compliant ranges from different clinicians.

While predicting the uncertainty of the CTV provides valuable insight, future work could investigate the incorporation of probabilistic information within the range. Generating a distribution of contours within the range would provide more granular information on the likelihood of certain areas belonging to the target volume. This probabilistic information could guide how the radiation dosage should be distributed over the target area to be most effective while minimising risk to healthy tissue. This could build upon prior work on stochastic segmentation models [2,10,16], and use the clinician-defined ranges to generate a set of multiple plausible contours for the clinical planning process.

Acknowledgment. O.T. and R.M. are funded through the European Union's Horizon Europe research and innovation programme under grant agreement 101080302. S.K. is supported by the CRUK Convergence Science Centre at The Institute of Cancer Research, London, and Imperial College London (A26234). B.G. and F.d.S.R. acknowledge the support of the UKRI AI programme, and the EPSRC, for CHAI - EPSRC Causality in Healthcare AI Hub (grant no. EP/Y028856/1). B.G. received support from the Royal Academy of Engineering as part of his Kheiron/RAEng Research Chair.

Disclosure of Interests. B.G. is a part-time employee of DeepHealth. No other competing interests.

References

1. World health organization cervical cancer. https://www.who.int/news-room/fact-sheets/detail/cervical-cancer. Accessed 02 June 2025

2. Baumgartner, C.F., et al.: PHiSeg: capturing uncertainty in medical image segmentation. In: Shen, D., et al. (eds.) MICCAI 2019. LNCS, vol. 11765, pp. 119–127. Springer, Cham (2019). https://doi.org/10.1007/978-3-030-32245-8_14
3. van den Berg, C.A., Meliadò, E.F.: Uncertainty assessment for deep learning radiotherapy applications. In: Seminars in Radiation Oncology, vol. 32, pp. 304–318. Elsevier (2022)
4. Bernstein, D., et al.: An inter-observer study to determine radiotherapy planning target volumes for recurrent gynaecological cancer comparing magnetic resonance imaging only with computed tomography-magnetic resonance imaging. Clin. Oncol. **33**(5), 307–313 (2021)
5. Bernstein, D., Taylor, A., Nill, S., Oelfke, U.: New target volume delineation and PTV strategies to further personalise radiotherapy. Phys. Med. Biol. **66**(5), 055024 (2021)
6. Isensee, F., Jaeger, P.F., Kohl, S.A., Petersen, J., Maier-Hein, K.H.: nnu-net: a self-configuring method for deep learning-based biomedical image segmentation. Nat. Methods **18**(2), 203–211 (2021)
7. Isensee, F., Kickingereder, P., Wick, W., Bendszus, M., Maier-Hein, K.H.: No new-net. In: Crimi, A., Bakas, S., Kuijf, H., Keyvan, F., Reyes, M., van Walsum, T. (eds.) BrainLes 2018. LNCS, vol. 11384, pp. 234–244. Springer, Cham (2019). https://doi.org/10.1007/978-3-030-11726-9_21
8. Joskowicz, L., Cohen, D., Caplan, N., Sosna, J.: Inter-observer variability of manual contour delineation of structures in CT. Eur. Radiol. **29**, 1391–1399 (2019)
9. Kinoshita, N., et al.: Quantification of uncertainties in reference and relative dose measurements, dose calculations, and patient setup in modern external beam radiotherapy. Radiol. Phys. Technol. **18**(1), 58–77 (2025)
10. Kohl, S., et al.: A probabilistic u-net for segmentation of ambiguous images. In: Advances in Neural Information Processing Systems, vol. 31 (2018)
11. Lazarus, E., Mainiero, M.B., Schepps, B., Koelliker, S.L., Livingston, L.S.: BI-RADS lexicon for us and mammography: interobserver variability and positive predictive value. Radiology **239**(2), 385–391 (2006)
12. Lee, C.Y., Xie, S., Gallagher, P., Zhang, Z., Tu, Z.: Deeply-supervised nets. In: Artificial Intelligence and Statistics, pp. 562–570. PMLR (2015)
13. Mackay, K., et al.: 1621 assessment of a novel approach for validating auto-contouring systems with an expert predicted acceptability range. Radiother. Oncol. **206**, S2439–S2442 (2025)
14. Menze, B.H., et al.: The multimodal brain tumor image segmentation benchmark (BRATS). IEEE Trans. Med. Imaging **34**(10), 1993–2024 (2014)
15. Mercieca, S., Belderbos, J.S., van Baardwijk, A., Delorme, S., van Herk, M.: The impact of training and professional collaboration on the interobserver variation of lung cancer delineations: a multi-institutional study. Acta Oncol. **58**(2), 200–208 (2019)
16. Monteiro, M., et al.: Stochastic segmentation networks: modelling spatially correlated aleatoric uncertainty. In: Advances in Neural Information Processing Systems, vol. 33, pp. 12756–12767 (2020)
17. Peltenburg, J.E., et al.: Interobserver variation in tumor delineation of liver metastases using magnetic resonance imaging. Phys. Imaging Radiat. Oncol. **30**, 100592 (2024)
18. Ronneberger, O., Fischer, P., Brox, T.: U-Net: convolutional networks for biomedical image segmentation. In: Navab, N., Hornegger, J., Wells, W.M., Frangi, A.F. (eds.) MICCAI 2015. LNCS, vol. 9351, pp. 234–241. Springer, Cham (2015). https://doi.org/10.1007/978-3-319-24574-4_28

19. Tudor, G., et al.: Geometric uncertainties in daily online IGRT: refining the CTV-PTV margin for contemporary photon radiotherapy. Br. Inst. Radiol. (2020)
20. Warfield, S.K., Zou, K.H., Wells, W.M.: Simultaneous truth and performance level estimation (staple): an algorithm for the validation of image segmentation. IEEE Trans. Med. Imaging **23**(7), 903–921 (2004)
21. Watadani, T., et al.: Interobserver variability in the CT assessment of honeycombing in the lungs. Radiology **266**(3), 936–944 (2013)
22. Zou, K., Chen, Z., Yuan, X., Shen, X., Wang, M., Fu, H.: A review of uncertainty estimation and its application in medical imaging. Meta-Radiol. **1**(1), 100003 (2023)

Diffusing the Blind Spot: Uterine MRI Synthesis with Diffusion Models

Johanna P. Müller[1(✉)], Anika Knupfer[1], Pedro Blöss[1], Edoardo Berardi Vittur[1], Bernhard Kainz[1,2], and Jana Hutter[1]

[1] Friedrich–Alexander University Erlangen–Nürnberg, Erlangen, DE, Germany
johanna.paula.mueller@fau.de
[2] Imperial College London, London, UK

Abstract. Despite significant progress in generative modelling, existing diffusion models often struggle to produce anatomically precise female pelvic images, limiting their application in gynaecological imaging, where data scarcity and patient privacy concerns are critical. To overcome these barriers, we introduce a novel diffusion-based framework for uterine MRI synthesis, integrating both unconditional and conditioned Denoising Diffusion Probabilistic Models (DDPMs) and Latent Diffusion Models (LDMs) in 2D and 3D. Our approach generates anatomically coherent, high fidelity synthetic images that closely mimic real scans and provide valuable resources for training robust diagnostic models. We evaluate generative quality using advanced perceptual and distributional metrics, benchmarking against standard reconstruction methods, and demonstrate substantial gains in diagnostic accuracy on a key classification task. A blinded expert evaluation further validates the clinical realism of our synthetic images. We release our models with privacy safeguards and a comprehensive synthetic uterine MRI dataset to support reproducible research and advance equitable AI in gynaecology. The code and data are available at https://github.com/ividja/SynthUterus.

Keywords: Uterus · Diffusion Models · Image Generation · MRI

1 Introduction

Generative models, particularly diffusion-based architectures, have demonstrated remarkable success across a wide range of applications in computer vision and medical imaging. However, despite their potential, key anatomical structures, such as the uterus and female pelvis, remain conspicuously absent from most publicly available models. While gynaecologists rely on their clinical expertise for diagnosis and treatment, making the interpretation process highly observer-dependent, the lack of high-quality uterine MRI datasets limits the development of tools that can support clinical education and improve diagnostic accuracy. Generative methods can be essential not only for training and reducing bias but also for enhancing the ability to detect complex or rare conditions like fibroids, adenomyosis, and congenital uterine anomalies. The scarcity of comprehensive uterine imaging datasets, compounded by privacy concerns, has hindered the development of robust diagnostic tools for these critical conditions. Given the high variability of female pelvic anatomy between individuals, by providing more diverse and representative data, generative models can help create diagnostic tools that assist clinicians in making faster, more accurate decisions, ultimately leading to improved patient outcomes.

From a machine learning perspective, this represents an opportunity to leverage the power of deep generative models, such as Denoising Diffusion Probabilistic Models (DDPMs) and Latent Diffusion Models (LDMs), to fill this gap. Diffusion models are particularly well-suited to medical image synthesis due to their ability to generate high-quality, anatomically realistic images by learning complex distributions from limited data. For gynaecologists, access to synthetic yet anatomically realistic uterine MRI scans can aid diagnosis by facilitating anomaly comparison and strengthening AI models trained on limited data, thereby supporting clinical workflows in data-scarce settings.

Contributions. In this work, we present a novel generative framework for uterine MRI synthesis, addressing the need for both data augmentation and the generation of anatomically correct images for clinical use. Our contributions include: (1) the development of a tailored approach for synthesising uterine MRIs with diffusion models, in 2D and 3D, (2) the introduction of both unconditional and conditioned models that enable generation of diverse uterine anatomies, (3) evaluation on a clinically relevant task such as classification.

2 Related Work

Uterus Imaging Datasets. Imaging plays a vital role in gynaecology and medical AI, yet publicly available datasets focused on the female pelvis, particularly high-resolution MRI, remain limited. Datasets such as UterUS [3] concentrate on transvaginal ultrasound and lack MRI data from adult, non-pregnant patients, omitting the pathological diversity needed for clinical relevance. The UMD dataset [10] represents a major advance, providing annotated sagittal T2-weighted pelvic MRIs with histologically confirmed uterine myomas, segmentations, and FIGO classifications to support diagnosis and treatment planning. However, it largely comprises pathological cases, limiting the utility of models that depend on normal anatomy for weakly-, self-, or unsupervised learning. Without sufficient healthy examples, such methods struggle to differentiate typical from atypical presentations, reducing clinical reliability and generalisability. Additional datasets like the Intrapartum Ultrasound Grand Challenge 2024 and the TCGA Uterine Corpus Endometrial Carcinoma Collection are highly specialised, highlighting the ongoing lack of comprehensive, balanced datasets covering both healthy and pathological uterine anatomy across imaging modalities.

Diffusion Models in Medical Imaging. Diffusion models have recently emerg-ed as powerful generative tools in medical imaging, enabling stable training and high-quality, anatomically coherent image synthesis. They have been applied successfully in brain MRI [6,13], chest CT [11], and digital pathology [15] for image generation, inpainting, and data augmentation. These methods enable the creation of realistic synthetic datasets that support downstream tasks such as classification, reconstruction and anomaly detection [1,2,9,18,19]. However, their use in pelvic and gynaecological MRI remains limited due to scarce publicly available datasets of uterine anatomy, with particularly few examples of healthy patients. Expanding diffusion-based synthetic data generation in this area could address data scarcity, reduce annotation demands, and facilitate robust AI development.

3 Method

Denoising Diffusion Probabilistic Models (DDPMs). We model the true data distribution $p_{\text{data}}(x)$ using a DDPM [7], which learns to reverse a fixed noising process defined by:

$$q(x_t \mid x_0) = \mathcal{N}(x_t; \sqrt{\bar{\alpha}_t} x_0, (1 - \bar{\alpha}_t)\mathbf{I}), \quad (1)$$

where x_t is a noisy version of the input image x_0 at diffusion step t, and $\bar{\alpha}_t$ is the cumulative product of variance schedule coefficients α_t. The denoising model $p_\theta(x_{t-1} \mid x_t)$ is parameterised by a U-Net with time-step embeddings and spatial self-attention. We minimise the DDPM loss:

$$\mathcal{L}_{\text{DDPM}}(\theta) = \mathbb{E}_{x_0,\epsilon,t}\left[\|\epsilon - \epsilon_\theta(x_t, t, c)\|_2^2\right], \quad (2)$$

where x_0 is the original clean image, $\epsilon_0 \sim \mathcal{N}(0, \mathbf{I})$ is the initial Gaussian noise added to x_0, ϵ is the noise added at timestep t, x_t is the noisy image at timestep t, c denotes conditioning information such as class labels or segmentation maps, and $\epsilon_\theta(x_t, t, c)$ is the model's predicted noise.

Latent Diffusion Models (LDMs). To scale the generative process to high-resolution outputs efficiently, we incorporated Latent Diffusion Models (LDMs) [17] for final-stage refinement. LDMs operate in a learned latent space $\mathcal{Z} \subset \mathbb{R}^{h \times w \times c}$ rather than the pixel space $\mathcal{X}$. A convolutional autoencoder $(\mathcal{E}, \mathcal{D})$ was trained to minimise:

$$\mathcal{L}_{\text{VAE}}(\phi, \psi) = \mathbb{E}_{x \sim p_{\text{data}}}\left[\|x - \mathcal{D}_\psi(\mathcal{E}_\phi(x))\|_2^2\right], \quad (3)$$

ensuring that $\mathcal{E}_\phi(x) = z$ retains all clinically relevant uterine features.

The diffusion model then operates in latent space as:

$$z_t = \sqrt{\bar{\alpha}_t} z_0 + \sqrt{1 - \bar{\alpha}_t}\epsilon, \quad \epsilon \sim \mathcal{N}(0, \mathbf{I}), \quad (4)$$

with loss function:

$$\mathcal{L}_{\text{LDM}}(\theta) = \mathbb{E}_{z_0,\epsilon,t}\left[\|\epsilon - \epsilon_\theta(z_t, t, c)\|_2^2\right], \quad (5)$$

where $z_0 = \mathcal{E}(x)$ and c again denotes conditioning inputs. Final reconstructions are obtained via $\hat{x} = \mathcal{D}(z_0)$.

Preprocessing. T2-weighted sagittal pelvic MRI scans were preprocessed to ensure anatomical consistency and facilitate multi-resolution modelling. Each volume $x \in \mathbb{R}^{H \times W \times S}$ was corrected for bias field inhomogeneity and standardised to zero mean and unit variance per scan. Using weakly supervised uterus localisation performed by a trained U-Net on a small set of annotated images, we extracted a region of interest (ROI) encompassing the uterus and adjacent structures. This ROI was then resampled to a standard in-plane resolution of 1.0 mm.

Text Conditioning. To enhance control and enable anatomically and clinically relevant synthesis, we incorporated text- and class-based conditioning into our diffusion models. Text conditioning uses structured natural language prompts, *e.g.*, keywords for uterine position (anteflexed, retroflexed, anteverted, retroverted), MRI parameters (*e.g.*, 1.5T, 3T), and sequence types (*e.g.*, TSE, HASTE). The input c is encoded via a pretrained text encoder (e.g., Transformer or CLIP), producing an embedding that modulates the denoising network via cross-attention. Class conditioning specifies categorical labels such as uterine position. This hybrid framework enables generation of anatomically plausible pelvic MRI slices and volumes aligned with clinical descriptors, supporting explicit control over synthesised image characteristics.

Privacy Filtering. To mitigate risks of patient reidentification, especially for the full pelvic scans, and prevent overfitting through memorisation we implemented a post-hoc privacy filter for all generated images $\hat{x}$. Each $\hat{x}$ was embedded into a perceptual space using a frozen encoder $f : \mathcal{X} \to \mathbb{R}^d$, trained independently from the diffusion model. For each training image x_i, we computed the cosine similarity:

$$\text{sim}(\hat{x}, x_i) = \frac{f(\hat{x}) \cdot f(x_i)}{\|f(\hat{x})\| \, \|f(x_i)\|}. \tag{6}$$

Generated samples were flagged and discarded if they exceeded a similarity threshold τ against any training image:

$$\max_i \text{sim}(\hat{x}, x_i) > \tau, \quad \text{with} \quad \tau = 0.95. \tag{7}$$

To detect higher-level near-duplicates, we compared structural embeddings from intermediate encoder layers and clustered them using approximate nearest neighbour search. This multi-scale filtering ensures accepted samples are sufficiently distinct from the training data, supporting patient anonymity and adherence to generative privacy standards.

4 Evaluation

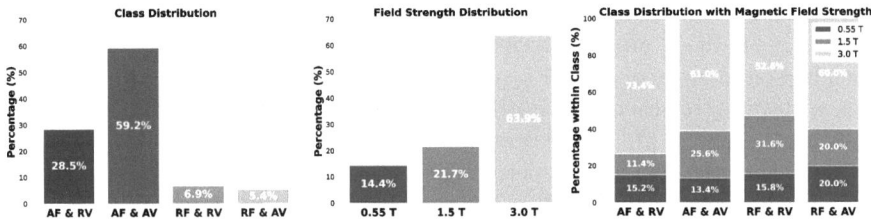

Fig. 1. FUNDUS dataset composition. (l.) Distribution of anatomical classes based on uterine orientation combinations - Anteflexed (AF), Retroflexed (RF), Anteverted (AV), and Retroverted (RV). (m.) Distribution of scanner magnetic field strengths (in Tesla). (r.) Breakdown of each anatomical class by scanner field strength.

Datasets. The UMD [12] dataset consists of sagittal T2-weighted pelvic MRI scans from 300 patients (ages 21–86) with histologically confirmed uterine myomas, acquired on a Philips 3T system. Pixel-level annotations were provided by experienced gynaecologists and radiologists for the uterine cavity, wall, myomas, and nabothian cysts. Each case is labelled according to FIGO classification (types 0–8). Images and masks are provided in NIfTI format and are publicly available via Figshare. The in-house FUNDUS dataset consists of 267 T2-weighted sagittal pelvic MRI scans of healthy individuals collected retrospectively at the University Hospital Erlangen (UKER), Germany. The age of the patients ranges from 11 to 82 years. The dataset is characterised by its variability in imaging parameters due to the lack of a standardised protocol for MRI of the abdomen and pelvis. These include differences in field strength (0.55 T, 1.5 T, 3 T), scanner type (Siemens, PHILIPS), resolution (208–832), sequence (TSE, HASTE) and use of contrast agents. In addition, natural anatomical variations during the menstrual cycle were recorded. Some individuals were scanned multiple times, revealing changes due to menstrual phase, bladder filling or age, further increasing the diversity of the dataset.

Metrics. Reconstruction quality (for encoders) and generation quality (for diffusion models) were evaluated using Learned Perceptual Image Patch Similarity (LPIPS) and Fréchet Inception Distance (FID). LPIPS quantifies perceptual similarity between individual image patches, capturing subtle, fine-grained differences, while FID compares the overall distributions of real and synthetic images to assess dataset-level realism. For both metrics, lower values indicate higher quality. Classification performance was measured using the Area Under the Receiver Operating Characteristic Curve (AUC) and macro-averaged F1-score (F1), reflecting discriminative ability and balanced class performance.

Training and Hyperparameters. All models were trained on NVIDIA A100 GPUs (40–80 GB memory). DDPMs followed the implementation from [14], and

LDMs used the framework by [16] with a Variational Autoencoder (VAE) with a 16× compression ratio and an EDM U-Net backbone [8]. Models were trained for up to 2000 epochs with early stopping based on validation loss (patience: 50) and class-weighted sampling. We used the AdamW optimiser with learning rates in [1e−5, 1e−3] and batch sizes between 1 and 64 (126 for Latent U-Net), depending on model size and GPU memory. Diffusion models used 1000 denoising steps with discrete schedules. Both DDPMs and LDMs used a perceptual loss weighting $\lambda_{\text{LPIPS}} \in [0.1, 1.0]$. Text and class conditioning used dropout rates sampled from [0.0, 0.2]. All hyperparameters were tuned via grid search on a held-out validation split.

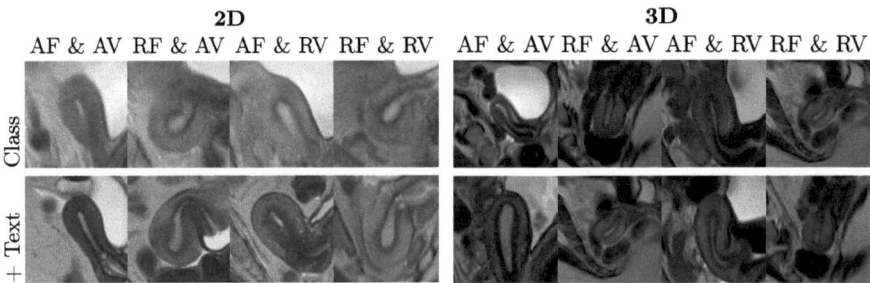

Fig. 2. Generated images from class-conditioned, and class- and text-conditioned DDPMs for 2D (left) and 3D (right) models. Uteri are shown in four orientation combinations: Anteflexed (AF), Retroflexed (RF), Anteverted (AV), and Retroverted (RV).

Downstream Clinical Task. We evaluated classification using a 2D ResNet-18 under multiple regimes: fully supervised on the ground truth (GT) dataset FUNDUS, supervised with a pretrained ResNet-18, weakly supervised with only 10% labelled data, and unsupervised via k-means clustering. These regimes were also applied to our synthetic datasets SynthUterus and SynthUterus (ROI), generated by class- and text-conditioned DDPMs capturing uterine positions and magnetic field strength of the scanners. Models were optimised with cross-entropy loss, producing softmax-normalised outputs, and evaluated on a held-out test set.

4.1 Results and Discussion

Image Reconstruction and Generation. Figure 3 (left): Using LPIPS (AlexNet), the AE trained on FUNDUS achieved a score of 0.17 on both full volumes and central slices (Z^0), while the VAE reached 0.15. Applying ROI cropping to FUNDUS increased LPIPS to 0.41 for the AE and 0.30 for the VAE. All UMD inputs were evaluated without cropping to ROI. We evaluated 2D and 3D DDPMs using FID and LPIPS across uterine orientation classes and conditioning setups (Table 1): class only, class + ROI, class + text (C+T), and C+T

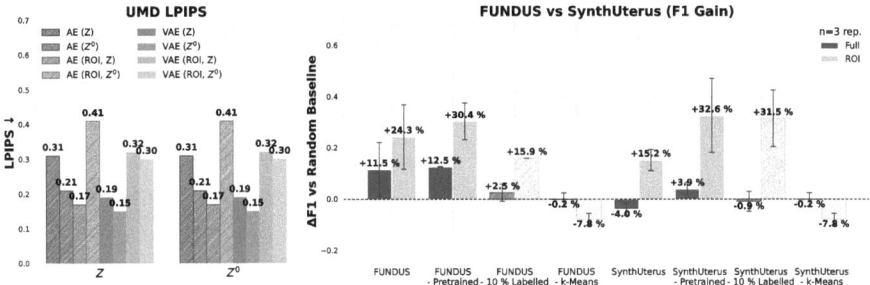

Fig. 3. Perceptual reconstruction quality (LPIPS) and classification (position) performance gain (Δ F1) across preprocessing strategies. Left: LPIPS scores for AE and VAE encoder models on the UMD test set under varying training preprocessing setups, tested on all slices of the volume and only the central slices. Lower values indicate better perceptual similarity. Right: Δ F1 relative to a random baseline on the FUNDUS and SynthUterus datasets using different training strategies. Preprocessing abbreviations: Z – full volume; Z^0 – central 3 slices; ROI – cropping to the uterus.

+ ROI. Example images for qualitative evaluation are shown in Fig. 2. All 2D models were trained on the central slices for evaluation, trained on all slices in the volume, FID and LPIPS increased by 10% at minimum. Text-conditioned models without class-conditioning performed worse than class-only conditioned models in an extended ablation study. The 2D DDPM with C+T + ROI conditioning consistently achieved the best results. ROI cropping alone also improved performance, especially when combined with semantic input. In 3D, the best results came from class + ROI, though overall quality lagged behind 2D models. In Table 2, the ablation study shows that conditioning with class and text information combined with ROI preprocessing consistently improves image quality across DDPM and LDM models, with 2D LDMs achieving the best overall FID and LP scores.

Synthetic Datasets. The SynthUterus datasets include 800 scans with 200 synthetic images per class for each uterine position and are balanced to match the FUNDUS dataset distribution (Fig. 1). Two versions were generated using class and text conditioned DDPMs: full images referred to as SynthUterus and uterus-focused region of interest crops referred to as SynthUterus ROI, capturing semantic and spatial details to improve training. Ten real and ten synthetic healthy pelvic ROI MRI samples were classified by three groups: non-expert AI researchers, less experienced radiologists and experienced pelvic radiologists. Their accuracies were 46.3%, 40% and 50% respectively, showing limited ability to distinguish real from generated images.

Image Classification. We evaluated classification performance across four training regimes: full supervision, pretrained ResNet-18, weak supervision with 10% labelled data, and unsupervised k-means, using both FUNDUS and SynthUterus datasets. Performance was reported in terms of improvement in F1 score over a random baseline on the FUNDUS test set, with $n = 3$ repetitions, see

Table 1. Ablation study on image generation quality across DDPM models and conditioning strategies by uterine orientation. FID: Fréchet Inception Distance; LP: Learned Perceptual Image Patch Similarity. Preprocessing as above. **1st-ranked**, 2nd-ranked model configuration, individually for 2D and 3D.

Model		ROI	Z^0	AF & AV		RF & AV		AF & RV		RF & RV	
				FID↓	LP↓	FID↓	LP↓	FID↓	LP↓	FID↓	LP↓
2D	+ Class	-	✓	7.89	0.52	7.46	0.52	7.55	0.50	8.16	0.51
		✓	✓	3.42	**0.38**	2.80	0.38	2.61	0.38	2.19	0.40
	+ C+T	-	✓	4.09	0.48	3.18	0.47	4.00	0.48	4.47	0.48
		✓	✓	**1.05**	0.40	**0.33**	**0.37**	**0.25**	**0.37**	**0.65**	**0.38**
3D	+ Class	-	-	27.12	0.72	24.88	0.71	25.77	0.71	**24.09**	0.71
		✓	-	24.66	**0.68**	**24.13**	0.70	23.61	0.69	24.60	0.70
	+ C+T	-	-	26.11	0.72	27.46	0.72	24.33	0.71	24.78	0.71
		✓	-	**24.51**	0.69	25.28	**0.70**	24.77	0.70	24.55	**0.69**

Table 2. Ablation study and average evaluation scores of DDPMs and LDMs across all uterine positions. FID: Fréchet Inception Distance; LP: Learned Perceptual Image Patch Similarity. Preprocessing as above. **1st-ranked**, 2nd-ranked configuration for each model.

Cond.		ROI	Z^0	DDPM (2D)		LDM (2D)		DDPM (3D)	
				FID↓	LP↓	FID↓	LP↓	FID↓	LP↓
Uncond.		-	✓	8.46	0.45	3.44	0.42	27.03	0.72
		✓	✓	1.90	**0.37**	2.17	0.35	25.45	0.70
+ Class		-	✓	7.77	0.51	2.13	0.39	25.46	0.71
		✓	✓	2.76	0.39	1.45	0.53	**24.25**	**0.69**
+ C+T		-	✓	3.93	0.48	1.97	0.43	25.67	0.72
		✓	✓	**0.57**	0.38	**1.35**	**0.32**	24.78	0.70

Fig. 3 (right). Models trained on SynthUterus ROI, consistently outperformed those trained on FUNDUS in weak-supervision settings, achieving a +32.6% gain with 10% labelled data over Random, compared to +15.9% for FUNDUS. Even under full supervision, SynthUterus achieved a modest boost (+2.5%) over FUNDUS if Resnet-18 was pretrained. The fully unsupervised k-Means clustering equally performed worse for both true and generated datasets.

Discussion. Our results demonstrate that semantic and spatial conditioning significantly enhance 2D diffusion-based MRI synthesis, enabling the production of anatomically coherent and high-quality images. Notably, the synthetic ROI dataset improved classification robustness and, in some cases, surpass models trained on real data under weak supervision and supervised with pretrained encoders. This underlines the potential of diffusion-generated data to support clinically relevant tasks, particularly where annotated data is scarce. While 3D DDPMs show promise, their performance is currently limited by longer training times and higher memory demands. Latent diffusion models remain sensitive to architectural choices; replacing the latent U-Net denoiser with transformer-based alternatives could improve anatomical fidelity and image realism. Nonetheless, both expert assessments and downstream evaluations reveal the potential for shortcut learning, where models might rely on superficial or spurious image features instead of meaningful anatomical structures. This highlights the critical need for robust validation, especially on held-out and multicentre datasets, to ensure generalisability and clinical relevance. Additionally, employing a standard pretrained encoder such as SwAV [4] resulted in a mean Image Retrieval Score $IRS_{\infty,\alpha}$ [5] below 0.10, indicating strong similarity among generated images. This may reflect a limited capacity of the encoder to distinguish between subtle uterine features and emphasise the need for higher diversity in image generation.

5 Conclusion

We present a diffusion-based framework for synthetic pelvic MRI generation conditioned on uterine position and descriptive text, including scanner field strength. This approach enables scalable, privacy-preserving data augmentation to address limited annotations and patient confidentiality. Our conditioned 2D DDPM achieves state-of-the-art image quality, with synthetic data matching or surpassing real data performance in weakly and fully supervised settings, supporting robust model development in data-scarce scenarios. By releasing our pipeline and models, we aim to promote reproducible research and accelerate progress in this clinical domain. Future work should focus on improving synthesis diversity through diversity modules and domain-specific encoders trained on multi-centre data, extending pathology conditioning to rare cases, incorporating radiology reports for richer conditioning, and rigorously evaluating privacy safeguards to ensure secure clinical deployment.

Acknowledgements. The authors gratefully acknowledge the scientific support and HPC resources provided by the Erlangen National High Performance Computing Center (NHR@FAU) under the NHR projects b143dc and b180dc. NHR funding is provided by federal and Bavarian state authorities. NHR@FAU hardware is partially funded by the German Research Foundation (DFG) – 440719683. This work was supported by the ERC Project MIA-NORMAL 101083647 and the ERC Starting grant EARTHWORM 101165242, DFG 513220538 and 512819079, DFG Heisenberg 502024488 and by the state of Bavaria (HTA).

References

1. Baugh, M., et al.: Image-conditioned diffusion models for medical anomaly detection. In: International Workshop on Uncertainty for Safe Utilization of Machine Learning in Medical Imaging, pp. 117–127. Springer, Cham (2024)
2. Behrendt, F., et al.: Leveraging the mahalanobis distance to enhance unsupervised brain MRI anomaly detection. In: International Conference on Medical Image Computing and Computer-Assisted Intervention, pp. 394–404. Springer, Cham (2024)

3. Boneš, E., Gergolet, M., Bohak, C., Lesar, Ž, Marolt, M.: Automatic segmentation and alignment of uterine shapes from 3D ultrasound data. Comput. Biol. Med. **178**, 108794 (2024). https://doi.org/10.1016/j.compbiomed.2024.108794
4. Caron, M., Misra, I., Mairal, J., Goyal, P., Bojanowski, P., Joulin, A.: Unsupervised learning of visual features by contrasting cluster assignments (2020)
5. Dombrowski, M., Zhang, W., Cechnicka, S., Reynaud, H., Kainz, B.: Image generation diversity issues and how to tame them. In: Proceedings of the Computer Vision and Pattern Recognition Conference (CVPR), pp. 3029–3039 (2025)
6. Dorjsembe, Z., Pao, H.K., Odonchimed, S., Xiao, F.: Conditional diffusion models for semantic 3d brain MRI synthesis. IEEE J. Biomed. Health Inform. (2024)
7. Ho, J., Jain, A., Abbeel, P.: Denoising diffusion probabilistic models. Adv. Neural. Inf. Process. Syst. **33**, 6840–6851 (2020)
8. Karras, T., Aittala, M., Aila, T., Laine, S.: Elucidating the design space of diffusion-based generative models. In: Proceedings of NeurIPS (2022)
9. Kazerouni, A., et al.: Diffusion models in medical imaging: a comprehensive survey. Med. Image Anal. **88**, 102846 (2023)
10. Li, D., Zhang, T., Xu, L., et al.: Multi-center annotated MRI dataset and benchmark for uterine myoma segmentation and classification. Sci. Data **11**(1), 192 (2024). https://doi.org/10.1038/s41597-024-03244-w
11. Liu, C., Shah, A., Bai, W., Arcucci, R.: Utilizing synthetic data for medical vision-language pre-training: bypassing the need for real images. arXiv preprint arXiv:2310.07027 (2023)
12. Pan, H., et al.: Large-scale uterine myoma MRI dataset covering all FIGO types with pixel-level annotations. Sci. Data **11**(1), 410 (2024)
13. Pinaya, W.H., Tudosiu, P.D., Dafflon, J., Da Costa, P.F., Fernandez, V., Nachev, P., Ourselin, S., Cardoso, M.J.: Brain imaging generation with latent diffusion models. In: MICCAI Workshop on Deep Generative Models, pp. 117–126. Springer, Cham (2022)
14. von Platen, P., et al.: Diffusers: state-of-the-art diffusion models (2022). https://github.com/huggingface/diffusers
15. Pozzi, M., et al.: Generating and evaluating synthetic data in digital pathology through diffusion models. Sci. Rep. **14**(1), 28435 (2024)
16. Reynaud, H., et al.: Echonet-synthetic: privacy-preserving video generation for safe medical data sharing. In: International Conference on Medical Image Computing and Computer-Assisted Intervention, pp. 285–295. Springer, Cham (2024)
17. Rombach, R., Blattmann, A., Lorenz, D., Esser, P., Ommer, B.: High-resolution image synthesis with latent diffusion models. In: Proceedings of the IEEE/CVF Conference on Computer Vision and Pattern Recognition, pp. 10684–10695 (2022)
18. Webber, G., Reader, A.J.: Diffusion models for medical image reconstruction. BJR| Artif. Intell. **1**(1), ubae013 (2024)
19. Yang, Y., Fu, H., Aviles-Rivero, A.I., Schönlieb, C.B., Zhu, L.: Diffmic: dual-guidance diffusion network for medical image classification. In: International Conference on Medical Image Computing and Computer-Assisted Intervention, pp. 95–105. Springer, Cham (2023). https://doi.org/10.1007/978-3-031-43987-2_10

Multi-step Segmentation of Pelvic Fractures: Handling Variable Fracture Counts Through Anatomical and Surface Analysis

Artur Jurgas[1,2(✉)], Maciej Stanuch[2], Marek Wodziński[1], and Andrzej Skalski[1,2]

[1] AGH University of Krakow, Krakow, Poland
[2] MedApp S.A, Krakow, Poland
arjurgas@agh.edu.pl

Abstract. Pelvic fractures pose a clinical challenge in women due to the complexity of the pelvic structure and adjacent organs. This paper introduces a step-by-step deep learning pipeline for segmenting pelvic fractures in CT imaging, specifically for female health. Using anatomical and fracture surface segmentation, our method addresses fracture pattern variability. We highlight the clinical impact on women's physical, sexual, and reproductive health and describe our technical methods. Our results show the potential for computer-aided imaging to enhance diagnostic accuracy and segmentation for women's pelvic trauma, especially in urgent clinical situations. Our code, models, and 54 newly annotated cases are available at https://github.com/Jarartur/multi-step-pelvic-fractures.

Keywords: Pelvic Fractures · Deep Learning · CT Imaging · Female Health · Segmentation

1 Introduction

Pelvic fractures, as presented in Fig. 1 and Fig. 2a, represent one of the most challenging and life-threatening injuries in trauma medicine across the population, with particularly devastating consequences for women. These injuries carry substantial morbidity and mortality risks, with studies showing that pelvic fractures are associated with significant complications and prolonged recovery periods [3,8]. Polytrauma patients with pelvic injuries face mortality rates reaching up to 42% [15]. For elderly women specifically, pelvic fractures present even more severe challenges, with research showing that 74% of patients with low-energy pelvic ramus fractures experience 1-year mortality rates of 16.3% and 5-year mortality rates of 58.1%—both significantly higher than age-matched controls [8].

The impact on women's health extends beyond immediate mortality concerns. Pelvic fractures in women are particularly debilitating due to the unique anatomical considerations of the female pelvis and its role in reproductive health [4,14]. Research shows that pelvic fractures constitute 7% of all fragility fractures and contribute to 5% of the expenses in managing osteoporotic fractures,

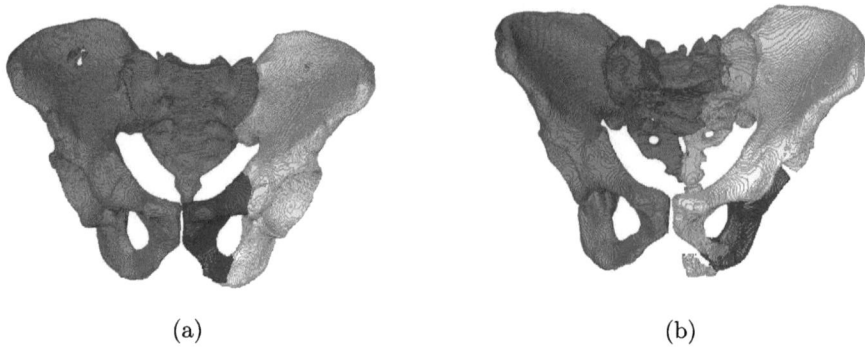

Fig. 1. Example of the variability of fracture counts in different images. It is not guaranteed that cases will have an identical number of fragments or that these fragments will be located in the same positions.

with over half of these incidents leading to a loss of independence among the elderly [14]. The incidence of pelvic fractures has increased significantly over the past three decades, particularly affecting postmenopausal women who face additional challenges due to decreased bone mineral density [14,18].

Women who suffer pelvic fractures typically endure longer hospital stays, remaining admitted for a median duration of 10 days, whereas those without genitourinary injuries stay for only 6 days. Additionally, these patients often require more intensive care unit admissions [4]. In terms of functionality, pelvic fractures result in lasting impacts, with 36% permanently needing enhanced ambulatory aids, and 20% requiring an increase in daily care [8]. These figures highlight the urgent necessity for quick and precise diagnostic and treatment strategies to enhance outcomes for women. Despite the critical nature of these injuries, effective segmentation algorithms have been challenging to develop due to limited comprehensive datasets. The complexity of pelvic anatomy, diverse fracture patterns, and varying imaging methods have complicated the formation of standardized datasets that encapsulate the full range of pelvic trauma [19,20], posing a significant barrier for researchers who require diverse, well-annotated datasets.

Although substantial progress has been made in medical image segmentation, particularly in scenarios where the number of target objects is known and consistent, significant challenges persist in segmenting a variable number of objects. Traditional techniques, while successful with a fixed object count, falter in unpredictably varying scenarios [2,22], a difficulty heightened in medical imaging by conditions that lead to unanticipated anatomical variations. Current deep learning models, although accurate under controlled conditions, often struggle with uncertainties in the object count, a critical issue in trauma imaging where the extent of injuries is unpredictable [17]. These fracture patterns contrast with fixed anatomical structures, presenting unique computational challenges that conventional segmentation techniques often cannot overcome [2,11,20].

Specifically, in pelvic fractures, fracture locations and the resulting bone fragments vary greatly within the pelvic ring [11]. This variability is influenced by factors such as the mechanism of injury, bone quality, and patient-specific anatomy [13,21]. Consequently, creating automated segmentation algorithms capable of accurately segmenting all fragments irrespective of their number or position remains a significant technical challenge.

Automated segmentation solutions enhance trauma care by boosting diagnostic speed and precision, facilitating rapid medical image analysis [10]. In trauma contexts, where quick decision-making is critical, these automated systems can be life-saving, providing consistent results and minimizing human errors. Furthermore, they can detect fractures under time constraints that may impede diagnostic accuracy otherwise. For their development a continued effort to prepare and publicly release training datasets remains crucial. One such example is the PENGWIN challenge [20] which this work expands on.

Contribution: We annotated 54 pelvis fracture cases and subsequently assessed our method against a leading technique in the domain. To aid in field progression, our model, code, and accompanying annotations are publicly released to encourage open scientific inquiry.

2 Methods

2.1 Overview

Our approach employs a multi-stage deep learning pipeline for the segmentation of pelvic fractures in CT scans, specifically tailored to the anatomical and clinical complexities of the female pelvis.

2.2 Data Acquisition and Preprocessing

For developing our model we used CT scans from the publicly available PENGWIN Challenge dataset [20]. Preprocessing steps included intensity normalization, where voxel intensities were clipped to the 0.5 and 99.5 percentile range, followed by mean subtraction and division by the standard deviation. All scans were resampled to an isotropic voxel spacing of 0.80 mm to ensure consistency across the dataset. Data augmentation techniques, such as random rotation and mirroring, were applied to improve model robustness and generalizability.

2.3 Anatomical Segmentation

The first stage of the pipeline employs an initial segmentation model from [12] which is a variation of the nnUNet architecture [9]. It is used to delineate the main pelvic structures: the left hipbone, right hipbone, and sacrum. This anatomical segmentation provides essential structural context, which is necessary for the accurate identification and localization of fracture surfaces in subsequent stages. A varied dataset comprising 1184 cases was employed to train this model, with the authors stating that it achieves a Dice score of 0.989 and a Hausdorff distance of 10.23 mm.

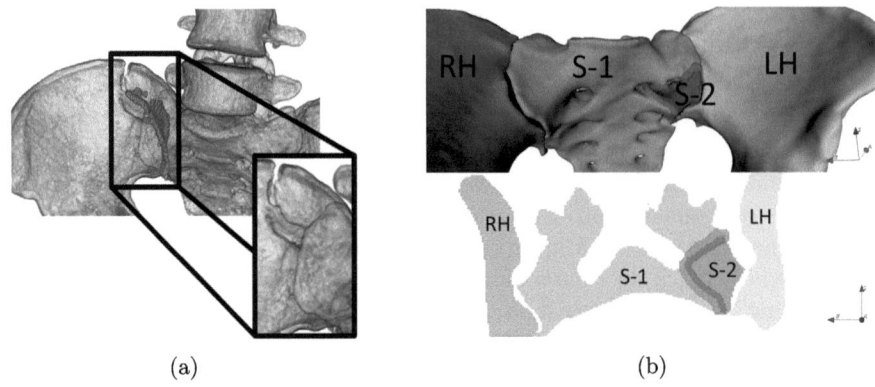

Fig. 2. The process of creating the training dataset. We use the original fragment labels to create surfaces between colliding bones in the same anatomical regions like sacrum and left/right hipbones. a) shows an exemplary fracture surface, while b) shows the method for creating fracture surfaces, with the fracture surface shown in blue. RH/LH denotes the right/left hip, while S-1/S-2 refers to sacral fragments. (Color figure online)

2.4 Fracture Surface Segmentation

A second model, based on nnUNet v2, is trained specifically to segment fracture surfaces, with a focus on the interfaces between bone fragments. Training labels for this model were generated by extracting the contours of bone fragments, shown in Fig. 2. Those contours were used to change the model's task from directly segmenting the fractures to segmenting the fracture surfaces, i.e., where two bone fragments collide. This tackles the problem of variable number of fractures and overcomes the problem of one label potentially symbolizing different parts of the bone (as the fracture labels were assigned in ascending order from the first fragment, so depending on where the fracture occured, the same label, e.g., first fragment could be assigned to a different anatomical part).

2.5 Post-processing

Following initial surface segmentation, several post-processing steps were applied to refine the results (see Fig. 3). Morphological operations were used to connect fragmented regions and bridge small gaps in the predicted fracture surfaces. Connected component labeling and filtering were then performed to identify and label individual bone fragments, discarding irrelevant or excessively small segments that could represent noise or artifacts. Anatomically-constrained label growing and merging were implemented to ensure that each fracture fragment was assigned to the correct anatomical region, thereby maintaining anatomical plausibility. Finally, distance-based label filtering was used to eliminate false positives and further improve segmentation quality.

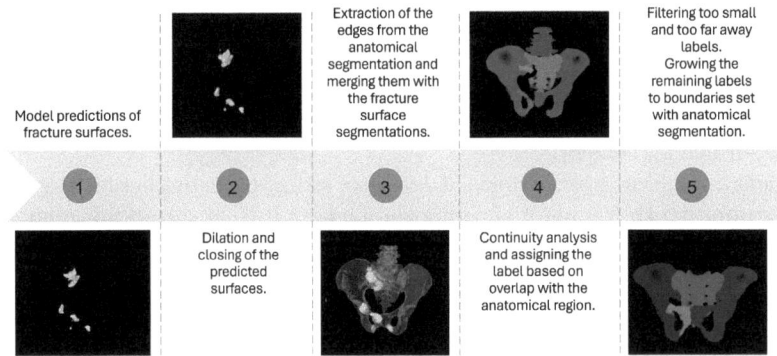

Fig. 3. Post-processing workflow. Starting from the primary fracture surface predictions, we superimpose these onto the anatomical segmentation. Following this, a continuity analysis is executed, whereby unique labels are allocated. Each label is then matched to its corresponding anatomical region according to the degree of overlap.

2.6 Ensembling and Inference

For robust prediction, we ensembled three folds of the nnUNet model. All post-processing steps were implemented in Python, utilizing SimpleITK for image processing and CuPy [16] for GPU acceleration to ensure efficient computation. This allowed for a great reduction in inference time of the post-processing step.

2.7 Evaluation

To rigorously assess our method, we extended the evaluation beyond the PENGWIN Challenge dataset. We independently annotated an additional 54 pelvic fracture cases from the CTPelvic1K dataset [12] (specifically its pelvic fractures subdataset), ensuring these cases did not overlap with the PENGWIN training or validation sets. This external test set provided a robust benchmark for generalizability.

To enhance the segmentation process, four additional annotators with expertise in biomedical engineering were recruited. Their task was to apply the annotation protocol as follows: they utilized the anatomical segmentation ground-truth from CTPelvic1K dataset as the initial mask, partitioned the segmentation into subregions for each fracture, and labeled fractures per the PENGWIN challenge convention (e.g., 1 for sacrum, 11 for left hipbone, 21 for right hipbone). Extra nine labels per region were preserved for potential fracture subregions, i.e. 2–10 for sacrum, 12–20 for left hipbone, and 22–30 for right hipbone. Cases with excessive fragments (>9) and with ambiguous fractures or other non-fracture issues were excluded from the CTPelvic1K dataset to maintain alignment with the original training set distribution.

We compare to the top performing method from the challenge, namely ABBC model from mic-dkfz team [1].

Segmentation performance was quantified using three key metrics: (i) Intersection over Union (IoU) to measure volumetric overlap between predicted and ground-truth fragments. (ii) Hausdorff Distance at 95% (HD95) to evaluate boundary accuracy. (iii) Average Symmetric Surface Distance (ASSD) to assess surface-to-surface agreement.

Fragment matching was performed by associating each predicted fragment with the ground-truth fragment showing the highest IoU, ensuring fair comparison despite variable fragment counts.

3 Results

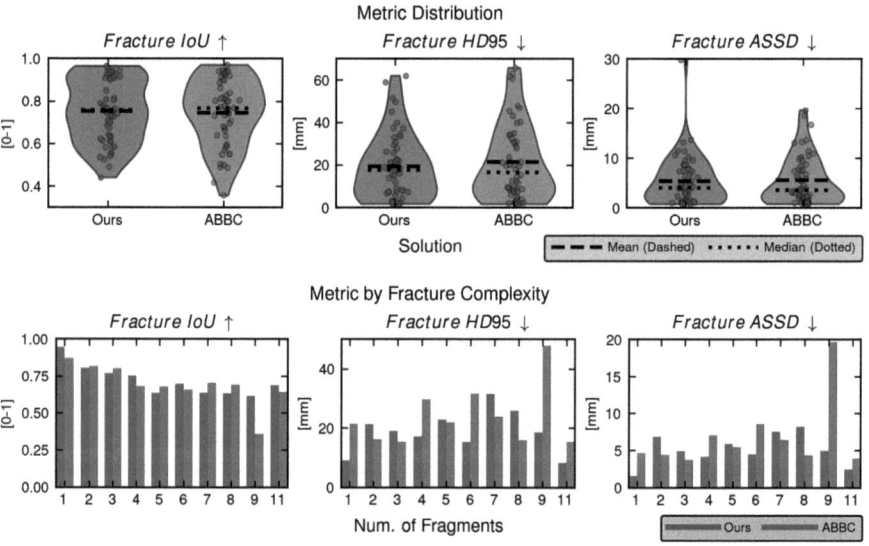

Fig. 4. Distribution of each method's final predictions. Individual measurement points are overlayed on top of the distributions. In the second row, for each metric we present the mean metrics of both methods binned according to the number of fragments present.

Our method shows a marginal performance advantage across all metrics, as summarized in Table 1. We observed slightly higher mean values for Intersection over Union (IoU), Hausdorff Distance at 95% (HD95), and Average Symmetric Surface Distance (ASSD) compared to the baseline approach. Critically, statistical analysis confirms this difference is not significant (p-values > 0.05). Overall, our solution performs comparably to the ABBC method. The practical equivalence in performance suggests both approaches achieve similar clinical utility despite architectural differences. Figure 4 presents the distribution of performance in individual predictions.

Table 1. Comparison of our method with ABBC across different fracture segmentation metrics along with their statistical significance, as tested on our additional 54 annotated acses.

Metric	Ours (Mean ± SD)	ABBC (Mean ± SD)	Wilcoxon p-value
Fracture IoU ↑	0.75 ± 0.15	0.74 ± 0.16	0.921
Fracture HD95 ↓	19.30 ± 15.46	21.43 ± 17.75	0.799
Fracture ASSD ↓	5.36 ± 4.97	5.56 ± 4.84	0.867

The ASSD showed only a moderate correlation with IoU ($|r| = 0.61$). In contrast, ASSD and HD95 were strongly correlated ($|r| = 0.88$). Notably, IoU values tended to decrease with an increasing number of fracture fragments, while ASSD and HD95 remained relatively stable (Fig. 4). This trend was especially pronounced in cases involving many small bone shards, which were often missed by the segmentation algorithm.

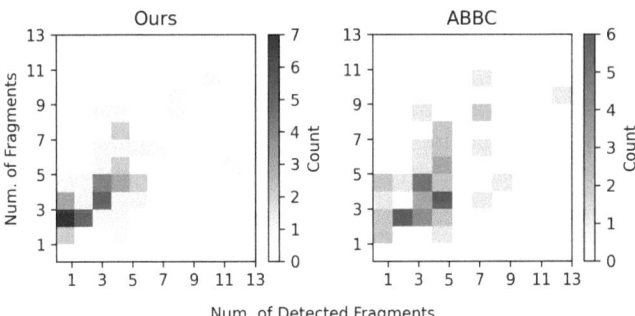

Fig. 5. Distribution of the number of detected fragments with regard to the ground-truth number.

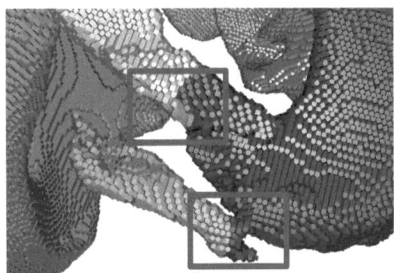

(a) Artifacts left from growing the fracture segmentations back to fill in the whole anatomical region.

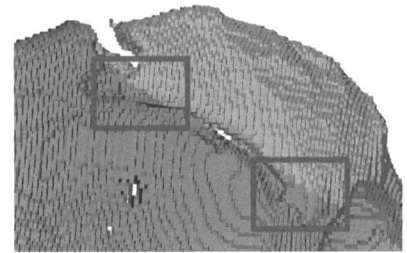

(b) Inaccurate border segmentation of a pronounced fracture site.

Fig. 6. Examples of failure in model's predictions.

Our algorithm, which uses thickened fracture surfaces to detect subtle fractures, often misses small areas near the edge of the fracture, as visible in Fig. 6. Although this method improves subtle fracture detection, it diminishes precision where boundaries are distinct. Tiny bone shards around main fragments are inconsistently segmented and present difficulties (Fig. 5).

4 Disscussion

Pelvic fractures in women are associated with profound and multifaceted health consequences that extend far beyond the immediate trauma. The anatomical variation of the female pelvis, combined with its proximity to vital organs and reproductive structures, means that pelvic injuries frequently result in significant hemorrhage, organ damage, and long-term dysfunction. Women are particularly vulnerable to complications such as sexual dysfunction, menstrual irregularities, and infertility following pelvic trauma [7]. These effects can severely impact quality of life, underscoring the need for precise and timely diagnosis as well as individualized management strategies.

Our multi-step segmentation pipeline addresses the challenges of pelvic fracture analysis by separately handling anatomical segmentation and fracture surface detection, thus accommodating the variable fracture patterns and fragment numbers prevalent in pelvic trauma, especially in women. This separation allows the pipeline to adapt to the unpredictability of fracture number effectively. Crucially, anatomically-constrained post-processing is applied to ensure segmentation outputs are not only accurate but clinically plausible, facilitating the transformation of automated analysis into actionable surgical and rehabilitation planning without risk of misleading clinicians with anatomically incorrect fragmentations. These constraints are particularly beneficial in complex cases, where distinguishing normal anatomical variations from pathological fragmentations requires precision.

In benchmarking against the PENGWIN Challenge dataset, our method demonstrated no statistically significant difference from the top-performing entry, achieving an average Intersection over Union (IoU) of 0.74 on real-life data. Notably this is a much lower score than the one on the leaderboard (0.93)—this highlights the need for more open testing of those methods on more diverse datasets. We hypothesize that this results from an increased average of fractures found in our test set, specifically 4.88 on average compared to 3.75 observed in the initial training data set. This level of performance suggests that the algorithm is reliable enough to serve as a valuable tool for clinicians during time-critical trauma diagnosis. However, before a broader clinical use can be achieved, additional improvement and validation must be done. Automated segmentation can improve clinical workflows, allowing faster and potentially more accurate assessment of pelvic fractures in the acute setting.

Despite this, pelvic fracture segmentation remains a partially unresolved issue. Detecting small bone shards, particularly those near larger fragments, presents significant challenges due to image noise, partial volume effects, and overlapping anatomical structures. In comminuted or "crushed" fractures where clear borders are absent, our method utilizes a thicker fracture surface to encapsulate relevant fragments, enhancing recall but potentially sacrificing precision for well-defined thin fractures. Balancing sensitivity and specificity remains an open research question. Importantly, our current reliance on thicker surfaces for model learning might compromise precision in thin fracture segmentation. Future research should investigate transformer-based architectures [5] or topology-preserving models [6] to better capture fine-grained fracture structures and improve generalizability. Although results are promising, further validation on larger, diverse datasets, especially those including gynecologic and obstetric complications, is crucial to ensure robustness of automated segmentation tools across the full spectrum of pelvic trauma in women.

Advanced computer-aided imaging offers significant potential for aiding early diagnosis, personalized treatment, and thorough rehabilitation for women experiencing pelvic trauma. Nonetheless, for these technologies to be successfully applied in clinical settings, continuous interdisciplinary cooperation among computer scientists, radiologists, surgeons, and specialists in women's health is essential. Such collaboration is crucial to ensure that technological innovations meet the nuanced, real-world needs of female patients. In an effort to further this field, we are releasing 54 additional annotated cases to expand the PENGWIN dataset. This enriched dataset aims to provide the community with a broader range of examples, especially those involving complex and subtle fracture patterns, thereby aiding the development and evaluation of more advanced algorithms.

Acknowledgments. We gratefully acknowledge Polish high-performance computing infrastructure PLGrid (HPC Center: ACK Cyfronet AGH) for providing computer facilities and support within computational grant no. PLG/2025/018194. We thank Lidia Potoczek, Weronika Solarska, and Zuzanna Pecka for their help annotating the dataset.

Disclosure of Interests. The authors have no competing interests to declare that are relevant to the content of this article.

References

1. Helmholtz Imaging DKFZ / Applied Computer Vision Lab / Challenges / abbc cdot GitLab (2024). https://codebase.helmholtz.cloud/hi-dkfz/applied-computer-vision-lab/challenges/abbc
2. Arnab, A. et al.: Pixelwise instance segmentation with a dynamically instantiated network. In: 2017 IEEE Conference on Computer Vision and Pattern Recognition (CVPR), pp. 879–888 (2017)
3. Ba, P.A., et al.: Definitive treatment of open pelvic fractures with external fixator. Int. J. Innovative Res. Med. Sci. **8**(05), 170–175 (2023)
4. Bjurlin, M.A., et al.: Genitourinary injuries in pelvic fracture morbidity and mortality using the national trauma data bank. J. Trauma Acute Care Surg. **67**(5), 1033 (2009)

5. Chen, J. et al.: TransUNet: transformers make strong encoders for medical image segmentation (2021)
6. Clough, J.R., et al.: A topological loss function for deep-learning based image segmentation using persistent homology. IEEE Trans. Pattern Anal. Mach. Intell. **44**(12), 8766–8778 (2022)
7. Gambrah, H.A., et al.: Sexual dysfunction in women after traumatic pelvic fracture negatively affects quality of life and mental health. J Sex Med **19**(12), 1759–1765 (2022)
8. Hamilton, C.B., et al.: Morbidity and mortality following pelvic ramus fractures in an older Atlantic Canadian cohort. Can. J. Surg. **62**(4), 270–274 (2019)
9. Isensee, F., et al.: nnU-Net: a self-configuring method for deep learning-based biomedical image segmentation. Nat. Methods **18**(2), 203–211 (2021)
10. Jesus, R. et al.: A vendor neutral archive with MONAI for automatic medical image analysis. In: 2023 IEEE 36th International Symposium on Computer-Based Medical Systems (CBMS), pp. 53–56 (2023)
11. Liu, J., et al.: An end-to-end geometry-based pipeline for automatic preoperative surgical planning of pelvic fracture reduction and fixation. IEEE Trans. Med. Imaging **44**(1), 79–91 (2025)
12. Liu, P., et al.: Deep learning to segment pelvic bones: large-scale CT datasets and baseline models. Int. J. Comput. Assist. Radiol. Surg. **16**(5), 749–756 (2021)
13. Liu, Y. et al.: Automatic intraoperative CT-CBCT registration for image-guided pelvic fracture reduction. In: 2024 IEEE International Symposium on Biomedical Imaging (ISBI), pp. 1–5 (2024)
14. Mohseni, M. et al.: SUN-395 pelvic bone density is lower than bone density of hip and femoral neck in postmenopausal women. J. Endocr. Soci. **4**(Supplement_1), SUN-395 (2020)
15. Morsund, L.A., et al.: Insidious, deadly, common - polytrauma with pelvic fracture. Emerg. Med. Serv. **10**(3), 192–195 (2023)
16. Okuta, R. et al.: CuPy: A NumPy-compatible library for NVIDIA GPU calculations
17. Oudoumanessah, G. et al.: Towards frugal unsupervised detection of subtle abnormalities in medical imaging (2023)
18. Peichl, P., et al.: Parathyroid Hormone 1–84 accelerates fracture-healing in pubic bones of elderly osteoporotic women. JBJS **93**(17), 1583 (2011)
19. Rahman, R., et al.: Enhancing fracture diagnosis in pelvic X-rays by deep convolutional neural network with synthesized images from 3D-CT. Sci. Rep. **14**(1), 8004 (2024)
20. Sang, Y. et al.: Benchmark of segmentation techniques for pelvic fracture in CT and X-ray: summary of the PENGWIN 2024 challenge (2025)
21. Utomo, G.P. et al.: Overview of pelvic ring fracture patients: observational study in the emergency department at Dr. Kariadi General Hospital, Semarang, Indonesia. 1 **8**(7), 4585–4593 (2024)
22. Zhong, X., et al.: Automatic image pixel clustering based on mussels wandering optimization. Int. J. Patt. Recogn. Artif. Intell. **35**(02), 2154005 (2021)

Visionerves: Automatic and Reproducible Hybrid AI for Peripheral Nervous System Recognition Applied to Endometriosis Cases

Giammarco La Barbera[1,2(✉)], Enzo Bonnot[1,2,3], Thomas Isla[1], Juan Pablo de la Plata[1,2], Joy-Rose Dunoyer de Segonzac[1], Jennifer Attali[4], Cécile Lozach[4], Alexandre Bellucci[5], Louis Marcellin[6,7], Laure Fournier[5], Sabine Sarnacki[1,2,8], Pietro Gori[2,3], and Isabelle Bloch[1,2,3,9]

[1] IMAG2, Institut Imagine, Université Paris Cité, Paris, France
[2] Replico SAS, Paris, France
[3] LTCI, Télécom Paris, Institut Polytechnique de Paris, Paris, France
giammarco.labarbera@replico.tech
[4] Department of Pediatric Imaging, Hôpital Necker Enfants-Malades, Assistance Publique-Hôpitaux de Paris (AP-HP), Université Paris Cité, Paris, France
[5] Department of Radiology, Hôpital Européen Georges Pompidou, AP-HP, Université Paris Cité, Paris, France
[6] Department of Gynecological Surgery and Oncology (Professor Chapron), Hôpital Cochin, AP-HP, Université Paris Cité, Paris, France
[7] Department of Development, Reproduction and Cancer (Professor Batteux), Institut Cochin, Paris, France
[8] Department of Pediatric Surgery, Hôpital Necker Enfants-Malades, AP-HP, Université Paris Cité, Paris, France
[9] Sorbonne Université, CNRS, LIP6, Paris, France

Abstract. Endometriosis often leads to chronic pelvic pain and possible nerve involvement, yet imaging the peripheral nerves remains a challenge. We introduce Visionerves, a novel hybrid AI framework for peripheral nervous system recognition from multi-gradient DWI and morphological MRI data. Unlike conventional tractography, Visionerves encodes anatomical knowledge through fuzzy spatial relationships, removing the need for selection of manual ROIs. The pipeline comprises two phases: (A) automatic segmentation of anatomical structures using a deep learning model, and (B) tractography and nerve recognition by symbolic spatial reasoning. Applied to the lumbosacral plexus in 10 women with (confirmed or suspected) endometriosis, Visionerves demonstrated substantial improvements over standard tractography, with Dice score improvements of up to 25% and spatial errors reduced to less than 5 mm. This automatic and reproducible approach enables detailed nerve analysis and paves the way for non-invasive diagnosis of endometriosis-related neuropathy, as well as other conditions with nerve involvement.

Keywords: Nerves Recognition · Hybrid AI · DWI · MRI · Endometriosis

1 Introduction

Endometriosis is a prevalent gynecological disease characterized by endometrial tissue outside the uterus, leading to chronic inflammation, immune dysfunction, and potential neurological involvement in the pelvic region. These neurological factors are difficult to diagnose with conventional imaging. Moreover, a better understanding of how pelvic nerve fibers are affected in endometriosis could help explaining the role they play in chronic pelvic pain [5,7]. Advanced techniques such as Diffusion Weighted MRI (DWI) and tractography [22] enable visualization of nerve fibers, but their application has mainly been limited to the central nervous system (CNS) [9,20,24], with limited studies in the peripheral nervous system (PNS) [4,19] and thus on endometriosis [18,26]. This is due to: (i) the challenge of accurately and reproducibly reconstructing PNS via tractography algorithms, primarily due to reliance on manual placement of regions of interest (ROIs) and significant inter-subject variability; (ii) the complexity of recognizing each individual nerve bundle, due to the abundance of streamlines and spurious fibers (such as muscle, tissue and noise) [12,17].

In this paper, we introduce "Visionerves", an original hybrid AI method that leverages anatomical knowledge for automatic nerve identification, eliminating the need for manual ROIs. By describing nerve trajectories relatively to other anatomical structures (segmented via deep learning from a standard MRI image) and modeling anatomical imprecision with fuzzy logic [3,13], our framework allows guiding the tractography algorithm, making the results more reproducible, and filtering out spurious (i.e. outliers) fibers by recognizing only nerve ones, via symbolic spatial reasoning. Furthermore, using a software such as 3DSlicer [8], Visionerves results (anatomical segmentation and nerve fibers) can be merged and rendered into 3D models, offering valuable insights into the relationships between lesions, surrounding organs, and nerve structures [23]. This approach could help explain the neuropathic component of chronic pain and paves the way for significant improvements in surgical and clinical planning. The presented method, applied in the pelvic region (from L5 to S3 nerve fibers) to 10 female adult subjects affected by endometriosis, yielded promising results, showing a good correlation with nerve reference reconstructions.

2 Related Work

Traditional methods employ the virtual dissection technique which requires manual placement of ROIs to select or exclude fibers [12,17,18], but this process is labor-intensive, time-consuming, and difficult to reproduce for complex tracts. Atlas-based approaches, commonly used in the brain, transfer labels via non-linear deformations and mappings [21], but the accuracy of the results depends on alignment and clustering quality, which is problematic in pathological cases [9,10]. Machine learning and deep learning methods, explored for the CNS [16,25], require large annotated datasets, are often hard to interpret, and can be affected by data biases such as site-specific protocol or scanner differences.

Moreover, they do not address the inherent vagueness of PNS tract definitions, where boundaries are inherently ambiguous and difficult to delineate.

Taking a different approach, WMQL [24] introduced a query language for defining brain white matter tracts using mathematical models of spatial relationships and logical operations. However, the method is limited to binary relations, rough representation of structures, and does not account for pathological deviations. A fuzzy set theory extension [6] addresses the inherent vagueness of anatomical definitions, but remains tailored to CNS fibers, not accounting for the more complex spatial relationships seen in the PNS. For these reasons, these methods offer valuable insights, but are insufficient to reconstruct and recognize convoluted and smaller nerves of the PNS, such as the nerves of the pelvic lumbosacral plexus, which are clinically significant in conditions like endometriosis.

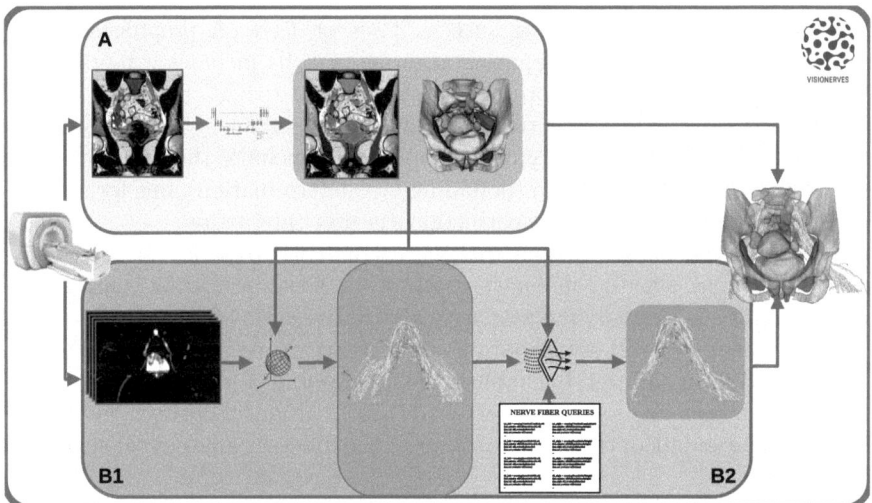

Fig. 1. The Visionerves framework (blue) from image acquisition on the left to the final 3D model merging anatomical structures and nerve fibers on the right. The method is composed of: phase A (green) - Anatomical Structure Segmentation - where a U-Net-based algorithm takes as input a morphological (e.g. T2-w) MR image and outputs an anatomical segmentation; phase B (red) - Peripheral Nerves Reconstruction (B1) and Recognition (B2) - where a tractography algorithm takes as input a DW image (together with output segmentation of phase A), and outputs a fibers reconstruction, which in turn is passed as input (together with nerve fibers queries and result of phase A) to our symbolic AI filtering method for recognizing the targeted nerves. (Color figure online)

3 The Visionerves Method

The proposed Visionerves method consists of two primary phases (Fig. 1): (A) anatomical structure segmentation from a morphological (e.g. T2-w) MR image (see Sect. 3.1); and (B) peripheral nerves reconstruction and recognition from multi-gradient DW image, leveraging the result of phase A (see Sect. 3.2). As described before, a final 3D model can be created, merging the extracted nerve information with the anatomical segmentation.

3.1 Phase A Anatomical Structure Segmentation

A U-Net-based algorithm inspired by the well-known nnU-Net [14] and its derivatives (nnDetection [1] for localization and nnInteractive [15] for error correction) is employed for rapid and fully automated modeling of anatomical structures from morphological MRI images, such as T2-w or T1-w. A preprocessing step (to have a standard dataset representation as in [14]) includes a reorientation of the images in the RAS coordinate system (left to right, posterior to anterior, inferior to superior), a correction of field heterogeneity, and a resampling to a common voxel size. The segmentation pipeline includes three custom U-Net subsystems: one for localization (bounding box determination), one for semantic segmentation, and one for error correction via user interaction.

This phase A of the pipeline enables fast and user-friendly 3D anatomical model generation, avoiding manual segmentation, however it is not central to our method and it can be easily replaced with alternative state-of-the-art approaches. For these reasons we will not elaborate on it further. Nevertheless it is important to mention that in addition to enabling the functioning of phase B, this part also allows for the visualization of the nerves in their anatomical context, leading to a better understanding of their relationships to the different anatomical structures.

3.2 Phase B Peripheral Nerves Reconstruction and Recognition

For the identification of the PNS, in contrast to previous works [20,24], we propose to represent and formalize anatomical knowledge, usually given in natural language, in first order logic, with the associated syntactic reasoning abilities. Taking inspiration from [6], we also propose to associate it with fuzzy semantics. Spatial relations between nerves and anatomical structures play an important role in the description of nerves. They are represented as predicates in the logic, for which a degree of satisfaction is computed using mathematical morphology and fuzzy sets [3]. These relations include distances, directions and connectivity with respect to segmented structures from phase A. This hybrid approach combines formal descriptions (syntactic part) with concrete representations in the spatial domain and as degrees of satisfaction taking values in $[0, 1]$ (semantic part). Fuzzy representations hence inherently solve the semantic gap, establishing links between abstract clinical concepts and image information.

Phase B1 Automatic Tractography for Reconstruction. The first part of phase B consists of fiber reconstruction via a tractography algorithm [22] applied to the multi-gradient DWI image. A preprocessing (as in [22]) includes denoising, Gibbs artifact removal, eddy currents and motion corrections, and correction of field heterogeneity. Following this, a tractography algorithm is applied (algorithm choice left to the user depending on DWI parameters and the studied body region). In order to narrow the reconstruction space as well as make this process automatic and reproducible, ROIs for seeding and inclusion zones (which are obligatory to be crossed in the specified order) are produced using either directly the segmented anatomical structures or by using spatial relations to define regions where they are satisfied (e.g. region "anterior of structure A" AND "to the right of structure B"). In this part, spatial relations are binarized, in order to be used in tractography algorithms. In addition, the created regions are large enough to not limit the reconstruction space too much, given the potential deviations from normal anatomy. It is important to note that, in order to have a good voxel matching between anatomical structures (produced from the MRI) and DWI, a registration might be necessary.

Phase B2 Symbolic AI for Recognition. Once the tractogram is reconstructed, we perform a filtering to recognize only the nerve fibers, differentiating them from muscle and tissue fibers as well as potential noise. The medical knowledge encoded in the logic is translated into queries used by the recognition algorithm. For each nerve bundle, a query representing its anatomical path is created using the spatial relations, with the possibility of combining the relations with AND/OR operators, creating exclusion zones with NOT operators, and ordering the nerve segments with THEN (i.e. "sequential" AND) operators. Once the query is built, its degree of satisfaction is assessed at each point along the fiber by mapping every point to the corresponding defined fuzzy regions. A fiber is considered to satisfy a query if it sequentially validates all specified spatial relations, where to validate means that the average of the non-zero fuzzy values along the fiber is higher than a specified threshold. All fibers that fulfill these criteria are then aggregated to form a bundle representing the targeted nerve. More details on the fuzzy logic modeling and on phase B2 can be found in [2].

4 Application on the Pelvic Region for Endometriosis

We applied our Visionerves method on the lumbosacral plexus in the 10 endometriosis cases, for whom a nerve fiber analysis could be a strong aid in the understanding of this disease as explained in Sect. 1. Furthermore, since this is a highly innervated region with different muscles and organs, it represents an ideal subject of application for our method.

4.1 Database

For the segmentation system of phase A, we used 168 T2-w MRI images of 131 patients (ranging from 2 months old to 20 years old) belonging to a proprietary database licensed by the Hôpital Necker-Enfants malades of Paris), with reference images manually annotated by expert surgeons and radiologists over the course of several years using 3DSlicer software [8]. Pelvic bones (L5 vertebra, hip bones and sacrum), muscles (piriformis, obturator and levator ani), visceral organs (bladder, colon and rectum) and reproductive organs (ovaries, uterus and vagina) were labeled, in addition to other regions of interest (sacral foramina from S1 to S3, sacral canal, intervertebral foramina of L5) facilitating nerve detection.

We then applied the complete Visionerves method (phases A and B) on 10 different adult female patients (5 diagnosed and 5 suspected endometriosis, both groups in an age range from 20 to 50 years old), gathered at Hôpital européen Georges-Pompidou of Paris. For each patient, a couple of T2-w MRI (reconstruction voxel size $0.5 \times 0.47 \times 0.47 \, mm^3$) and multi-gradient DWI image (acquisition voxel size $3.3 \times 2.3 \times 3.6 \, mm^3$, NEX 1, 50 directions, b-value 600) was acquired in a 3T GE Signa Architect machine during a preliminary research (for a future prospective study) and used retrospectively after anonymization. Nerve reference reconstructions were created using the method of phase B1 plus the use of a ROI mask, in order to select the fibers passing through, exclusively and completely, within it. This further constrains the search area to the region we consider to represent the true pathway of fiber passage. Such a ROI mask was produced under the supervision of expert surgeons and radiologists via manual segmentation of tubes enclosing each bundle of nerve fibers (given the difficulty of accurately segmenting these structures). All the manual annotations detailed in this paragraph were performed using 3DSlicer software [8].

Finally the nerve queries were written with the help of clinical experts, leveraging anatomy books [11], literature [18] and knowledge, and aiming to make them generalizable across different cases. For example a query for recognizing the left S2 nerve is (the parameters defining the relations and threshold values are not mentioned here for the sake of readability):

S2_left =crossing(SacralHoleS2Left) then anterior_of(PiriformisMuscleLeft)
then left_of(LevatorAniMuscles) then not posterior_of(Sacrum)
then not (crossing(SacralHoleS1Left) or crossing(SacralHoleS3Left))
then not left_of(PiriformisMuscleLeft)
then not anterior_of(ObturatorMuscleLeft)
then not between(ObturatorMuscleLeft, ObturatorMuscleRight)

4.2 Results and Discussion

The networks in phase A were implemented from scratch using Tensorflow 2.16. We used 89 T2-w images for training, 16 as validation set and 63 as test set. All images were preprocessed as described in Sect. 3.1 with a common voxel size of $0.88 \times 0.88 \times 0.88 \, mm^3$. The method showed high quality segmentation of the pelvic structures described in Sect. 4.1 with Dice indices exceeding 85% for dense structures and Average Surface Distance less than 2 mm for elongated or small structures. The pelvic region was consistently localized by the first network and the U-Net-based error correction proved effective for minor pelvic structures, providing satisfying results for clinicians in around 2 min in worst case scenarios. Although the error correction phase reduces the level of automation of phase A, it serves to decouple potential segmentation errors from directly propagating into the results of phase B.

Table 1. Quantitative results of phase A of the Visionerves method in average (and standard deviation) for 10 endometriosis cases on different anatomical structures using Dice and Average Symmetric Surface Distance (ASSD). Results are shown before the use of the U-Net-based error correction. Bones are L5 vertebra, hip bones and sacrum; muscles are piriformis, obturator and levator ani; visceral organs are bladder, colon and rectum; reproductive organs are ovaries, uterus and vagina; specific ROIs are sacral foramina from S1 to S3, sacral canal and intervertebral foramina of L5.

Structure	Bones	Muscles	Visceral organs	Reproductive organs	Specific ROIs
Dice [%]	95.7	91.3	89.1	86.4	86.5
	(0.14)	(0.54)	(0.92)	(0.78)	(1.26)
ASSD [mm]	0.22	0.36	0.97	0.93	0.43
	(0.09)	(0.42)	(1.18)	(0.62)	(0.51)

The results of the complete Visionerves method on the 10 subjects with both T2-w and DWI acquisitions are shown in Table 1 for phase A (segmentation). These results are reported for completeness, even though segmentation is not the central focus of our method; they are shown before error correction, which was rarely necessary. Phase B results (reconstruction and recognition) are shown in Table 2 and were obtained using the 10 nerve reference reconstructions available from our patient cohort. After preprocessing, nerve bundles were extracted using raw tractography. The sacral or intervertebral foramen corresponding to each nerve (for each side) served as the seed labelmap, and fiber selection was constrained to those containing at least one point within the region traversed by the sciatic nerve (where all the four analyzed fiber bundles are confluent, see Fig. 2 for a better understanding). This region was constructed using the binarized spatial relations that we defined in Sect. 3.2. This phase was executed using MRTrix3 software [22] and we used a FOD-based algorithm with deterministic tracking, called "SD STREAM" [21], with minimum FOD amplitude for seeds of 0.15, FOD cut-off of 0.10, maximum angle of 45° and step size of 3 mm. This raw tractogram is referred as just "Tractography" in Table 2, and represents the current state of the art in PNS nerve recognition for traditional methods. Learning-based approaches could not be evaluated, primarily due to the challenges associated with detailed manual nerve segmentation in the T2-w images, and, more critically, the infeasibility of training a neural network given the only 10 cases with DWI and the lack of publicly available pre-trained models. We then applied our filtering method based on symbolic AI using the nerve queries defined as in Sect. 4.1 (see also Fig. 1) to the raw tractograms produced.

Table 2. Quantitative results of the Visionerves method (pre- and post-filtering) in average (and standard deviation) for 10 endometriosis cases on 4 different lumbosacral nerves (divided by sides) using Dice, precision, Average Symmetric Surface Distance (ASSD), Average Symmetric Centerline Distance (ASCD) and Absolute (Euclidean) Length Difference (ALD).

Nerve Bundle	Visionerves	Dice [%]	Precision [%]	ASSD [mm]	ASCD [mm]	ALD [mm]
L5 left	Tractography	49.56 (19.22)	35.09 (18.69)	9.66 (4.42)	31.67 (19.33)	30.64 (33.73)
	+ Filtering	**70.70 (16.26)**	**63.65 (17.35)**	**5.02 (4.38)**	**14.27 (16.11)**	**26.49 (30.52)**
L5 right	Tractography	55.81 (14.29)	40.21 (14.21)	6.30 (3.63)	18.28 (12.53)	**22.25 (27.78)**
	+ Filtering	**64.86 (9.85)**	**58.74 (14.31)**	**3.49 (2.38)**	**10.01 (8.89)**	24.98 (30.65)
S1 left	Tractography	56.37 (21.52)	42.37 (21.95)	6.02 (3.48)	14.14 (8.34)	36.12 (22.75)
	+ Filtering	**74.31 (11.95)**	**70.02 (16.47)**	**2.37 (1.80)**	**7.20 (7.00)**	**21.37 (23.47)**
S1 right	Tractography	60.40 (24.97)	47.79 (27.36)	6.59 (4.39)	13.44 (11.44)	**14.98 (18.03)**
	+ Filtering	**74.46 (19.94)**	**69.65 (25.02)**	**2.12 (2.54)**	**5.81 (5.32)**	15.03 (18.34)
S2 left	Tractography	50.96 (18.43)	36.57 (20.23)	7.27 (3.11)	19.30 (15.20)	35.76 (35.40)
	+ Filtering	**69.32 (12.48)**	**59.45 (17.39)**	**3.52 (2.27)**	**11.95 (18.01)**	**32.40 (27.03)**
S2 right	Tractography	56.78 (17.69)	41.83 (17.67)	6.37 (4.11)	13.54 (8.82)	25.30 (17.36)
	+ Filtering	**70.71 (10.05)**	**61.19 (12.66)**	**3.01 (2.61)**	**6.37 (5.75)**	**17.77 (17.68)**
S3 left	Tractography	44.54 (18.73)	30.55 (16.40)	7.48 (3.32)	17.47 (7.07)	37.68 (32.23)
	+ Filtering	**54.78 (15.95)**	**56.90 (21.35)**	**3.19 (1.83)**	**7.14 (2.82)**	**30.61 (21.72)**
S3 right	Tractography	39.49 (18.56)	26.32 (15.11)	9.66 (4.40)	21.69 (12.07)	33.70 (27.81)
	+ Filtering	**54.06 (18.77)**	**55.26 (23.43)**	**4.28 (3.54)**	**6.88 (2.67)**	**28.55 (22.80)**

These results are referred as "+ Filtering" in Table 2. Since the Dice score is not well adapted to the thin and tubular structure of the nerves, we also used the precision score (recall was not considered, as it cannot exceed the performance achieved by tractography) and multiple distance metrics that are the Average Symmetric Surface Distance (ASSD), the Average Symmetric Centerline Distance (ASCD) and the Absolute Length Difference (ALD). In order to make these measurements, each fiber bundle was transformed into a single labelmap.

Results show that just using tractography, even guided via ROIs for seeding and inclusion, is not enough to eliminate all spurious fibers. By contrast, the proposed approach via symbolic AI allows Dice results to be increased by at least 15% and precision by at least 25% for most fibers, indicating proper elimination of false positives with nearly no loss of true positives. Distance metrics (more suitable for evaluation of elongated structures) decrease drastically to half a centimeter for the entire bundle surface and a centimeter when considering the centerline. The difference in length remains around 2 cm, indicating that some fibers are not tracked all the way to the end of the portion of the fiber associated with the sciatic nerve. According to clinical experts, these distances are acceptable (to a certain extent) for clinic use, in particular when examined along with a visual assessment. Notably, Dice and precision scores are lower for S3 due to its smaller fiber diameter, making these evaluation measures less suitable; however, distance-based measures remain comparable to those of other nerve bundles.

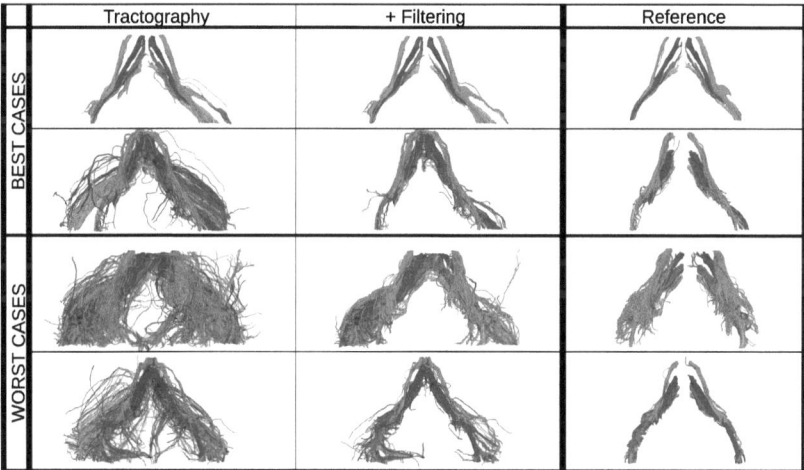

Fig. 2. Qualitative results of the Visionerves method (before and after recognition filtering) for the two best cases and two worst cases of the 10 endometriosis cases. Nerve reference reconstructions are produced as described in Sect. 4.1. Color code for nerve bundle: L5 in green, S1 in blue, S2 in magenta and S3 in cyan. (Color figure online)

Some qualitative results are presented in Fig. 2: for the two best cases, except for a few spurious fibers, the bundles overlap almost perfectly, while in the two worst cases most false positives are still effectively filtered (moreover on one case reference nerves are also highly disorganized). Only one case (third row) appears anatomically incorrect, but the reference nerves are also very disorganized. Interestingly, the two best-performing cases correspond to patients with confirmed endometriosis, whereas the worst-performing cases involve patients with suspected endometriosis (who exhibited symptoms of menorrhagia and pelvic pain). It remains unclear whether these suboptimal results are due to the choice of the tractography algorithm, its parameter settings or to intrinsic limitations of the imaging data. A more in-depth study needs to be conducted. Moreover, the filtering parameters and threshold values may probably need to be adjusted in cases where the raw tractogram already appears very disorganized.

5 Conclusion and Perspectives

In this work, we introduced Visionerves, a novel hybrid AI framework that leverages anatomical knowledge for the automatic and reproducible recognition of peripheral nerves. By integrating fuzzy spatial reasoning with symbolic AI and multi-modal MRI, our method addresses key limitations of traditional tractography, most notably its reliance on manual intervention and lack of reproducibility. For a preliminary assessment we applied Visionerves in the pelvic region on 10 endometriosis cases. Results demonstrated significant improvements over conventional tractography approaches confirming that our method can substantially reduce spurious fibers while maintaining the structural integrity of the nerve reconstructions.

By enabling the reproducible and individualized extraction of nerve bundles, Visionerves paves the way for assessing nerve-specific diffusion and morphological characteristics. This is particularly valuable in endometriosis, where these fiber properties may enable diagnosis in suspected cases of nerve involvement without the need for surgical biopsy. The S2 and S3 would be the principal nerves studied for this pathology since they are part of the pudendal plexus that is innervating the external genitalia and the perineum. Even though L5 and S1 further constitute the sciatic nerve, they are still of interest due to their proximity to the uterus and ovaries. Other conditions with possible nerve involvement may also benefit from our method (e.g. pelvic cancers), where Visionerves can also be used for pre-surgical planning and longitudinal follow-up.

In order to reach clinically acceptable results, in future work we plan to: (i) extend the database, including also healthy subjects and other pathologies, in order to enable more informed selection of hyperparameters during both phase B stages; (ii) refining query formalization (e.g. new spatial relations), and automate its generation from textual anatomical descriptions and its parametrization in cases where the raw tractogram is full of spurious fibers; (iii) exploring alternative validation criteria for fiber selection or adopt a solution where threshold values are adjusted based on a general "anatomical coherence score" that can be adjusted by the user, such as in [6]. Ultimately, we will test Visionerves on other pelvic nerve fibers (e.g. S4, pudendal, obturator) and other regions, (e.g. skull base, head and neck, brachial plexus), where conventional tractography remains particularly challenging. Once an anatomical segmentation of a region and the trajectories of the nerves in that region are defined, the Visionerves method can be applied in a straightforward manner, leveraging the existing comprehensive set of spatial relations, which can be easily expanded if needed.

Acknowledgments. This work has been funded and supported by Ligue contre le cancer, Fondation Béatrice Denys and Prématuration IP Paris. This work was performed using HPC Jean-Zay resources from GENCI–IDRIS (Grant 2025-AD011015418). We would like to thank Fatiha Tacine for her assistance with the organization and retrieval of the acquisitions at the Hôpital européen Georges Pompidou. We would like to thank also Alice Sorrentino for her assistance with the organization and segmentation of the acquisitions at the Hôpital Necker-Enfants malades.

Data Use Declaration. The 131 patients used in phase A were included under a license granted by the Hôpital Necker-Enfants malades for acquisitions during protocol n°2015-101705-44. The 10 endometriosis patients used for testing the Visionerves framework were included under preliminary acquisitions of a future research clinical protocol n°2024-100538-39 approved by the Hôpital européen Georges-Pompidou.

Disclosure of Interests. The authors declare that a patent application has been filed, related to the method presented in this paper. This disclosure is made in the interest of transparency and does not affect the integrity or objectivity of the research.

References

1. Baumgartner, M., Jäger, P.F., Isensee, F., Maier-Hein, K.H.: nnDetection: a self-configuring method for medical object detection. In: de Bruijne, M., et al. (eds.) MICCAI 2021. LNCS, vol. 12905, pp. 530–539. Springer, Cham (2021). https://doi.org/10.1007/978-3-030-87240-3_51
2. Bloch, I., Bonnot, E., Gori, P., La Barbera, G., Sarnacki, S.: First order logic with fuzzy semantics for describing and recognizing nerves in medical images. In: IEEE International Conference on Fuzzy Systems (FUZZ-IEEE) (2025)
3. Bloch, I., Ralescu, A.: Fuzzy Sets Methods in Image Processing and Understanding: Medical Imaging Applications. Springer, Cham (2023)
4. Cage, T., et al.: Visualization of nerve fibers and their relationship to peripheral nerve tumors by diffusion tensor imaging. Neurosurg. Focus **39**(3), E16 (2015)
5. Chapron, C., Marcellin, L., Borghese, B., Santulli, P.: Rethinking mechanisms, diagnosis and management of endometriosis. Nat. Rev. Endocrinol. **15**(11), 666–682 (2019)
6. Delmonte, A., Mercier, C., Pallud, J., Bloch, I., Gori, P.: White matter multi-resolution segmentation using fuzzy set theory. In: IEEE International Symposium on Biomedical Imaging (2019)
7. Fauconnier, A., Chapron, C.: Endometriosis and pelvic pain: epidemiological evidence of the relationship and implications. Hum. Reprod. Update **11**(6), 595–606 (2005)

8. Fedorov, A., et al.: 3D Slicer as an image computing platform for the quantitative imaging network. Magn. Reson. Imaging **30**(9), 1323–1341 (2012)
9. Garyfallidis, E., et al.: Recognition of white matter bundles using local and global streamline-based registration and clustering. Neuroimage **170**, 283–295 (2018)
10. Gori, P., Durrleman, S., Colliot, O., Mangin, J.F., Ayache, N.: A prototype representation to approximate white matter bundles with weighted currents. In: Medical Image Computing and Computer-Assisted Intervention, pp. 289–296 (2014)
11. Gray, H.: Anatomy of the Human Body. Lea and Febiger (1918)
12. Haakma, W., et al.: Diffusion tensor magnetic resonance imaging and fiber tractography of the sacral plexus in children with spina bifida. J. Urol. **192**(3), 927–933 (2014)
13. Hudelot, C., Atif, J., Bloch, I.: Fuzzy spatial relation ontology for image interpretation. Fuzzy Sets Syst. **159**(15), 1929–1951 (2008)
14. Isensee, F., Jaeger, P., Kohl, S., Petersen, J., Maier-Hein, K.: nnU-Net: a self-configuring method for deep learning-based biomedical image segmentation. Nat. Methods **18**(2), 203–211 (2021)
15. Isensee, F., et al.: nnInteractive: redefining 3D promptable segmentation. arXiv preprint arXiv:2503.08373 (2025)
16. Knoedler, M., Feibus, A., Lange, J., Venkatesh, R., Landman, J.: Individualized physical 3-dimensional kidney tumor models constructed from 3-dimensional printers result in improved trainee anatomic understanding. Urology **85**(6), 1257–1261 (2015)
17. Lemos, N., Melo, H., Sermer, C., et al.: Lumbosacral plexus MR tractography: a novel diagnostic tool for extraspinal sciatica and pudendal neuralgia? Magn. Reson. Imaging **83**, 107–113 (2021)
18. Manganaro, L., et al.: Diffusion tensor imaging and tractography to evaluate sacral nerve root abnormalities in endometriosis-related pain: a pilot study. Eur. Radiol. **24**(1), 95–101 (2014)
19. Muller, C., et al.: Integrating tractography in pelvic surgery: a proof of concept. J. Pediatr. Surg. Case Rep. **48**, 101268 (2019)
20. Smith, R., Tournier, J.D., Calamante, F., Connelly, A.: Anatomically-constrained tractography: improved diffusion MRI streamlines tractography through effective use of anatomical information. Neuroimage **62**(3), 1924–1938 (2012)
21. Tournier, J.D., Mori, S., Leemans, A.: Diffusion tensor imaging and beyond. Magn. Reson. Med. **65**(6), 1532–1556 (2011)
22. Tournier, J., Smith, R., Raffelt, D., et al.: MRtrix3: a fast, flexible and open software framework for medical image processing and visualisation. Neuroimage **202**, 116–137 (2019)
23. Vinit, N., Blanc, T., Bloch, I., Sarnacki, S., Agon, C., Romero, G.: Robotics and 3D modeling for precision surgery in pediatric oncology. EJC Paediatr. Oncol. **4**, 100181 (2024)
24. Wassermann, D., et al.: The white matter query language: a novel approach for describing human white matter anatomy. Brain Struct. Funct. **221**(9), 4705–4721 (2016). https://doi.org/10.1007/s00429-015-1179-4
25. Wasserthal, J., Neher, P., Maier-Hein, K.: TractSeg - fast and accurate white matter tract segmentation. Neuroimage **183**, 239–253 (2018)
26. Zijta, F., et al.: Evaluation of the female pelvic floor in pelvic organ prolapse using 3.0-Tesla diffusion tensor imaging and fibre tractography. Eur. Radiol. **22**(12), 2806–2813 (2012)

A Prospective Dual-Modality Tool for Monitoring Uterine Peristalsis: Integrating Dynamic MRI and Electrohysterography

Maria Camila Bustos Vivas[1,2(✉)], Smiti Tripathy[1,2], and Jana Hutter[1,2]

[1] Radiology Department, Uniklinikum Erlangen, Erlangen, Germany
maria.v.bustos@fau.de
[2] Smart Imaging Lab, Friedrich-Alexander-Universität Erlangen-Nürnberg, Erlangen, Germany

Abstract. This paper presents a first step towards a novel approach that combines simultaneous transabdominal electromyography (EMG) with dynamic echo-planar imaging multi-echo gradient-echo (EPI-MEGE) magnetic resonance imaging (MRI) for monitoring uterine peristaltic motion. Uterine peristalsis (UP) influences crucial processes such as menstruation, sperm transport, and embryo implantation. Current monitoring methods focus only on mechanical or electrical activity, making comparing and extrapolating results between different modalities difficult. The proposed protocol combines dynamic EPI-MEGE MRI and transabdominal EMG to capture the anatomical and electrophysiological features of UP simultaneously. Electrohysterographic (EHG) signals obtained from recorded EMG supported the spatiotemporal information of MRI by integrating the synchronized electrical activity of uterine muscles. Safety testing in a phantom confirmed that the electrode temperature during EPI-MEGE MRI acquisition remained within acceptable limits for human application. Three healthy volunteers underwent EPI-MEGE MRI acquisition with simultaneous transabdominal EMG. Electrode placement strategies proved to be reproducible and anatomically consistent. MRI frames enabled the visualization of the uterus anatomy and contractions, while bowel gas affected the spatial resolution, and the bladder filling influenced the uterus positioning over time. Results showed the feasibility of a non-invasive and simultaneous method for assessing uterine contractility, combining dynamic MRI scans with synchronized EHG.

Keywords: Uterine Peristalsis · EHG · dynamic MRI

1 Introduction

Uterine contractility originates from electrical activity within the myometrial cells. Changes in the ion permeability of cell membranes induce action potentials in the smooth muscle. A single spike can trigger an individual contraction, whereas multiple high-frequency spikes produce a sustained contraction. The characteristics of these contractions depend on the number of synchronized active cells and the frequency and duration of bursts of spike action potentials [5,12]. The resulting subtle wave-like movements known as uterine peristalsis (UP) influence crucial processes such as menstruation, sperm transport, and embryo implantation [15].

Despite its clinical significance, monitoring uterine peristalsis (UP) non-invasively and dynamically in clinical settings remains challenging [12]. Current methods typically focus on either mechanical or electrical activity, making it difficult to compare and extrapolate results across different modalities [7]. We propose a novel protocol combining dynamic MRI and transabdominal EMG to capture simultaneously the anatomical and electrophysiological features of UP.

The paper reviews related work in Sect. 2, describes the proposed method in Sect. 3, presents experimental results in Sect. 4, and finishes with discussions and future research considerations in Sects. 5 and 6.

2 Related Work

The frequency, intensity, and direction of UP change throughout the menstrual cycle. Propagation can occur retrograde (cervix-to-fundus) or anterograde (fundus-to-cervix) [12]. During the peri-ovulatory phase, high-frequency retrograde activity enhances sperm transport. In contrast, anterograde propagation helps to expel menstrual blood. During the luteal phase, a quiescent state supports implantation. Contraction frequency increases from the follicular to periovulatory phase and decreases during the luteal phase to reach its lowest value during menses [4,13,19]. Any deviation from this established process may have physiological significance [18]. Abnormal uterine contractility, particularly hyper-contractility, is associated with pathological conditions such as adenomyosis, endometriosis, and leiomyoma [7,11,12].

Various techniques are associated with different stages of the physiological cascade underlying UP, including intrauterine pressure catheters, which are invasive and might interfere with natural UP [6]. Transabdominal electromyography (EMG) provides a non-invasive approach to extract electrohysterographic (EHG) signals and characterize uterine muscle activity [5,12]. Among imaging modalities, transabdominal ultrasound provides a broad view of the uterus and surrounding anatomy, particularly useful when transvaginal ultrasound (TVUS) is not an option, such as in premenarchal patients. However, image quality can decrease due to the abdominal wall and distance from the uterus [17]. TVUS videos allow for analysis of UP, but the technique is invasive and only captures secondary endometrial movements [4,12].

In recent years, magnetic resonance imaging (MRI) has emerged as a promising non-invasive and reproducible method [18]. It captures dynamic changes in the junctional zone (JZ) as temporal signal reductions and has demonstrated the relationship between dynamic abnormalities and uterine pathologies [11]. The JZ appears differently on MRI than on TVUS, and histopathological ex-vivo changes make correlating imaging findings with pathology challenging [7]. Furthermore, factors such as hormonal fluctuations, uterine orientation, and bladder filling influence UP, limiting the ability to extrapolate findings between modalities [13,18].

Recently, a non-invasive imaging modality was able to estimate electrical activation patterns in a 3D uterus model created from a single anatomical MRI scan [19]. This approach maps the electrical activity over time on a static 3D model, which does not account for observable uterine movements. Consequently, there is a need for a non-invasive, dynamic, and multi-modal technique to obtain synchronized insights into the electrical and mechanical dynamics of UP.

3 Methodology

The proposed technique considered the female pelvis's complex anatomical and physiological conditions illustrated in Fig. 1 to obtain spatial and electrophysiological information of uterine muscle layers from a simultaneous MRI and transabdominal EMG acquisition protocol.

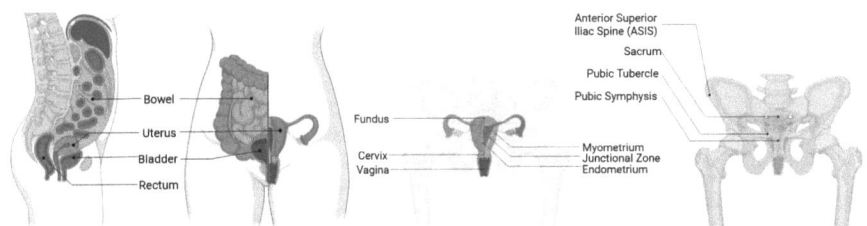

Fig. 1. Female Pelvic Anatomy and Uterine Structure. The uterus is situated between the bladder and rectum and can be anteverted, retroverted, anteflexed, or retroflexed. It consists of the fundus, corpus, isthmus, and cervix, with the corpus containing three smooth muscle layers: endometrium, junctional zone, and myometrium. The uterus is located within the pelvis, formed by the hip bones connected by the pubis symphysis at the front and the sacrum and coccyx at the back. Modified from: [14,20].

3.1 Experimental Setup and Acquisition Protocol

Using a 0.55 T MAGNETOM Free.Max scanner (Siemens Healthineers, Erlangen, Germany) with a blanket-like BioMatrix 9ch Contour-M body coil, we acquired dynamic MRI data while recording synchronized transabdominal EMG signals via an eight-channel BrainAmp ExG MR, an ExG AUX Box, a SyncBox, and special MRI-conditional multirode bipolar electrodes (Brain Products,

Gilching, Germany). The connection between the SyncBox and the MRI scanner clock output generates synchronization markers, which indicate the acquisition of each MRI frame.

Participants must empty their bladder before the protocol and prepare a clean, shaved area on the abdomen and pelvis for placing electrodes. They also provide information about their menstrual cycle phase. The use of abrasive gel reduces the impedance at the skin-electrode interface, ensuring that the value is below 10 $k\Omega$. The patient laid supine on the scanner table, with the body coil above the electrodes, while keeping the BrainAmp ExG MR and its battery outside the scanner bore as illustrated in Fig. 2.

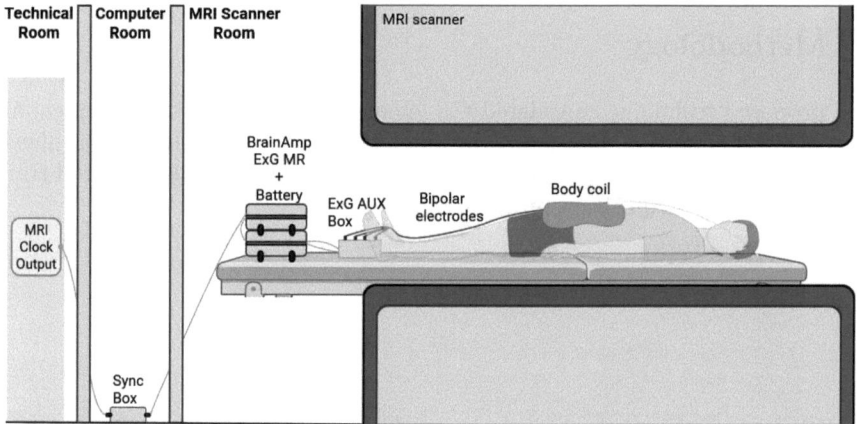

Fig. 2. Setup for dual-modality data acquisition. The bipolar electrodes on the abdomen below the body coil are connected to the ExG AUX Box between the participant's legs. The BrainAmp ExG MR and its battery should remain at the end of the table outside the scanner bore. The SyncBox in the computer room is connected to the BrainAmp ExG MR and the scanner clock. Created with BioRender.com

A single-shot, echoplanar imaging, multi-echo gradient echo (EPI-MEGE) sequence, with the following parameters: TR = 1700 ms, TEs=[31, 79, 127] ms, flip angle = 90°, FOV = $290 \times 290 \, \text{mm}^2$, voxel size = $3 \times 3 \times 6 \, \text{mm}^3$, bandwidth= 1184 Hz/Px, in-plane acceleration=2, slices=8, produces a dynamic MRI scan of 250 frames. A low-field 0.55 T MRI system helps to mitigate off-resonance artifacts resulting from B_0 field inhomogeneities that can be generated in the abdominal region. The sequence does not employ inversion radiofrequency (RF) pulses and must stay within a maximum limit of RMS B_{1+} of 1.5 µT to avoid RF-field induced heating of electrode lead wires and cables. All cables must remain fixed and untwisted, avoiding loops. Brain Products Recorder Software collects eight EMG signals at a sampling rate of 5 kHz.

3.2 Phantom-Based Safety Validation

A temperature test will ensure that the parameters of the EPI-MEGE MRI sequence do not produce a temperature increase that poses risks for the patient or degrade the electrodes. The use of a cylindrical plastic phantom allows for evaluating the feasibility of the proposed setup in humans. The phantom is filled with a solution that contains 3.75 g of $NiSO_4 \cdot 6H_2O$ and 5 g of NaCl per 1000 g of water (Siemens Healthineers, Erlangen, Germany). Wet towels surrounding the phantom simulate the skin, and the abrasive gel ensures good conductivity at the interface between the phantom and the electrodes. Temperature probes monitor changes in temperature along the surface of three monopolar electrodes with cable lengths of 30 cm, 60 cm, and 90 cm during EPI-MEGE acquisition.

3.3 Electrode Positioning

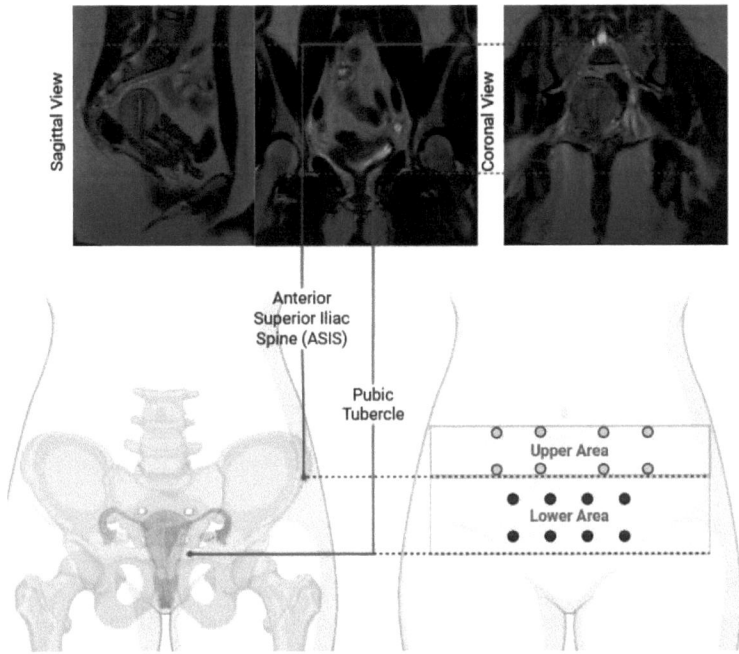

Fig. 3. Electrode positioning for transabdominal EMG recording. Sagittal and coronal 2D turbo spin echo abdominal scans illustrate the pelvic anatomy. The sagittal view reveals the orientation of the uterus, and the coronal view displays the anterosuperior iliac spine (ASIS) and the pubic tubercle, dividing the abdomen into the upper region (yellow) and the lower region (blue). Created with BioRender.com. (Color figure online)

Three healthy volunteers gave their written informed consent before participating in the study. The anterosuperior iliac spine (ASIS) and the pubic bone point to the area where a fiducial marker should be placed on the abdominal surface to locate the uterus using the localizer scan, as shown in Fig. 3. After confirming the uterus orientation, the protocol continues outside the scanner bore.

The strategy divides the abdominal area into two regions: the upper section extending from the umbilicus to the ASIS, and the lower section ranging from the ASIS to the pubic tubercle. Each part has four electrodes placed in a 4X2 array and parallel aligned to the mid-body axis. A minimum inter-electrode distance of three centimeters considers the average dimensions of an adult female uterus, 8 cm (L) × 5 cm (W) × 4 cm (T) [2], ensuring sufficient coverage along the uterus' longitudinal axis and reducing any potential interference from nearby organs. The ground electrode sits over the ASIS at one of the hip bones. After verifying the electrode impedance, the protocol continues with the placement of the body coil and the reinsertion of the patient table.

3.4 EMG Signal Processing

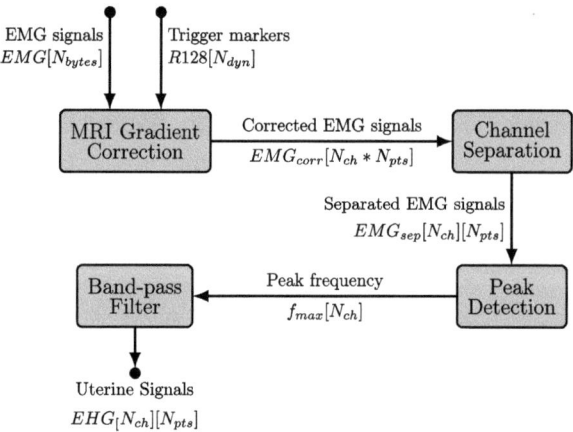

Fig. 4. EHG Signal Extraction. MRI gradient correction for each EPI-MEGE MRI scan starts with the recorded transabdominal EMG signals with a size N_{bytes} and the corresponding trigger markers indicating the acquisition of N_{dyn} MRI dynamics. The analysis continues separately for each channel after extracting the N_{ch} signals, each signal of size N_{pts}. The power spectral density (PSD) shows the frequency at the highest peak within the uterine peristalsis frequency range for each signal. Selecting the frequency at the highest peak for each signal results in an array of frequency values (f_{max}). These values define the frequency center of a zero-phase band-pass filter of width ±0.005 Hz for each channel. The linear second-order Butterworth band-pass filter filters forward and backward the N_{ch} signals to isolate the EHG signals without phase distortion.

The acquisition protocol records eight transabdominal EMG signals. Utilizing a band-pass filter to extract EHG signals provides an electrical representation of uterine contractility from surface abdominal recordings. First, trigger markers indicating each frame acquisition help to mitigate gradient-field-related artifacts in the transabdominal EMG recording. Since each channel captures the signal between the corresponding pair of bipolar electrodes, the result after extraction is one corrected transabdominal EMG signal per channel. The power spectral density (PSD) calculated using Welch's method, with a window length of 2^{21} samples and 75 % overlap, reveals whether there are frequency peaks within the normal range of UP (0.005âĂŞ0.05 Hz) [12]. For every channel, this value represent the center of a linear second-order Butterworth band-pass (BP) filter of width ±0.005 Hz [16]. Applying a combined filter both forwards and backwards to the corrected transabdominal EMG signals helps isolate EHG signals and prevents phase distortion.

3.5 Preliminary Data Synchronization

The SyncBox ensures phase synchronization between the sampling rate of the EMG recording and the MRI scanner. Synchronization markers were obtained to indicate the onset of the gradient artifact, time-locked to the acquisition of each frame. Brain Products Analyzer software allows users to extract the time positions for all markers to align EMG signals with the MRI frames (Fig. 4).

4 Results

4.1 Dual-Modality Acquisition Protocol

The fiducial marker allowed verifying the position of the uterus in the sagittal view for all volunteers. In all cases, the ASIS and the pubic tubercle served as anatomical landmarks for guiding the electrode positioning. Participants underwent successful simultaneous transabdominal EMG and EPI-MEGE acquisitions.

Fig. 5 shows frames 73 and 85 of the 2nd echo for EPI-MEGE MRI scan. The images reveal that the electrodes generated artifacts in the anterior abdominal wall; however, this does not affect the visualization of the abdominal organs. The three smooth muscle layers of the uterus are visible, and therefore, the motion patterns in the JZ (low signal band) can be appreciated. Bowel and bladder dynamics are also visible in the MRI frames.

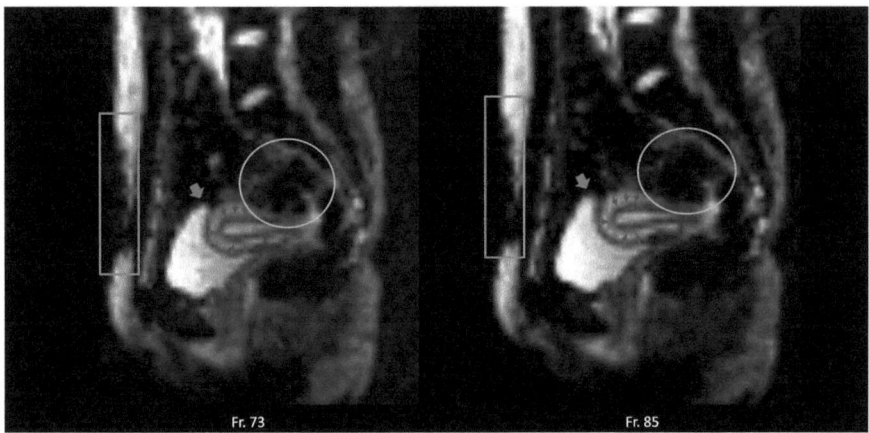

Fig. 5. Dynamic EPI-MEGE MRI. Two sagittal frames of the second echo of one participant highlight image artifacts created by the electrodes (green box), bowel gas (yellow region), bladder dynamics (blue narrow), and peristaltic motion in the JZ (red arrows). (Color figure online)

A nearest view of the uterus in multiple frame of the 2nd echo for the same volunteer display the peristaltic motion in Fig. 6. The red arrows indicate the movements of the JZ (low signal layer) over time. The transabdominal EMG signal recorded from channel eight, located in the lower abdominal region, captures the electrical activity at a specific spatial point. Meanwhile, the extracted EHG signal reflects the electrical activity from the uterus at the same point. The synchronization markers, represented as dashed blue lines, connected the point in the EHG signal with the corresponding MRI frame.

After gradient-field-related artifacts correction [1], the analysis continues separately for each channel signal. Figure 7apresents the PSD for each channel for one of the participants. For each channel, the selection of the power peak is based on the uterine peristalsis frequency range (green band), avoiding the frequency band of the detrusor muscle in the bladder (blue band) at $0.033 \pm 0.008\,\text{Hz}$ [19]. Figure 7bshows the PSD for all channels for the three volunteers. In all cases, the PSD displayed a peak within the frequency range associated with UP [12], indicating that transabdominal EMG is able to record EHG signals. The frequency at the highest peak in the region of interest represents the frequency center of the second-order Butterworth BP filter for each channel. Synchronization markers allowed the time-alignment of the extracted EHG signals with the MRI scans based on their time positions. An illustrative example of the EHG signal from one of the lower region channels, along with the corresponding MRI frames, is shown in Fig. 6.

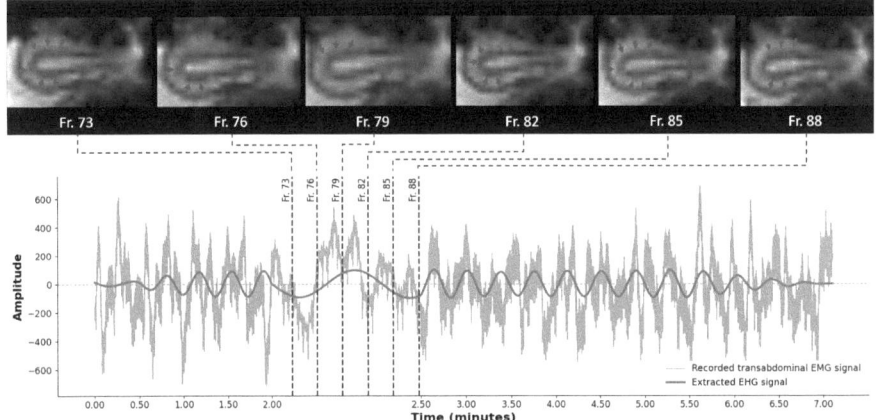

Fig. 6. Dynamic MRI and EHG signal Synchronization. Multiple frames of the second echo highlight peristaltic motion in the JZ (red arrows). The recorded transabdominal EMG (gray signal) and extracted EHG signal (red signal) from channel number eight (lower region) are below. The synchronization markers, represented as dashed blue lines, connected the point in the EHG signal with the corresponding MRI frame. (Color figure online)

4.2 Phantom Safety Testing

The temperature probes monitored temperature changes of three multirode monopolar electrodes with cable lengths of 30 cm, 60 cm, and 90 cm during EPI-MEGE acquisition at the electrode surface. The temperature was stable during the whole acquisition, with the temperature range not exceeding 24°C, below the CEI 60601-2-33 standard threshold of 43°C for skin contact [3]. The results suggest that following the mentioned safety recommendations enables the implementation of the proposed dual-modality acquisition protocol in human subjects to simultaneously record EMG while conducting EPI-MEGE acquisitions.

5 Discussion

The proposed non-invasive acquisition protocol combining dynamic MRI with simultaneous transabdominal EMG allows for the capture of anatomical and electrophysiological features of UP. The electrode positioning strategy demonstrated reproducibility and anatomical consistency [10]. Additionally, implementing the protocol with the human participants resulted in no adverse effects. Dynamic EPI-MEGE MRI scans allowed the visualization of the pelvic anatomy and motion patterns of abdominal organs in low-field. The bowel, uterus, bladder, and rectum were visible in the images. However, the resolution of the EPI-MEGE is surpassed by CINE sequences often employed [11,18]. The bladder filling dynamically influenced the position of the uterus [15,17]. Signal loss observed in the uterus in some frames is likely due to off-resonance artifacts resulting from

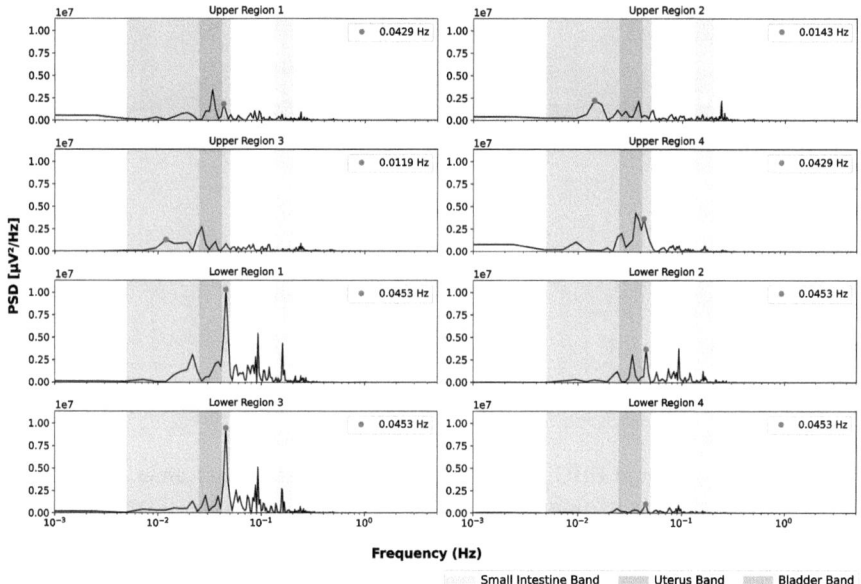

(a) PSD plots for all channels of one participant.

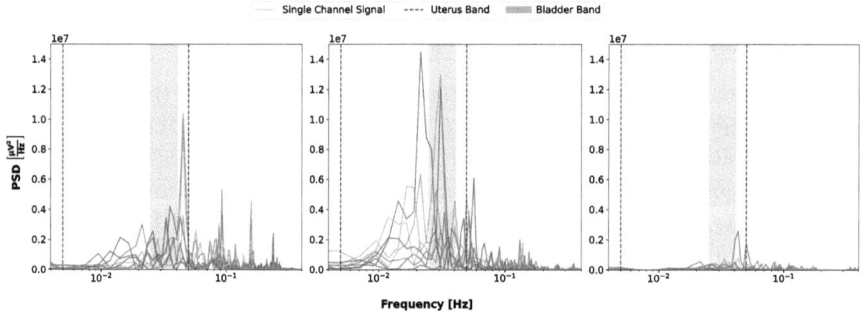

(b) PSD plots for all participants.

Fig. 7. Power spectral density (PSD) plots. (a) Each subplot shows the PSD for each channel signal for one of the volunteers. The color bands indicate the frequency range associated with the uterus (green), bladder (blue), and small intestine (yellow). The cyan point represents the selected peak for each signal channel. (b) Each subplot displays the PSD of eight-channel signals recorded from each volunteer. The dashed lines indicate the frequency band associated with the uterus, and the blue band represents the frequency band associated with the bladder. (Color figure online)

B_0 field inhomogeneities, even in a 0.55 T system [9]. These inhomogeneities might occur because air in the bowel and rectum has a different magnetic susceptibility compared to the surrounding tissues. This difference leads to local magnetic field distortions which increase with the strength of the magnetic field

[8]. The dual-modality acquisition protocol facilitated the visualization of pelvic organ dynamics and the extraction of uterine electrical activity, establishing a foundation for future advancements in non-invasive monitoring of UP. Future research will aim to include a larger, more diverse population with variability in the orientation of the uterus and to add menstrual cycle information in the analysis. CINE sequences will be explored to enhance spatial resolution and minimize off-resonance artifacts, considering the safety requirements of the Brain Products EMG system. This includes avoiding inversion RF pulses and adhering to the maximum limit of RMS B_{1+} of $1.5\,\mu\text{T}$. Ultimately, the proposed methodology will be integrated into a comprehensive protocol designed to monitor and evaluate uterine layer peristalsis through the acquisition of multiple dynamic MRI sequences and simultaneously electrophysiological signals in real time.

6 Conclusion

This study introduced a novel non-invasive acquisition protocol that combines dynamic MRI with transabdominal EMG to gather anatomical and electrophysiological data simultaneously. The protocol underwent validation through phantom and in-vivo experiments, demonstrating its feasibility and safety for human application. The extraction of EHG signals from the transabdominal EMG recordings allowed the synchronization of the EPI-MEGE dynamics with the electrical activity in the uterine muscle. Despite limitations in spatial resolution and susceptibility to bowel gas artifacts, the protocol effectively identifies the mechanicoelectrical features of UP and ensures a reproducible electrode placement strategy.

Acknowledgments. The authors thank Cilia and Lena from Brain Products for helping the project meet safety requirements. This work was supported by the High Tech Agenda of the Free State of Bavaria, DFG Heisenberg funding [502024488] and an ERC Starting grant EARTHWORM [101165242].

Disclosure of Interests. The authors have no competing interests to declare that are relevant to the content of this article.

References

1. Allen, P.J., Josephs, O., Turner, R.: A method for removing imaging artifact from continuous EEG recorded during functional MRI. Neuroimage **12**(2), 230–239 (2000)
2. Ameer, M.A., Fagan, S.E., Sosa-Stanley, J.N., et al.: Anatomy, abdomen and pelvis: uterus. In: StatPearls [Internet]. StatPearls Publishing (2022). https://www.ncbi.nlm.nih.gov/books/NBK470297/
3. Reis, J.E., et al.: Reconstruction of the 12-lead ECG using a novel MR-compatible ECG sensor network. Magn. Reson. Med. **82**(5), 1929–1945 (2019)
4. Eytan, O., Halevi, I., Har-Toov, J., Wolman, I., Elad, D., Jaffa, A.J.: Characteristics of uterine peristalsis in spontaneous and induced cycles. Fertil. Steril. **76**(2), 337–341 (2001)

5. Garfield, R.E., Maner, W.L.: Physiology and electrical activity of uterine contractions. Semin. Cell Dev. Biol. **18**(3), 289–295 (2007)
6. Hadar, E., Biron-Shental, T., Gavish, O., Raban, O., Yogev, Y.: A comparison between electrical uterine monitor, tocodynamometer and intra uterine pressure catheter for uterine activity in labor. J. Maternal-Fetal Neonatal Med. **28**(12), 1367–1374 (2015)
7. Harmsen, M.J., et al.: Uterine junctional zone and adenomyosis: comparison of MRI, transvaginal ultrasound and histology. Ultrasound Obstet. Gynecol. **62**(1), 42–60 (2023)
8. Haskell, M.W., Nielsen, J.F., Noll, D.C.: Off-resonance artifact correction for MRI: a review. NMR Biomed. **36**(5), e4867 (2023)
9. Hori, M., Hagiwara, A., Goto, M., Wada, A., Aoki, S.: Low-field magnetic resonance imaging: its history and renaissance. Invest. Radiol. **56**(11), 669–679 (2021)
10. Jossou, T.R., et al.: Electrodes in external electrohysterography: a systematic literature review. Biophys. Rev. **13**(3), 405–415 (2021). https://doi.org/10.1007/s12551-021-00805-w
11. Kido, A., et al.: Cine MR imaging of uterine peristalsis in patients with endometriosis. Eur. Radiol. **17**(7), 1813–1819 (2007)
12. Kuijsters, N.P.M., Methorst, W.G., Kortenhorst, M.S.Q., Rabotti, C., Mischi, M., Schoot, B.C.: Uterine peristalsis and fertility: current knowledge and future perspectives: a review and meta-analysis. Reprod. Biomed. Online **35**(1), 50–71 (2017)
13. Kunz, G., Noe, M., Herbertz, M., Leyendecker, G.: Uterine peristalsis during the follicular phase of the menstrual cycle: effects of oestrogen, antioestrogen and oxytocin. Hum. Reprod. Update **4**(5), 647–654 (1998)
14. National Cancer Institute: Pelvis, female, anatomy (2025)
15. Paramasivam, S., Proietto, A., Puvaneswary, M.: Pelvic anatomy and MRI. Best Pract. Res. Clin. Obstetrics Gynaecol. **20**(1), 3–22 (2006)
16. Rebollo, I., Tallon-Baudry, C.: The sensory and motor components of the cortical hierarchy are coupled to the rhythm of the stomach during rest. J. Neurosci. **42**(11), 2205–2220 (2022)
17. Roach, M.K., Andreotti, R.F.: The normal female pelvis. Clin. Obstet. Gynecol. **60**(1), 3–10 (2017)
18. Soares, D.M., Junior, H.W., Bittencourt, L.K., Lopes, F., Oliveira, M.A.P.: The role of cine MR imaging in the assessment of uterine function. Arch. Gynecol. Obstet. **300**(3), 545–553 (2019)
19. Wang, S., et al.: Noninvasive imaging of 4D electrical activation patterns of uterine peristalsis during normal menstrual cycles. NPJ Women's Health **2**(1) (2024)
20. Wong, L.C.Y., Chiu, W.K., Russ, M., Liew, S.: Review of techniques for monitoring the healing fracture of bones for implementation in an internally fixated pelvis. Med. Eng. Phys. **34**(2), 140–152 (2012)

Real-Time Automated Analysis and Reporting of Uterine MRI

Deepak Bhatia[1,2(✉)], Jordina Aviles Verdera[1,2], Michael Kitzberger[1,2], Smiti Tripathy[1,2], Maria Camila Bustos Vivas[1,2], Lieselotte Kratzsch[1,2], Anika Knupfer[1,2], and Jana Hutter[1,2,3]

[1] Smart Imaging Lab, University Hospital Erlangen and Friedrich-Alexander University Erlangen-Nuremberg, Erlangen, Germany
deepak.bhatia@fau.de
[2] Institute for Diagnostic Radiology, University Hospital Erlangen, Erlangen, Germany
[3] Institute for Women's Health, University Hospital Erlangen, Erlangen, Germany

Abstract. Inter-observer variability, lack of standardization, the necessity to document incidental findings, and the clinical demand for rapid diagnostic support limit the efficiency and reliability of pelvic MRI, emphasizing the need for automated analysis of uterine MRI scans. This work introduces a real-time, deep learning-based tool designed to automatically generate structured analysis reports directly from sagittal T2-weighted pelvic MR images. Utilizing real-time scanner interfacing and state-of-the-art 3D nnU-Net architecture with a Residual Encoder preset trained on a publicly available dataset, the proposed system accurately segments the uterine wall, uterine cavity, uterine fibroids, and Nabothian cysts. Post-processing of the predicted segmentation enables the generation of comprehensive structured HTML reports that include precise uterine volumetric measurements and detailed lesion assessments for fibroids and Nabothian cysts. The performance of the tool was validated on two independent datasets from different clinical sites, varying in magnetic field strength, and scanner vendor. Its real-time inference capability was also confirmed. The segmentation model showed reliable performance uterine wall, uterine cavity and uterine myoma (mean dice coefficient of 0.82, 0.77 and 0.78 respectively) and a mean dice coefficient of 0.43 for Nabothian cysts. Reports were consistently generated in real-time within an average time of 60 s. By providing immediate, standardized, and reproducible analyses, the developed tool is well-positioned for seamless integration into clinical radiological workflows.

1 Introduction

Uterine MRI is a critical tool for diagnosing and evaluating a broad spectrum of pathologies, encompassing malignant conditions such as endometrial and cervical cancers, as well as benign disorders including fibroids, cysts, adenomyosis, and endometriosis [1,18,20,21]. Structural abnormalities and uterine morphometric parameters have significant diagnostic implications. Sevindik et al. [22]

showed that specific uterine dimensions, such as corpus length, fundal thickness, and anteroposterior diameter, differ notably between fertile and infertile women. These measurements are also commonly used to estimate uterine and uterine myoma volumes in clinical practice [3,14]. Volumetric measurements provide comprehensive morphological assessments, essential for evaluating pathological enlargement due to conditions such as fibroids or other abnormalities [3,14]. Additionally, focal or global thickening of the endometrium and junctional zone is a characteristic of adenomyosis [1,30]. Thus, quantitative uterine metrics (size, shape, volume) hold clinical value in reproductive health assessments and therapeutic decision-making.

Uterine fibroids (also known as Uterine myomas, or leiomyomas) are common benign pelvic lesions in women which often result in symptoms like heavy menstrual bleeding and pelvic pain, affecting approximately one-third of women in their reproductive years [12,24]. Large or multiple fibroids can enlarge the uterus, exert pressure on neighboring organs (leading for example to urinary frequency or constipation), and contribute to infertility or adverse pregnancy outcomes [12,24]. Nabothian cysts are benign, mucus-filled cysts, often encountered incidentally during imaging. Although typically asymptomatic, large cysts can occasionally cause discomfort or require differential diagnosis from other cervical lesions [18]. Accurate assessment of uterine morphology and lesions is in general important in accurately diagnosing and managing symptomatic pelvic diseases and plays a role in the evaluation of infertility [3,14,22,25].

While ultrasound is widely used, the non-invasive nature of MRI, superior soft-tissue contrast, and ability to evaluate the entire pelvis with multiplanar imaging, increasingly position it as an essential diagnostic tool for the aforementioned diseases [1,19,21]. It can effectively visualize the distinct anatomical layers of the uterus and detect even small myomas [1,5]. Yet, uterine MRI remains challenging due to variability in uterine anatomy and dynamic physiological changes related to reproductive phases, uterine peristalsis, and external factors such as intrauterine devices, bowel motility or gas [13,17,22,26,30]. Manual pelvic MRI analysis is both time-consuming and subjective, prone to inconsistencies. The absence of standardized reporting further exacerbates these inconsistencies. Automated deep learning-based analysis methods overcome these limitations, offering reproducible, objective segmentation, and precise volumetric evaluations [10,11,16,25]. Furthermore, real-time integration of AI analysis during MRI scans enables adaptive imaging strategies, such as triggering additional sequences or optimizing acquisition planes based on initial findings [4,23,27,29]. Immediate access to information such as uterine volume, shape data, and identification and characterization of benign findings, including fibroids and Nabothian cysts, allows responsive adjustments during the scan, can reduce follow-up imaging and enhance MR-guided interventions such as MR-HIFU treatment or laparoscopic myomectomy [2,4,15].

In this study, we introduce a deep learning-based tool for uterine MRI that provides a real-time AI analysis of T2-weighted sagittal MRI volumes in the form of a standardized report, detailing uterine volumetry, the presence or absence of uterine fibroids and Nabothian cysts, and their locations and volumes if present. The tool provides objective morphometric data in an easy-to-read structured report that can supplement clinical impressions and can easily be integrated into routine uterine MRI clinical workflows.

2 Methods

In the following, the entire workflow of the proposed tool, from data acquisition to automatic segmentation, identification, and quantification of incidental findings and generation of an automatic real-time compatible standardized report will be detailed. An overview of the workflow is provided in Fig. 1.

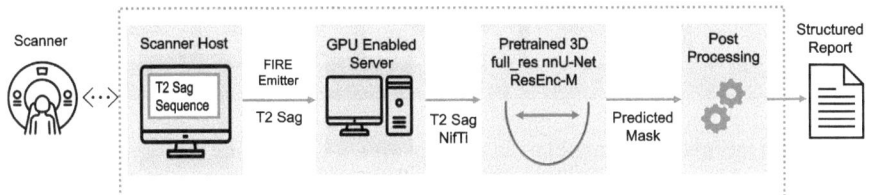

Fig. 1. Schematic overview of the workflow implemented in the proposed tool, illustrating the process from data acquisition to generation of individual structured report containing segmentation visualizations, volumetry results and information on incidental findings.

2.1 Data

For training and evaluation of the proposed tool, we used two distinct datasets comprising T2-weighted sagittal pelvic MRI volumes acquired using a range of clinical MRI scanners from various vendors. These datasets include detailed pixel-level annotations for four clinically relevant classes: uterine wall (including the cervical wall), uterine cavity, uterine myomas, and Nabothian cysts. A description of the annotated labels is illustrated in Fig. 2. The first dataset (**Dataset I**) is a large-scale publicly available collection of T2-weighted annotated sagittal MRI volumes from 300 patients diagnosed with uterine myomas, with Nabothian cysts present in 127 of these cases [19]. The dataset includes all nine categories of uterine fibroids as defined by the International Federation of Gynecology and Obstetrics (FIGO) system [6,19]. This dataset contains both 3T and 1.5T images. Annotations for the above stated four categories were generated by a multidisciplinary team of uterine myomaâŞtreating physicians and experienced radiologists, ensuring both high clinical relevance and annotation reliability [19]. Of the 300 cases, 240 were used for training and validation, while the remaining 60 cases were used for testing. The second dataset (**Dataset II**) comprises 30 cases, curated specifically for out-of-distribution evaluation to assess the generalizability of the proposed tool. It includes T2-weighted sagittal MRI volumes acquired using scanners from different vendors, clinical sites, and magnetic field strengths ranging from 3T to 0.55T. The images at 0.55T were acquired using a Siemens MAGNETOM Free.Max scanner (Siemens Healthineers, Erlangen, Germany). This dataset contains an equal mix of healthy cases and cases diagnosed with uterine myomas and Nabothian cysts. Only images free from visible large scale imaging artifacts were maintained and annotations for this dataset were generated using the same structural definitions as described above for Dataset I.

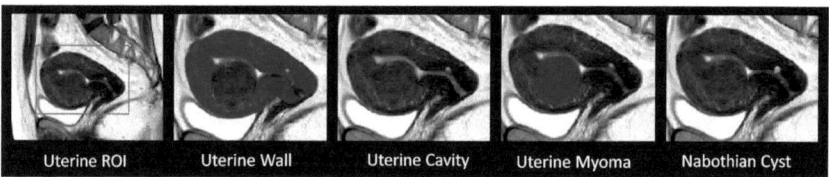

Fig. 2. Illustration of annotated labels, uterine wall in red, uterine cavity in green, uterine myoma in blue and Nabothian cysts in yellow on an exemplary dataset. Modified from [19] (Color figure online).

2.2 Automated Segmentation and Volumetric Analysis

We implemented the segmentation part of the proposed tool using the nnU-Net-v2 package by training the *3D full-resolution* U-Net with the latest residual encoder "ResEnc-M" preset [7,9]. All training procedures followed the default nnU-Net-v2 settings without manual intervention. In line with the self-configuring design of the nnU-Net, the framework automatically determined the hyperparameters and data augmentation strategy for the dataset. Standard nnU-Net preprocessing was applied, and the model was optimized using the default training schedule and loss functions provided by nnU-Net-v2 [7,9]. We trained five independent models using a five-fold cross-validation scheme and ensembling models by averaging their softmax output maps at inference [7,9]. Our models were trained from scratch for 1000 epochs using a NVIDIA Tesla V100 GPU.

To derive volumetric measurements from the predicted segmentation masks, we computed the physical volume of each segmented class by summing the number of voxels assigned to that label and multiplying by the voxel dimensions extracted from the image metadata. The final volumes are reported in cubic centimeters (cm^3), according to clinical conventions. To identify and enumerate individual lesions, we applied 3D connected component analysis to the predicted masks of the uterine myoma and Nabothian cyst classes using functions from the SciPy package in Python [28]. Each spatially contiguous cluster of labeled voxels was treated as a distinct lesion, enabling computation of lesion-wise statistics.

2.3 Automatic Report Generation

The entire workflow, from image acquisition to report generation, is fully automated via a command-line interface connected by Fire, enabling real-time execution [4,29]. The tool is launched with a single command, which initiates the real-time transfer of T2-weighted sagittal MRI RAW data slice-by-slice, converted to ISMRMRD format and streamed offline from the scanner computer to a GPU-enabled server. The slices are stacked together and converted into a NifTi file for further processing. The above described pre-trained 3D segmentation model based on the nnU-Net-v2 ResEnc-M architecture then performs inference on the NifTi file, generating segmentation masks for the uterine wall, uterine cavity, uterine myoma, and Nabothian cysts [7,9]. Following segmentation, post-processing steps as mentioned in Sect. 2.2, compute volumetric measurements for each class and identify and enumerate individual lesions. Finally, a structured HTML report is automatically generated using Python, summarizing volumetric statistics and lesion counts, and representative slices with maximum individual structure volumes selected and visualized with predicted segmentation masks. The report is saved in a designated output directory, making it instantly available for clinical review. An illustration of this workflow is shown in Fig. 1.

2.4 Evaluation

We evaluated the proposed tool in terms of segmentation accuracy and processing time. Segmentation performance was assessed using two widely adopted metrics: the Dice Similarity Coefficient (DSC), which measures overlap between predicted and ground-truth masks, and the Intersection over Union (IoU), which quantifies the ratio of intersection to union between the predicted and reference regions. Both metrics were computed per structure for each individual case in the hold-out test set of Dataset I (n = 60) and in Dataset II (n = 30), and then averaged across individual anatomical labels within each dataset. Additionally, the proposed tool was run in two participants in real-time after informed consent was obtained, with inference durations recorded and averaged to quantify the end-to-end processing time from image acquisition to report generation.

3 Results

Table 1 summarizes the segmentation performance metrics, including Dice similarity coefficient (DSC) and Intersection over Union (IoU), for the uterine wall, uterine cavity, uterine myoma, and Nabothian cysts on the hold-out test set from Dataset I and on out-of-distribution Dataset II. The tool achieved high DSCs of 0.81 and 0.74 for the uterine wall and uterine cavity on Dataset I and yielded slightly higher scores of 0.83 and 0.79 on Dataset II. For uterine myoma, the tool achieved a DSC of 0.69 on Dataset I and improved to 0.86 on Dataset II, while for Nabothian cyst the tool yielded DSCs of 0.46 on Dataset I and 0.39 on Dataset II. IoU values followed the same trend across structures and datasets, with the uterine wall and uterine cavity achieving the highest overlaps and uterine myoma and Nabothian cysts yielding comparatively lower scores. Overall, segmentation scores for the uterine wall, uterine cavity, and uterine myoma were slightly higher on Dataset II compared to Dataset I. Figure 3 illustrates a qualitative comparison between ground truth masks and predicted masks for both a healthy and a pathological case. The tool was successfully employed in real-time conditions on two participants, with images acquired using different T2-weighted sagittal sequences on a Siemens MAGNETOM Sola 1.5T scanner (Siemens Healthineers, Erlangen, Germany). The average processing time from the completion of image acquisition to report delivery was under 60 s. An exemplary generated report is shown in Fig. 4.

Table 1. Segmentation performance (mean ± SD) on hold-out test set from Dataset I, and on Dataset II reported using Dice Similarity Coefficient (DSC) and Intersection Over Union (IOU).

Structure	Dataset I (n = 60)		Dataset II (n = 30)	
	DSC (mean ± SD)	IOU (mean ± SD)	DSC (mean ± SD)	IOU (mean ± SD)
Uterine Wall	0.81 ± 0.17	0.71 ± 0.17	0.83 ± 0.08	0.72 ± 0.10
Uterine Cavity	0.74 ± 0.19	0.62 ± 0.19	0.79 ± 0.09	0.66 ± 0.11
Uterine Myoma	0.69 ± 0.29	0.59 ± 0.28	0.86 ± 0.08	0.76 ± 0.12
Nabothian Cyst	0.46 ± 0.35	0.37 ± 0.30	0.39 ± 0.25	0.27 ± 0.19

4 Discussion

The proposed tool delivers real-time, standardized quantitative report of uterine structures and anomalies with minimal user input. Automating the segmentation and volumetric analysis of uterine structures reduces observer variability, enhances workflow efficiency, and enables reproducible assessment of uterine morphology and pathology from MRI. This marks a significant advance over current clinical practice, where volume estimates typically rely on either the prolate ellipsoid formula, based on orthogonal linear dimensions or manual slice-by-slice contouring. Both methods are time-intensive and suffer from inter-observer variability, especially in cases involving multiple lesions or distorted anatomy [3,25]. Our approach mitigates these limitations and brings the additional advantage of delivering results immediately at the point of care. The tool estimates total volumes for key anatomical regions such as the uterine wall and uterine cavity and identifies individual lesions such as uterine fibroids and Nabothian cysts, reporting their counts and spatial locations. By automating a time-intensive and variable process, the tool enhances efficiency, standardization, and diagnostic precision in routine gynecological imaging. While the segmentation accuracy in terms of Dice scores is modest, the performance is comparable with existing

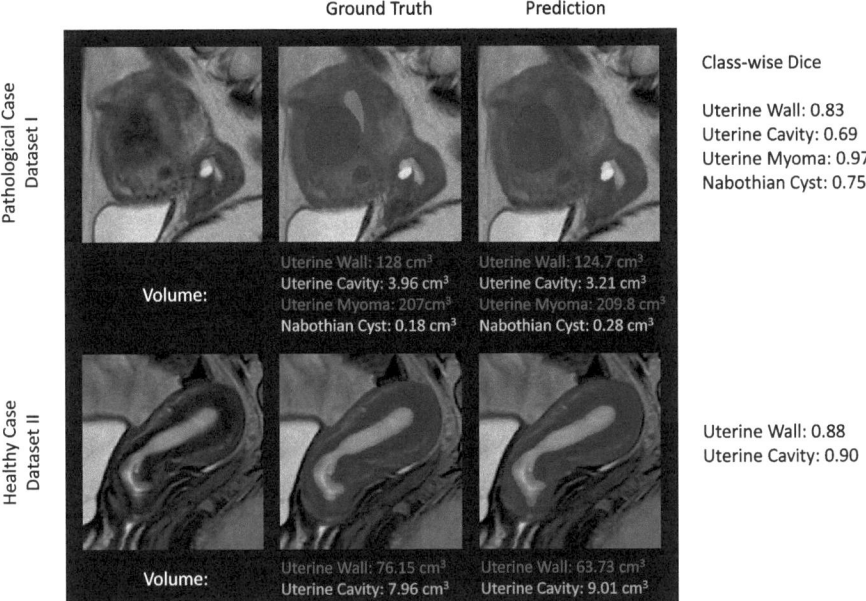

Fig. 3. Qualitative comparison of segmentation results, showing ground truth and predicted masks for a pathological case from Dataset I (top row) and a healthy case from Dataset II (bottom row). The ground truth masks and predicted masks highlight anatomical structures including the uterine wall (red), uterine cavity (green), uterine myoma (blue), and Nabothian cyst (yellow). (Color figure online)

methods tackling similar multiclass uterine MRI segmentation for the uterine wall and uterine cavity [10,11]. The overall lower Dice scores, particularly for Nabothian cysts and uterine myomas, primarily reflect the inherent difficulty of the task: Dataset I includes substantial anatomical variability, ranging from very large myomas with minimal healthy tissue to very small myomas, as well as small or absent Nabothian cysts. This variability led to partial or missed predictions in challenging cases, disproportionately reducing the average Dice score. In contrast, Dataset II contains predominantly healthy uteri and mild benign findings with clearer anatomical boundaries and fewer such small, difficult-to-detect structures. Combined with higher image quality and fewer artifacts, these characteristics facilitated more accurate segmentation, resulting in improved Dice scores on Dataset II. Importantly, this is the first tool to provide multiclass segmentation of the uterine body, related incidental findings, and real-time volumetric reporting. Dataset II, featuring cases from multiple clinical sites, scanners, and magnetic field strengths, introduced realistic domain shifts. Despite these challenges, the tool maintained comparable segmentation quality across domains, demonstrating robustness and generalizability beyond the training distribution. The immediate availability of segmentation results and quantitative metrics during MRI acquisition not only eliminates the need for separate post-processing but

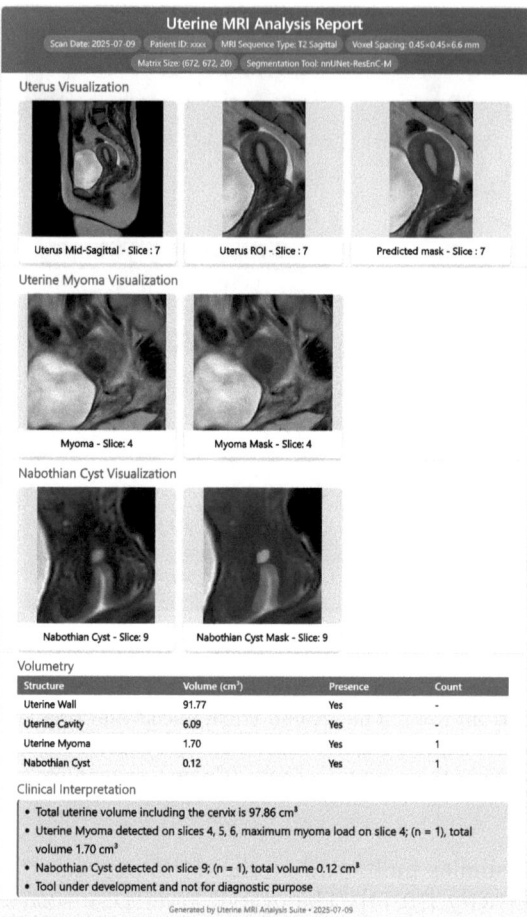

Fig. 4. Example of an automated uterine MRI analysis report showing segmentation masks and volumetric measurements for the uterine wall, uterine cavity, myomas, and Nabothian cysts, each visualized on the slice with maximum volume. Key findings such as lesion count, localization, and total uterine volume are summarized, with the report generated in under 60 s after image acquisition using the proposed tool.

also allows adaptive scanning in real time. Radiologists and clinicians can leverage these on-the-fly results to optimize acquisition planes or trigger additional sequences when ambiguous findings are detected [23]. This capability facilitates same-session review and decision-making for procedures such as fertility evaluation or surgical planning [2], ultimately helping reduce interpretive delays, recall rates, healthcare costs, and patient anxiety while improving diagnostic confidence.

The proposed tool, however, has several limitations. Firstly, the anatomical definitions were restricted, as our segmentation did not include a layered subdivision of the uterus (e.g., endometrium, junctional zone, myometrium) [1,11]. Furthermore, the labels used for the uterine wall and uterine cavity encompassed both the uterus and cervix, preventing cervix-specific volumetry from being reported separately [11]. The current evaluation was limited to segmentation performance assessed by standard metrics, which appropriately measures boundary delineation but does not fully capture the clinical utility of the tool. Given that the method also performs instance-level detection of myomas, a more comprehensive evaluation including detection accuracy is required. Additionally, the tool currently operates only on sagittal MRI volumes, with no support yet for axial or coronal planes. These limitations will be systematically addressed in future iterations of the tool, with the goal of refining anatomical granularity, expanding clinical utility, and improving robustness. The report will be expanded to include separate cervix and uterine biometry such as uterine length, width, anteroposterior diameter, and fundal thickness, and uterocervical angle, which are known to influence fertility outcomes [22]. Further efforts will focus on improving the segmentation and detection of uterine myomas and Nabothian cysts through targeted, region-specific training approaches [8,11].

5 Conclusion

We present a fully automated tool for uterine MRI analysis that integrates deep learning-based 3D segmentation with real-time structured report generation. The system works towards rapid and reproducible quantification of key uterine structures and lesions, producing clinician-friendly outputs that include volumes, lesion counts, and contextual metrics. By automating a time-intensive and variable process, the pipeline prepares the way for increased efficiency, standardization, and diagnostic precision in routine gynecological imaging. Real-time generation of results through the tool during the MRI scan facilitates rapid decision-making in clinical settings, particularly in the evaluation of uterine anomalies, preoperative planning, and reproductive health.

Acknowledgments. The authors thank all women for participating in this study. This work was supported by the High Tech Agenda of the Free State of Bavaria, DFG Heisenberg funding [502024488] and an ERC Starting grant EARTHWORM [101165242].

Disclosure of Interests. The authors have no competing interests to declare that are relevant to the content of this article.

References

1. Agostinho, L., Cruz, R., Osório, F., Alves, J., Setúbal, A., Guerra, A.: MRI for adenomyosis: a pictorial review. Insights Imaging **8**(6), 549–556 (2017). https://doi.org/10.1007/s13244-017-0576-z
2. Anneveldt, K., et al.: Lessons learned during implementation of MR-guided high-intensity focused ultrasound treatment of uterine fibroids. Insights Imaging **12**, 1–13 (2021). https://doi.org/10.1186/s13244-021-01128-w

3. Bérczi, V., et al.: Outlier data in volume calculations of uterine fibroids comparing ellipsoid formula and voxel-based segmentation. BMC Med. Imaging **25**(1), 1–8 (2025). https://doi.org/10.1186/s12880-025-01672-7
4. Chow, K., Kellman, P., Xue, H.: Prototyping image reconstruction and analysis with fire. In: SCMR 24th Annual Scientific Sessions. Virtual Meeting (2021)
5. Dueholm, M., Lundorf, E., Hansen, E.S., Ledertoug, S., Olesen, F.: Accuracy of magnetic resonance imaging and transvaginal ultrasonography in the diagnosis, mapping, and measurement of uterine myomas. Am. J. Obstet. Gynecol. **186**(3), 409–415 (2002). https://doi.org/10.1067/mob.2002.121725
6. Fraser, I.S., Critchley, H.O., Broder, M., Munro, M.G.: The figo recommendations on terminologies and definitions for normal and abnormal uterine bleeding. In: Seminars in Reproductive Medicine, vol. 29, pp. 383–390. Thieme Medical Publishers (2011). https://doi.org/10.1055/s-0031-1287662
7. Isensee, F., Jaeger, P.F., Kohl, S.A.A., Petersen, J., Maier-Hein, K.H.: nnU-Net: a self-configuring method for deep learning-based biomedical image segmentation. Nat. Methods **18**(2), 203–211 (2021). https://doi.org/10.1038/s41592-020-01008-z
8. Isensee, F., Jäger, P.F., Full, P.M., Vollmuth, P., Maier-Hein, K.H.: nnU-net for brain tumor segmentation. In: Crimi, A., Bakas, S. (eds.) BrainLes 2020. LNCS, vol. 12659, pp. 118–132. Springer, Cham (2021). https://doi.org/10.1007/978-3-030-72087-2_11
9. Isensee, F., et al.: nnu-net revisited: a call for rigorous validation in 3D medical image segmentation. In: International Conference on Medical Image Computing and Computer-Assisted Intervention, pp. 488–498. Springer, Cham (2024). https://doi.org/10.1007/978-3-031-72114-4_47
10. Khaghani, J., Basar, S., Chodakiewitz, Y., London, S., Attariwal, R., Hashemi, S.: A deep learning-based tool for analyzing the female reproductive system in MR images. In: ISMRM Annual Meeting. ISMRM, Concord, CA (2024)
11. Khaghani, J., Khallaghi, S., Basar, S., Chodakiewitz, Y., Attariwala, R., Hashemi, S.: An AI-based solution for MR image analysis of the female reproductive system. In: ISMRM Annual Meeting. ISMRM, Concord, CA (2024). https://doi.org/10.1002/ca.24045
12. Khan, A.T., Shehmar, M., Gupta, J.K.: Uterine fibroids: current perspectives. Int. J. Women's Health 95–114 (2014). https://doi.org/10.2147/ijwh.s51083. https://pubmed.ncbi.nlm.nih.gov/24511243/
13. Kido, A., Togashi, K., Kataoka, M.L., Nakai, A., Koyama, T., Fujii, S.: Intrauterine devices and uterine peristalsis: evaluation with MRI. Magn. Reson. Imaging **26**(1), 54–58 (2008). https://doi.org/10.1016/j.mri.2007.06.001
14. Kurban, L.A.S., Metwally, H., Abdullah, M., Kerban, A., Oulhaj, A., Alkoteesh, J.A.: Uterine artery embolization of uterine leiomyomas: predictive MRI features of volumetric response. Am. J. Roentgenol. **216**(4), 967–974 (2021). https://doi.org/10.2214/AJR.20.22906
15. Liu, F., Chen, M., Pan, H., Li, B., Bai, W.: Artificial intelligence for instance segmentation of MRI: advancing efficiency and safety in laparoscopic myomectomy of broad ligament fibroids. Front. Oncol. **15**, 1549803 (2025). https://doi.org/10.3389/fonc.2025.1549803
16. Liu, X.Y., et al.: Deep learning assisted detection and segmentation of uterine fibroids using multi-orientation magnetic resonance imaging. Abdominal Radiol. 1–12 (2025). https://doi.org/10.1007/s00261-025-04934-8

17. Neumann, W., Uhrig, T., Malzacher, M., Kossmann, V., Schad, L.R., Zoellner, F.G.: Risk assessment of copper-containing contraceptives: the impact for women with implanted intrauterine devices during clinical MRI and CT examinations. Eur. Radiol. **29**(6), 2812–2820 (2018). https://doi.org/10.1007/s00330-018-5864-6
18. Omi, M., et al.: Preoperative diagnosis of cervical cystic lesions using magnetic resonance imaging: a retrospective study. BMC Womens Health **24**(1), 460 (2024). https://doi.org/10.1186/s12905-024-03304-8
19. Pan, H., et al.: Large-scale uterine myoma MRI dataset covering all figo types with pixel-level annotations. Sci. Data **11**(1), 410 (2024). https://doi.org/10.1038/s41597-024-03170-x
20. Patel, S., Liyanage, S.H., Sahdev, A., Rockall, A.G., Reznek, R.H.: Imaging of endometrial and cervical cancer. Insights Imaging **1**, 309–328 (2010). https://doi.org/10.1007/s13244-010-0042-7
21. Salman, S., Shireen, N., Riyaz, R., Khan, S.A., Singh, J.P., Uttam, A.: Magnetic resonance imaging evaluation of gynecological mass lesions: a comprehensive analysis with histopathological correlation. Medicine **103**(32), e39312 (2024). https://doi.org/10.1097/MD.0000000000039312
22. Sevindik, B., Unver Dogan, N., Secilmis, O., Uysal, E., Fazliogullari, Z., Karabulut, A.K.: Differences in the anatomical structure of the uterus between fertile and infertile individuals. Clin. Anat. **36**(5), 764–769 (2023)
23. Silva, S.N., et al.: Automatic flow planning for fetal cardiovascular magnetic resonance imaging. J. Cardiovasc. Magn. Reson. **27**(1), 101888 (2025). https://doi.org/10.1016/j.jocmr.2025.101888
24. Stewart, E.A., Cookson, C., Gandolfo, R.A., Schulze-Rath, R.: Epidemiology of uterine fibroids: a systematic review. BJOG Int. J. Obstetrics Gynaecol. **124**(10), 1501–1512 (2017). https://doi.org/10.1111/1471-0528.14640
25. Theis, M., et al.: Deep learning enables automated MRI-based estimation of uterine volume also in patients with uterine fibroids undergoing high-intensity focused ultrasound therapy. Insights Imaging **14**(1), 1 (2023). https://doi.org/10.1186/s13244-022-01342-0
26. Tong, A., et al.: Recommendations for MRI technique in the evaluation of pelvic endometriosis: consensus statement from the Society of Abdominal Radiology endometriosis disease-focused panel. Abdom. Radiol. **45**(6), 1569–1586 (2020). https://doi.org/10.1007/s00261-020-02483-w
27. Verdera, J.A., et al.: Heron: High-efficiency real-time motion quantification and re-acquisition for fetal diffusion MRI. IEEE Trans. Med. Imaging (2025). https://doi.org/10.1109/tmi.2025.3569853
28. Virtanen, P., et al.: Scipy 1.0: fundamental algorithms for scientific computing in python. Nat. Methods **17**(3), 261–272 (2020). https://doi.org/10.1038/s41592-019-0686-2
29. Xue, H., et al.: Gadgetron inline AI: effective model inference on MR scanner. In: Proceedings of the 27th Annual ISMRM Meeting and Exhibition, p. 4837 (2019)
30. Zand, K.R., Reinhold, C., Haider, M.A., Nakai, A., Rohoman, L., Maheshwari, S.: Artifacts and pitfalls in MR imaging of the pelvis. J. Magn. Reson. Imaging **26**(3), 480–497 (2007). https://doi.org/10.1002/jmri.20996

Author Index

A

Abhishek, Kumar 23
Arlt, Tillmann 71
Arndt, Sebastian 71
Attali, Jennifer 113
Aviles Verdera, Jordina 137

B

Baumgärtner, Georg Lukas 71
Bayasi, Nourhan 3
Bellucci, Alexandre 113
Bernstein, David 82
Bhatia, Deepak 137
Bloch, Isabelle 113
Blöss, Pedro 93
Bonnot, Enzo 113
Bui, Tran Quang Khai 57
Bustos Vivas, Maria Camila 125, 137

C

Chakraborty, Sayoni 34
Coskunuzer, Baris 34

D

de la Plata, Juan Pablo 113
de Segonzac, Joy-Rose Dunoyer 113

E

El-Nahry, Yasmin 71

F

Fayyad, Jamil 3
Fournier, Laure 113

G

Glocker, Ben 82
Gori, Pietro 113
Gracey, Lia 13

H

Hamarneh, Ghassan 23
Hamm, Charlie Alexander 71
Hong, Charmgil 46
Hutter, Jana 71, 93, 125, 137
Huynh, Phat K. 57
Huynh, Xuan-Loc 57

I

Isla, Thomas 113

J

Jurgas, Artur 103

K

Kainz, Bernhard 93
Kawahara, Jeremy 23
Kim, Sooha 82
Kitzberger, Michael 137
Knupfer, Anika 93, 137
Koung, Philmore 34
Kratzsch, Lieselotte 137

L

La Barbera, Giammarco 113
Le, Minh Huu Nhat 57
Lindholz, Maximilian 71
Lozach, Cécile 113

M

Mackay, Katherine 82
Marcellin, Louis 113
May, Matthias 71
Mechsner, Sylvia 71
Mehta, Raghav 82
Moon, Jihyun 46
Müller, Johanna P. 93

N
Najjaran, Homayoun 3
Nguyen, Quan 57
Nguyen, Tat-Bach 57
Nguyen, Thanh-Minh 57

P
Penzkofer, Tobias 71
Pham, Huy-Thach 57

R
Reeves, Carlie 13
Ribeiro, Fabio De Sousa 82
Ruppel, Richard 71

S
Sarnacki, Sabine 113
Schmidt, Robin 71
Schulze-Weddige, Sophia Elisabeth Ellen 71
Siegler, Lisa 71
Skalski, Andrzej 103
Stanuch, Maciej 103
Stepansky, Leonard 71
Stothers, Duncan 13

T
Taylor, Alexandra 82
Todd, Omar 82
Tripathy, Smiti 125, 137

V
Vittur, Edoardo Berardi 93
Vu, Anh Mai 57

W
Wodziński, Marek 103

X
Xu, Sophia 13

Y
Yu, Ziyang 3

MIX
Papier aus verantwortungsvollen Quellen
Paper from responsible sources
FSC® C105338

If you have any concerns about our products,
you can contact us on
ProductSafety@springernature.com

In case Publisher is established outside the EU,
the EU authorized representative is:
**Springer Nature Customer Service Center GmbH
Europaplatz 3, 69115 Heidelberg, Germany**

Printed by Libri Plureos GmbH
in Hamburg, Germany